FOOTSTEPS OF OUR FOREFATHERS:

What they Suffered and what they Sought.

DESCRIBING LOCALITIES, AND PORTRAYING PERSONAGES AND EVENTS CONSPICUOUS IN THE STRUGGLES FOR RELIGIOUS LIBERTY.

BY JAMES G. MIALL.

HAMPDEN MANOR, THE SEAT OF THE PATRIOT HAMPDEN.

Thirty-six Illustrations by Anelay, from Sketches by the Author, ENGRAVED BY DICKES, LONDON.

BOSTON:
GOULD AND LINCOLN,
59 WASHINGTON STREET.
1852.

PRESS OF G. C. RAND, CORNHILL, BOSTON.

PREFACE.

The design of the following work is to exhibit, in a form as little repulsive as the nature of the subject will allow, some of the phenomena of Religious Intolerance, especially as it has been displayed in a Protestant form, and to indicate the mistaken principle in which these melancholy results have had their origin.

It has been no part of the author's aim to advocate any distinctive form of doctrine or polity; but rather to show how *any* religious system, whether Episcopal, Presbyterian or Congregational, may become vitiated and perverted by its alliance with the powers of the state, and by the assumption, exclusiveness and worldly pride, which such a connection invariably engenders.

The author will rejoice if his work shall produce, especially in the minds of the young, a juster estimate of the value of that spiritual freedom for which their ancestors longed, suffered, and even died; though they did not always clearly understand the true nature of that liberty which alone could have met their wants, and which, in the degree in which it exists, is, for the most part, the measure of the religious prosperity, and of the moral and social well-being, of nations.

To those friends who have aided in such inquiries as were important to the writer's object,—who have opened sources of information, or yielded to him their generous hospitality during the progress of his search,—cordial thanks are offered.

CONTENTS.

1*

CHAPTER VII.

CHAPTER VIII.

CHAPTER IX.

CHAPTER X.

CHAPTER XI.

CHAPTER XII.

Illustrations.

PAGE

CHAPTER I.

THE LIGHT OF A DARK AGE.

"Fame's lasting register
Shall leave his name enrolled as great as those
Who at Philippi for their country fell."

Lines to the Memory of A. Marvell, 1678.

WICLIF'S CHURCH AT LUTTERWORTH.

No part of England is more rich in historical associations than its midland counties. Though neither statues nor obelisks mark the spots where our ancestors struggled for freedom or for truth, the scenes are sacred; and Buckinghamshire, Huntingdonshire, Northamptonshire and Leicestershire, offer points not less memorable than were Platæa, Marathon and Thermopylæ, in Grecian story. Our first journey with the reader shall be taken to the last of the counties we have named, and to the secluded, yet not altogether inconsiderable, town of Lutterworth. The traveller is here in the centre of England. Not far distant is Leicester, where Richard III. buckled on his armor for the battle of Bosworth, — a conflict which delivered the country from a cruel tyrant and a disputed succession; and which, ending the wars of the Roses, introduced a new era. In the same town Wolsey breathed out his troubled spirit, when Protestantism, headed by Anne Boleyn, became for the moment triumphant, and the cardinal began to stand in the way of his master. There, too, John Bunyan's life was spared, when an accidental circumstance substituted a comrade in his place; and so saved the future saint from death, that he might devote a rich genius to the cause of religion and of truth. Not far from Lutterworth, in the village of Thurcaston, Hugh Latimer was born. And on another side of the town stand the height and village of Naseby, memorable for that great conflict which displayed the military prowess of Cromwell, changed the fortunes of a great empire, and proved the ruin of a despotic tyrant and a perjured prince.

The scenery about Lutterworth is not of the highest order. But the country, though flat, is fertile; consisting of rich, level grazing land, interspersed with good trees. If, in visiting the town, the traveller shall expect many memorials of the past, he will be disappointed; few antiquarian curiosities remain. Five centuries are, in truth, a huge period in the history of man, and most human structures crumble down before it. "The lines where beauty lingers" are altogether swept away, so far as the town itself is concerned; and for the characteristic buildings of the period most in his mind, — for the sharp gables with overhanging stories, and every rich adornment of carved wood and florid plaster, — the visitant must draw upon his imagination. Instead of these, he will find only buildings constructed with the most mathematical precision, and of the reddest of red brick. Lutterworth is, in short, a quiet, well-to-do-looking town, exhibiting everywhere modern neatness and respectability, but totally unlike what it must have been in 1350; when, with more picturesqueness, it must have contained much squalid poverty, wretched ventilation, and deplorable agriculture. On the whole, though with some restiveness, we prefer the place as it is.

But Lutterworth contains one building worth all the rest; having, it is true, little about it likely to prove attractive to a stranger, but full of interest when one is aware that this is the ancient church of John Wiclif.—The name of the reformer was spelt in many different ways, like those of Shakespear, Rawleigh and others, and perhaps was not written uniformly even by its possessor. We choose the form in which the name appears when the reformer was appointed papal delegate, in 1374.

A grave, quiet sanctity, renders the old church at Lutterworth attractive, and even imposing. The walls are rent, patched, and buttressed. The windows, dim with age, admit a struggling and murky light. The old porch seems to have been constructed for the days when marriages were not yet celebrated within ecclesiastical edifices, but at their entrance. On the rectory side of the building, a low portal, which seems specially appropriated to the officiating clergyman, receives interest from the thought that by it, probably, Wiclif passed to the performance of his sacred duties. Though close to the town, the grave-yard is quiet and secluded; and when, towards evening, the overhanging trees are casting their thick shadows over the venerable pile, the gloom and silence answer well to the dusky memories of the period which renders the scene memorable.

The exterior of the church is, however, its greatest attraction; the interior is scarcely worthy of its associations. A slovenly, semi-Grecian, but altogether barbaric hand, has been busy at the processes of restoration,—removing, repairing and enlarging, Wiclif's pulpit, and leaving the interior of the church in a state of miserable and most unmeaning transformation. But the vestry still retains the table on which the reformer was once wont to dispense a primitive hospitality,—a fine piece of old oak; and the vestment which he wore when officiating at the altar is still preserved, embroidered with angels, and now shut up in a glass case, like some relics of saints in continental churches. The first view of this popish habiliment is somewhat startling; for the world has learned almost to regard Wiclif as a Protestant,—which he was in fact, but not then in name; and, as one looks upon the time-worn garment, it becomes invested with very peculiar associations, reminding us of him who has grown too large for his system, but is still obliged to keep within its narrow limits, and compelling us to pity the contest—the terrible contest—going on still, in many a mind, conscientious as Wiclif's was, between the claims of position on the one hand, and of convictions on the other. Those dingy rafters, too, over head, look as if they might once have echoed to the reformer's voice. But this is rendered somewhat doubtful by the fact that, in 1703, a violent storm blew down the ancient spire—a tapering and very lofty cone, surmounted by a ball—into the nave, leaving it to be replaced by a structure bearing no kind of resemblance to the original erection. Though somewhat out of place, it may illustrate one peculiarity of a state church—its want of ready adjustment to circumstances as they arise—to observe that the necessary repairs consequent on this accident involved the then existing rector—the Rev. H. Meriton—in a prolonged chancery suit. He had collected money by brief, for the purpose of repairing the edifice, which the high wind had nearly destroyed. But, though personally above suspicion, he had applied part of that money to the repairing of the church; a condition "not in the bond." The troubles incident on this litigation shortened the poor man's life.*

To this living of Lutterworth, John de Wiclif, so called from the place of his birth, on the banks of the Tees, Yorkshire, was presented by the crown in the year 1375, when about fifty years of age. He held the rectory about ten years. The services which led to his appointment may be briefly told.

Wiclif, one of the best scholars of his time, had attained great distinction as the most advanced man in the University of Oxford

* Nichols' Hist. and Ant. of Leicestershire.

(which has not always been in arrear of the age). He had signalized himself by the offensive war he had carried on, in behalf of that university, against the mendicant friars. The fashion of monkery, which had been extremely popular during the reigns of the Anglo-Norman kings, had been for some time on the wane; and the disgust excited by the venality and licentiousness of the religious houses had called into existence the begging orders, who, abjuring monastic establishments, professed poverty, and, as wandering priests, subsisted on the alms of the devout. Yielding, in their turn, however, to the temptations of the times, these wandering friars soon began to wallow in the mire of corruption which had swallowed up their predecessors. These friars were divided into four principal orders, and indeed were, by the constitutions of Pope Gregory X., limited to that number: the *Dominicans*, established by St. Dominic, founder of the Inquisition; the *Franciscan* or *Gray friars*, established by St. Francis of Assisa, called also Cordeliers from the knotted cord which they wore suspended from their girdles; the *Carmelites* or *White friars*, and the *Augustinian* or *Austin friars*. Many cities were divided and mapped out among these four orders, each of which was licensed to beg within a given district; whence the mendicants were called "limitours." The doctrine of these friars was, that the Founder of the Christian religion was himself a beggar, and that mendicancy was a gospel ordinance. Every reader of Milton is familiar with the passage which Bentley would fain have expunged as an interpolation.

"Embryos and idiots, eremites and friars
White, black and gray, with all their trumpery.
* * * Then might ye see
Cowls, hoods and habits, with their wearers tossed
And fluttered into rags; then reliques, beads,
Indulgences, dispenses, pardons, bulls,
The sport of winds: all these, upwhirled aloft,
Fly o'er the backside of the world far off,
Into a limbo large and broad, since called
The paradise of fools." — *Par. Lost*, III.

Such was the popularity of these mendicants, that the confessionals of the ordinary clergy were at one time almost forsaken, whilst penitents of all classes crowded for absolution to these religious drones. Chaucer has thus painted one of them:

"For he had power of confession,
As said himself, more than a curate,
For of this order he was licenciate.
Full swetely heard he confession,
And pleasant was his absolution;
He was an easy man to give penance,
And well he knew to have a good pittance.*
* * * *
Therefore, instead of weeping and prayers,
Men might give money to the poor friars."

Prol. to Cant. Tales.

The powers and privileges claimed by some of these orders were enormous. Salvation, they said, was certain to those who died invested with the scapulary of their order. It was usual for persons of infirm health, or at the point of death, to seek admission among the mendicants, and to desire that their bodies might be interred in the old garments of the friars, or at least near some of the order, that thus they might be safe at last. St. Eloy gave the following advice to his parishioners: "Redeem your souls from destruction while you have the means in your power. Offer presents and titles to churchmen; come more frequently to church; humbly implore the patronage of the saints; for, if you do these things, you may come with security in the day of retribution to the tribunal of the Eternal Judge, and say, Give to us, O Lord, for we have given to Thee."†

Among the mendicant friars, the Franciscans surpassed all others in the privileges they claimed, holding their powers independently of the bishops, and possessing unlimited authority to grant indulgences as a compensation for their vows of poverty. Their authority was principally appealed to in all questions affect-

* Plenty of provisions. † Mosheim.

ing the See of Rome. But each of these orders waged incessant warfare with the rest, and the contests between the Franciscans and Dominicans were most exasperated. Nor were the members of the same fraternity at peace among themselves. In the mean time, however, they all lived by continual benevolences, and often by gross exactions. Chaucer's lines may be accepted as a general portrait of the class:

"Specially, above everything,
Excited he the people in his preaching
To trentals,* and to give for God's sake
Wherewith men might holy houses make.

* * * *

And when this friar had said all his intent
With *qui cum Patre*,† forth his way he went.
Where folks in church had given what he list,
He went his way, no longer would he rest,
With scrip and tipped staff, uplifted high,
In every house began to pore and pry,
And begged meal and cheese, or else corn.
The fellow had a staff tipped with horn,
And wrote always the names as he stood
Of all folk that gave him any good.
Aside that he would for him pray,
'Give us a bushel wheat, or meal, or rye,
A holy cake, or a piece of cheese,
Or else what you will, we may not choose.
A God's halfpenny, or a mass penny,
Or give us of your bran if you have any.
Bacon or beef, or such thing as you find.' "

Nor was the morality of these friars more unimpeachable. The virtue of the clergy in general may be pretty decisively inferred from a petition presented to parliament by the clergy in 1449, which prayed that all cases of rape, committed by priests before the following 1st June, might be pardoned, on condition that a noble (6*s.* 8*d.*) should be paid to the king on behalf of every priest in the kingdom. Nor did the mendicants greatly differ

* A service of thirty masses. † The last words of the church service.

from the priests. One of them is described by Chaucer (and the portrait corresponds with a multitude of insinuations scattered about his works) as "a wanton and a merrie," having his tippet stuffed full of presents "for to given faire wives;" "he sings a merrie note;" he knows "ful wel the tavernes in every town;" he could "rage as it hadde been a whelp;" and

> "Wan that he had his song,
> His eyen twinkled in his hed aright
> As dow the sterres in a frosty night."

Such are only specimens.

The Dominicans had, on their first introduction into England, settled at Oxford. But, in the course of a few years, their disorders and encroachments had so enormously increased, as to reduce the number of university students from thirty thousand to six thousand. Parents feared to send their children to the schools, lest they should become corrupted by the friars. Fitz-Ralph, the Chancellor of Oxford, and afterwards Archbishop of Armagh, had appealed against them to the pope, but the death of the prelate suspended the proceedings.

It was at this crisis that Wiclif, on behalf of the university in which he held the post of divinity professor, entered the lists of controversial warfare. Brought up in the most rigid school of Aristotle and St. Thomas Aquinas, of Ockham and Duns Scotus, Wiclif was well versed in all the dialectical subtleties of the day. But he was more; — his remarkable acquaintance with the Scriptures — a matter not altogether neglected by the schoolmen of his day — had procured for him the title of the *evangelical* doctor, as Aquinas had been called the *angelical*, from his discussions of the properties of angels. Whatever Wiclif's merits as a schoolman, his distinction in this controversy arose from the plain sense and daring pungency of his diatribes. His words were strong, though careless; he spared no epithets, he rounded no periods. It is beside our purpose to enter further into the nature of this controversy. It will be sufficient to remark that Wiclif's part in it gained him speedy preferment. He was constituted warden, first of Balliol College, and afterwards of Canterbury Hall, by the presentation of Islip, Archbishop of Canterbury. Islip soon after died, and his successor in office, who was favorable to the religious orders, deposed Wiclif from his post. Wiclif appealed to the pope, and ultimately lost his appointment.

Every one must have observed how frequently it happens, in excited states of society, that slight circumstances are attracted, as by a kind of magnetic influence, to range themselves about great principles. Whilst Wiclif was awaiting the papal decision on his wardership, a concurrent movement of much greater importance was agitating the community. The pope, Urban V., not satisfied that one-third of the property of England had already passed over to the church, had demanded of Edward III. the tribute promised by King John, in token of his feudal subjection to the successors of St. Peter. But the demand came a day too late, and the House of Commons, which had now become one of the powers of the realm, united with the spirited monarch in repudiating the claim. Up to this time, the church had been the superior and the state the inferior power; but now lords spiritual and temporal united with the commons in repudiating the claims of the papacy, and in declaring themselves ready to uphold the monarch in resistance to its offensive demands. Wiclif, who was already known to the court, and who had been promoted to the office of king's chaplain, entered warmly into this controversy, and his name, now graced by the title of D. D., appears second on the list of English delegates selected by the parliament to remonstrate with the pontiff at Bruges.

In this embassy he was associated with men of the highest rank and station, and, among others, with John of Gaunt, his future patron, third son of Edward III. To this great man, the Duke of Lancaster, much of the management of the kingdom was confided, in the latter part of this and the commencement of the succeeding reign; and he was the only member of the royal family who took a conspicuous part in the stormy religious controversies of those times. It would interest us much to know the details of the proceedings of the great reformer during this memorable period. Bruges, that old continental city, memorable still for the traces which it preserves of the mediæval ages, — a kind of Venice of the north, whose merchants were princes resolutely maintaining freedom of thought and action, — was doubtless the scene of many debates and movements of the highest importance. But the records have mainly perished. About the same time, an energetic effort was made by the parliament to dispossess churchmen of the high secular offices they were then in the habit of holding, and to confine the clergy to their more spiritual duties. Wiclif entered into this controversy with characteristic ardor.

The consequence of these movements was, that the Bishop of Winchester relinquished his post of chancellor, and the Bishop of Exeter resigned that of treasurer.

Though the mission of Wiclif to Bruges was productive of little direct service, it was of unspeakable benefit in maturing the views of the reformer himself. Something, indeed, was done in support of the celebrated statute against "provisors," passed in 1350; but the increasing age and infirmities of the king rendered him less an object of dread than he had been heretofore, and Wiclif saw in the pope's conduct, throughout the whole transaction, a worldly ambition on the one hand, and a paltry evasiveness on the other, which stimulated him to attack the Romish hierarchy with increased severity. Removed from his mastership at Oxford, he was at this time, by way of amends, constituted prebendary of Worcester, and rector of Lutterworth.

Chaucer's description of the good parish priest has been frequently supposed to be a representation of the manner in which Wiclif fulfilled the duties of his cure. Certain it is that Chaucer, like the reformer, was attached to the party of the Duke of Lancaster, and sympathized strongly with many of Wiclif's opinions. But that the portrait of the clergyman was designed to represent any individual, is without sufficient evidence. Wiclif is represented as going about the country, clad in a long frieze gown, preaching whenever he could find or make an opportunity. In thus occupying himself, he was intent on correcting a special deficiency of the times. Not many years before, Archbishop Pecham, after complaining of the almost universal disuse of preaching, made some attempt at an improvement. He drew out a list of topics, to be expounded in the regular course of pulpit instruction, such as the decalogue, the articles of faith, the seven leading virtues, the seven deadly sins, &c. Each preacher was required to deliver four sermons to his parishioners during the year; and the sort of aid which the archbishop proposed to give may be well understood by those who are familiar with the technical terms, "cramming" and "grinding." Wiclif, however, was a preacher for himself, and in earnest. He devoted his time, also, most assiduously, to the humbler duties of his sacred office. His place was, every morning, by the sick-bed of the sufferer, or in the home of the mourner. A considerable number of his sermons are still extant,—probably preserved by the care of his curate,—replete with vehement attacks upon incompetent and indolent priests, exhorting to the study of God's Word in opposition to popes and prelates, vindicating the freedom of Christian men, and dilating, with fervid earnestness, on those various points of doctrine or practice which would be enforced by a Christian teacher in perilous times.

Plain speaking like this roused, we may well suppose, the reformer's enemies into action. The seclusion of Lutterworth proved no asylum to Wiclif. Scarcely was he settled in his new rectory, when, at the instigation of Courtenay, Bishop of London, a haughty and intolerant churchman, but fully accredited by the pope in the movement, the reformer was cited to appear before him, at the church of St. Paul's, in London.

What would not a historian and antiquarian of the present day sacrifice to know the details of a journey from Lutterworth to London five hundred years ago, or to look upon the picture of the metropolis at that date? Instead of the well-adjusted towns and quiet homesteads which the traveller now passes, on his way to the great city, the route would then be marked by the presence of castles of strength, whilst the few inhabitants were fain to place cottages or other property beneath their gigantic protection. Extensive forests yet stretched themselves across the country, the haunts of the successors of Robin Hood and his associates; and such a man as the reformer would be only safe with a military escort to protect him, not only from such marauders, but from open and avowed enemies. Except castles, nothing more distinguished the period than the churches which were springing up in all the larger towns, marked by the features of a true, though then somewhat modern, style of architecture. Arrived in London, possibly to make his "hostelrie" at the Tabard Inn, in Southwark, the traveller from Leicestershire would gaze with unconcealed eagerness upon a metropolis then rarely visited. The old, ugly, but venerable bridge, now supplanted, was then the only one which spanned the river; the stream, at ebb tide, flowing down its arches almost with the force of a cataract. Though on this bridge the church of St. Thomas was conspicuous, yet it was, as yet, unencumbered with the numerous buildings afterwards attaching themselves to it like limpets; and chivalry, then the prevailing fashion, held occasional joustings on its narrow area. The order of the Templars had been recently suppressed; but that of the Knights of St. John survived, and maintained its splendors in a building adjacent to the ancient gate, yet standing. "The pomp and circumstance of glorious war" was witnessed everywhere. Mingling with the crowd in the streets, less dense than that of 1851, the spectator might discern the mailed baron, with his armed retinue of bowmen and lancers, or the gay lady, wearing the embroidered jacket, not much unlike the "polka" of a more modern day, though sometimes accompanied by the long strips of linen which dangled from her elbows, or fluttered like pennons in the breeze, whilst her head was enveloped in an inflated but not ungraceful head-tire, and surmounted by a woollen cap. Ecclesiastics of high rank were then little distinguishable from the military barons; the man of peace was not to be found amidst those mounted and armed retainers. Sometimes, amidst the crowd, who were dressed in sober, and often wretched habits, might be discerned the men of some of the less strict orders, or the monk, with his bald tonsure, and often jolly form; and not unfrequently the eye might rest upon the bare head, brown coat and long rosary, of the Franciscan friar, or the solemn, black-hooded stateliness of the Dominican. The civic honors of London were then in their infancy, and were guarded by the citizens with a jealousy pertaining to semi-barbarous times, whilst the people were at all times ripe for conflict, or even for revolt. A peculiar feature of the period was, that the city was then beginning to be remarkable for its opaque and dense atmosphere, derived from the use of coals, then recently introduced. The sides of the Thames were not then, as now, crowded with houses of merchandise. Stately palaces, well fortified, stood on the Strand side of the river, among which the Savoy, the castellated residence of the Duke of Lancaster, was very conspicuous. A large Dominican friary stood in Blackfriars; another, of equal pretensions, near to the Temple, belonged to the Carmelites, and was called Whitefriars; the Franciscans had an edifice in Newgate-street, whilst a fourth, in the vicinity of what is now the Bank, was devoted to the Austins, or Augustines. The plague, which had recently desolated Europe, had been extremely fatal in London, and had caused considerable improvements in the city. But it was close, ill-ventilated, and inconvenient; and the inhabitant of Chester can well understand, from certain parts of his own city, what was its general appearance.

To this city, and, when arrived there, to one of the courts in the vicinity of Old St. Paul's, Wiclif, now an accused man, made his way. He had sought protection from the Duke of Lancaster, who, nothing loth, accompanied him on his trial, together with Earl Percy, the Marshal of England. On their arrival at St. Paul's, they met an excited crowd. The Duke of Lancaster was suspected to be hostile to the liberties of the city of London, and was extremely unpopular amongst its inhabitants, and the representations made by the hierarchy had greatly inflamed the minds of the people. Wiclif made his way with much difficulty into the presence of his judges. He found Courtenay extremely annoyed at the powerful defenders who stood at his side. When the earl marshal employed his authority to gain Wiclif a place, the following excited conversation occurred:

Bishop Courtenay. Lord Percy, if I had known what maisteries you would have kept in the church, I would have kept you out from coming hither.

Duke of Lancaster. He shall keep such maisteries here, though you say nay!

Lord Percy. Wiclif, sit down, for you have many things to answer to, and you need to repose yourself on a soft seat.

Bishop. It is unseasonable that one cited before his ordinary should sit down during his answer. He must and shall stand!

Duke of Lancaster. The Lord Percy his motion for Wiclif is but reasonable. And as for you, my lord bishop, who are grown so proud and arrogant, I will bring down the pride, not of you alone, but of all the prelatcy in England!

Bishop. Do your worst, sir!

Duke of Lancaster. Thou bearest thyself so brag upon thy parents,* which shall not be able to help thee; they shall have enough to do to help themselves.

Bishop. My confidence is not in my parents, nor in any man else, but only in God, in whom I trust; by whose assistance I will be bold to speak the truth.

Duke. Rather than I will take these words at his hands, I would pluck the bishop by the hair out of the church!

How often have great interests been jeoparded by such rash and excited advocates! John of Gaunt had little sympathy with Wiclif's opinions, as matters of truth. He regarded them only as implements of a party, and he soon after this period grew cold on Wiclif and his cause. His last words, however, though spoken in an undertone, were caught up by the by-standers, and a tumult ensued. The trial was suspended; the mob proceeded to violence.

* Courtenay's father was Duke of Devonshire, a powerful noble.

"They broke open," says Fox, "the Marshalsea, and freed all the prisoners; and, not content with this, a vast number of them went to the duke's palace, in the Savoy, where, missing his person, they plundered his house." At the same time, a clergyman, mistaken for the earl marshal, was put to death.

The protracted and vigorous reign of Edward III. was now ended, and the weak-minded Richard of Bordeaux had succeeded him on the throne. One of the earliest questions debated by parliament in this reign was, whether it was not lawful for the nation to forbid the exit of its treasure to foreign ecclesiastics. The judgment of Wiclif was appealed to, who, as a divine grounding his opinions solely on the lessons of God's Word, gave his conclusion strongly in the affirmative. In his published reply he says, "Temporal lords may lawfully and meritoriously take away the goods of fortune from a delinquent church." "In the paper subsequently published he repeats that the use of church censures, and of the authority of the magistrate, to extort from the people a revenue for the priesthood, are customs unknown to the better ages of the church, and to be numbered among the corruptions consequent on her endowment under Constantine. He even proceeds so far as to say, that a state of things might arise in which to deprive the church of her wealth would be a more Christian act than to have bestowed it upon her." *

Though the church had been baffled in its first endeavor to punish the boldness of Wiclif, it resolved to make a new attempt to exterminate these new and dangerous heresies. The pope wrote letters to the king and the higher ecclesiastics, demanding the seizure of the reformer's person, and the suppression of his tenets. The rector of Lutterworth was once more summoned. The Duke of Lancaster had now lost much of his political influence, and on this occasion Wiclif was alone.

But it was better as it was. The people, who had now extensively learned Wiclif's doctrines, constituted a surer protection.

* Vaughan's Tracts and Treatises of Wycliffe, XLVII.

The queen mother, widow of the Black Prince, sent a message to the court of Lambeth, before which Wiclif was cited, forbidding further proceedings. Muzzled thus by a power greater than their own, the baffled authors of the citation could only vent their rage in angry growls.

But the great discovery was already made. Digging amidst these ruins of a hieroglyphical system, now beginning to be obsolete, Wiclif had found the explanatory stone, the key to the whole mystery; and, after him, Luther had nothing left to do but to show its important application. Errors and truth were alike expounded by one simple principle, THE SUFFICIENCY OF SCRIPTURE. Wiclif seized the truth, and it became in his hand a thunderbolt. His blood was up, and he wrote daringly, and, for himself, dangerously. It is not for ordinary minds to conceive of the impetuosity of an ardent soul which has caught fire from a "present truth," especially if it happen to be one which has been long undiscovered. It is more than a conviction, — it is an inspiration. Colder men may censure; unbelieving ones may doubt. Prudence may summon a halt, and fear may draw back aghast. But such a man sees his goal, and opposition only stimulates the high purpose of his noble nature. Rushing onward to the conflict, Wiclif was not always careful on what or on whom he trod. But he uplifted his standard, and, fearful as have been the attacks upon it, it has never been removed. He set up the truth which the experience of centuries has but served to maintain, that, whether against popes or cardinals, against law churches or ecclesiastical organizations, the only test of truth is the Word of God.

But the mortal man failed where the spiritual one was impregnable. Bulls from Rome denounced him; a hostile and furious clamor pursued his steps, and in the midst of the irritation consequent on these combined hostilities his overtasked frame gave way. He fell ill at Oxford, where he had still continued to deliver his lectures. His sickness emboldened his old enemies, the mendicants, and they sent a deputation to his chamber, imagining that he would attribute his illness to a judicial providence, and be ready to recant. But they had mistaken their man. Wiclif listened in silence to the admonitions addressed to him; and, when they were concluded, beckoned his servants to raise him in his bed. Then, fixing his eyes on those who were around him, he said, with emphasis, "I shall not die, but live, and declare the evil deeds of the friars." It was like a voice from another world! The mendicants fled, and time soon brought to pass the sick man's prediction.

The influence of the doctrines which Wiclif promulgated was at this time extremely great. Even popish writers have confessed that more than half of the population of England were Lollards; * and Walsingham, the papal advocate of the period, declares that the Londoners were nearly all such. It must not be supposed that up to this time heretical opinions, as they were termed, had been absolutely unknown in England, though they certainly had met with remarkably little encouragement here. In matters of religious freedom, Britain had been hitherto far behind its continental neighbors. Its submission to the pope was more abject, its dread of heresy more obstructive to free inquiry. Though from this circumstance it persecuted less than others, it was not, however, entirely guiltless of human blood. In the year 1159, a band of German exiles had appeared in this country, who, though they did not claim the character of ecclesiastics, denied or ignored many of the favorite doctrines of the Church of Rome. They appear only to have made a single convert; but they were condemned to be branded in the forehead, whipped through the streets, and denied the smallest offices of life. Thus wounded, naked, desolate, they died miserably. During the reign of John, mention is also made of a company of Albigenses, who were burned alive. The doctrines of Wiclif appear to have been the first which made any considerable impression on the population. The name "Lollard" has been attributed by some to Walter Lolhard, who suffered death for his opinions in the city of Cologne. But this is altogether an

* Knighton Troysd. Script. x. col. 2664.

error. The origin of the word is the German *Lullen*, whence the English verb to lull. The term "Lollard" was thus expressive of one who praised God by sacred songs. It did not denote any particular class of opinions, but was applied generally to all those who made, or were supposed to make, professions of unusual piety. The attention received by the sick and dying, from various religious persons, at the time when the fearful plague of 1345 was desolating Europe and taking off half its inhabitants, and when the religious orders had fled in terror from its advance, had tended greatly to render the name "Lollard" popular among the people. Though not himself the originator, therefore, of this body as a sect, Wiclif's teachings had largely contributed to strengthen their opinions, and to increase their numbers.

It appears, from the first act in our parliamentary history, which was one levelled against the followers of Wiclif, and providing for their arrest, that the great reformer and his "poor priests" were accustomed, without license from their ordinary, to preach daily as they perambulated the country, in churches and church-yards, in markets and in fairs, and wherever a congregation could be assembled. Two of the names which figure in these proceedings were Dr. Hereford and Master John Ashton. The former probably aided Wiclif in his translation; the other was an active Lollard missionary, who, by simplicity of character, conversation and preaching, was distinguished among the rest. The question "why poor priests have no benefices," which is the title of one of Wiclif's tracts, is thus easily answered. They were the protestors — the dissenters of their day. One of these "poor priests" — William Thorp — is described as having principally labored in the northern counties.

Knighton observes that in the year 1382 the number of Wiclif's followers had greatly increased; and that, "starting like saplings from the root of a tree, they were multiplied, and filled every place within the compass of the land." As Knighton was an inhabitant of Leicester, thus much may, at least, be inferred, — that Wiclif's doctrines had taken a strong hold on the inhabitants of the midland counties. The sympathetic influence of similar religious sentiments is always remarkable; and persons were struck by the singular correspondence, in modes of speech and peculiarities of opinion, among these Lollards, wherever they were found. Like most sincere converts to important truths, they were eager and prompt for controversy, fervent in their appeals and their remonstrances, and inclined, on all occasions, to act aggressively on the old system. It will interest many modern readers to know that a renunciation of war was one of the principles of the Lollard creed; and that, whilst they claimed from the civil power that they should be protected in their just rights, they regarded moral suasion as the only means of establishing truth.*

On his recovery from the illness which we have just mentioned, Wiclif now set about that great work on which his fame as a reformer may most securely rest, — the translation of the Scriptures into the vernacular tongue. Before the reformer's time, portions of the Word of God had been rendered into the vulgar language, usually accompanied, however, by comments. It was Wiclif's great ambition to liberate gospel truth from the bondage of an unknown tongue, and thus to make his appeal to private judgment, — the true means of determining the accuracy of the doctrines he had so laboriously taught. A concurrence of circumstances rendered the period at which this translation was issued very remarkable. It was in a secondary, though not unimportant sense, "the fulness of the time." The good seed scattered in Europe by the Albigenses had not wholly perished; the English language was becoming fixed and definite; the influence of Rome was perceptibly on the wane; and the seat of the papacy had been removed from the Eternal city. The constitution of England had begun to develop itself in its existing form; and the love of liberty, both in action and thought, was taking firm root in the minds of the multitude. In the apprehension of Romanists, therefore, Wiclif's Bible was like a firebrand thrown amongst a mass of

* Vaughan's Wycliffe, p. 190.

combustibles. Knighton says: "In this way the gospel pearl is cast abroad and trodden under foot of swine; and that which was before precious to both clergy and laity is rendered, as it were, the common jest of both. The jewel of the church is turned into the sport of the people; and what was hitherto the principal gift of the clergy and divines is made forever common to the laity." In subsequent times it was usual, when a heretic was burned, to fasten round his neck such portions of Wiclif's translation as were found in his possession.

The excitement which followed the issuing of this edition of the Scriptures was intense. A bill was brought into parliament to suppress the whole work, under the plea that it would prove ruinous to all religion. The friends of Wiclif argued that, as the translation of the Scriptures into Latin had been followed by no less than sixty different heretical opinions, though none of those heresies had been charged on that translation, there could be no argument against the English Bible which did not hold against the Latin one. The bill for the suppression was thrown out by a large majority.

Every reader of history will remember the insurrection which, headed by Wat Tyler, menaced the royal authority in the early part of the reign of Richard II. The opportunity of calumniating the reformer was too tempting to be lost; and, though at that period other European states exhibited similar convulsions, the disaffection was eagerly traced to Wiclif and his writings. It is a penalty which every one who attacks abuses must be content to bear, that, whatever disorders or convulsions may simultaneously arise, which can be by possibility connected with his doctrines, the stigma will be fixed on himself. It is always convenient to transfer blame from the evils themselves to the individual who has exposed them. But in this connection Walsingham has himself recorded the confession of one of the leaders of the rebellion, that the destruction of the hierarchy was contemplated in that insurrection only to make way for the promotion of the mendicants. At the same time the House of Commons, in an address to the king, declared that the late riots were but the natural consequence of years of oppression and misgovernment.* It is beside our purpose to detail the attack which Wiclif next made on the doctrine of transubstantiation, in his lectures before the University of Oxford, in 1381. It may be sufficient to observe that, in the course of the quarrel, the reformer, having appealed, as before, to the Duke of Lancaster, was informed that the best advice that prince could give him was to abandon his novelties, and to submit quietly to his ecclesiastical superiors. Courtenay was now Archbishop of Canterbury. He summoned Wiclif to a convocation, at the monastery of the Grayfriars in London, to answer for his new and dangerous opinions. Wiclif declined to appear, declaring that, as a member of the University, he was not subjected to episcopal jurisdiction; but the court proceeded, in his absence, to condemn his sentiments. Whilst they were debating these points an earthquake occurred, by which the monastery was violently agitated. The bishops threw down their papers, and declared that their discussion was displeasing to God, and that they would proceed no further. Courtenay with some difficulty calmed their fears. Wiclif was accustomed jestingly to call this the "Council of the Herydene," — that is, earthquake. The resolution of the convocation was, that some of Wiclif's opinions were erroneous, and some heretical. Courtenay, upon this, preferred a bill in parliament to imprison preachers of heresy. The Lords passed it; but the Commons, jealous of the powers of the clergy, refused their concurrence. Disappointed in his act of parliament, Courtenay obtained letters patent from the king to the same effect; but this measure was vehemently opposed by the Commons, and Richard II. was compelled to yield. The archbishop, however, succeeded, after some difficulty, in obtaining the expulsion of Wiclif from the University of Oxford. The contest which was at this time going on between two rival popes, and the appointment of Spenser, Bishop of Norwich, as general of an army, in the war made by

* Hallam, vol. III., p. 93.

Pope Urban against Pope Clement, led Wiclif once more to take up his pen. Though he was now advanced in years, age had not abated the vigor of his style. He asks the pope, "How dare you make the token of Christ on the cross (which is a token of peace, mercy, and charity) a banner to lead on to slay Christian men for the love of two false priests, and to oppress Christendom worse than Christ and his apostles were oppressed by the Jews? When will the proud priest of Rome grant indulgences to mankind to live in peace and charity, as he now does to fight and slay one another?"

Roused by such remonstrances, Urban summoned him to Rome; but the citation came too late. A stroke of palsy had already fallen upon the old man, and his enemies regarded him as no longer an object of terror. His public work was done; but yet that venerable form, hoary with age, and bearing an expression of fine benevolence, was to be seen amidst the public worshippers in the parish church at Lutterworth, where he sometimes preached. But his end was near. "It was reported," one of them tells us, "that he had prepared accusations and blasphemies, which he intended, on the day he was taken ill, to have uttered in his pulpit against Thomas à Becket, the saint and martyr of the day; but by the judgment of God he was suddenly struck, and the palsy seized all his limbs; and that mouth, which was to have spoken huge things against God and his saints and holy church, was miserably drawn aside, and afforded a frightful spectacle to the beholders. His tongue was speechless, and his head shook, showing plainly that the curse of God was upon him." The fact is, that whilst he was attending divine service in the church at Lutterworth, he was seized with a fresh attack of paralysis, which, on the third day, terminated his valuable life.

Lutterworth still preserves among its relics the chair in which the proto-reformer of England is reported to have died. It now occupies a place by the communion-table of the old church. It is a venerable relic, apparently of the period to which it professes to belong. Wiclif's portrait is to be seen in his vestry. It has no merit as a work of art; but corresponds with sufficient closeness to the portraits given of him as authentic, — one of which is that in the possession of the Duke of Dorset, — and to the fine one prefixed to Vaughan's Life of the reformer. In all of them he is represented as of a manly and noble form, wearing a flowing gown, and bearing on his head a velvet cap. His face, graced by a long, white beard, exhibits mingled penetration, firmness, intelligence, and goodness. Wiclif died on the 31st of December, 1384, and his body was buried in the chancel of his own church.

WICLIF'S CHAIR.

Many of the opinions of this great reformer were illustriously in advance of his times. It would be superfluous to cite his observations on the multifarious subjects which employed his pen; but some of his opinions are so decidedly cognate to the objects of the present treatise, as to justify a few short extracts.

Respecting the sufficiency of the Word of God: — "Poor priests and true men would willingly yield obedience to God and to holy church, and also to each man on earth, inasmuch as he teacheth truly the commandments of God and things which may profit the souls of men. And no more ought any man to obey, even to Christ himself, both God and man. If any worldly prelate asketh more obedience than this, he surely is antichrist, and Lucifer's minister."

With regard to the liberty of preaching the truth: — "Almighty Lord God, most merciful, and in wisdom boundless, since thou sufferedst Peter and all apostles to have so great fear and cowardice, at the time of thy passion, that they flew all away for dread of death and for a poor woman's voice; and since, afterwards, by the comfort of the Holy Ghost thou madest them so strong that they were afraid of no man, nor of pain, nor death; help now, by gifts of the same Spirit, thy poor servants who all their life have been cowards, and make them strong and bold in thy cause, to maintain the gospel against antichrist and the tyrants of this world."

Wiclif strongly advocated the removal of spiritual men from all secular duties, and from the temptations of inordinate wealth. "By this means, the poor commons would be discharged of many heavy rents. * * * And thus, by restoring lordships to secular men, as is done by Holy Writ, and by reducing the clergy to meekness and wilful poverty and ghostly travail, as lived Christ and his apostles: sin should be destroyed in each degree of holy church, and holiness of life brought in, and secular laws strengthened, and the poor commons aided, and good government, both temporal and spiritual, come again."—"Lordly dominion is plainly forbidden by the apostles, and wilt thou venture to usurp the same? If a lord, thine apostleship is lost; if an apostle, thy lordship is no more, for certainly one or the other must be relinquished. If both are sought, both shall be lost. Or shouldst thou succeed, then judge thyself to be of that number respecting whom God so greatly complains, saying, They have reigned, but not through me; they have become princes, but I have not known them. * * This, then, is the true form and institution of the apostolic calling—lordship and rule are forbidden, ministration and service are commanded."

On courage for truth's sake:—"Let a man stand in virtue and truth, and all the world overcometh him not; for if they overcome him with these, then they overcome God and his angels, and then they should make him to be no God. Thus good men are comforted to put away fear, since be they never so few nor feeble, they believe that they may not be discomfited. Thus the words of Christ make his knights to be hardy."

His views of compulsory payments may be gained from the following passage:—"True it is that tithes were due to priests and deacons under the old law, and so bodily circumcision was then needful to all men, but it is not so now, under the law of grace.

Christ, however, was circumcised, and yet we read not where he took tithes as we do; nor do we read in all the gospels that he paid them to the high priest, or bade that any other man do so. Lord, why should our worldly clergy claim tithes, and offerings, and customs, from Christian people, more than did Christ and his apostles, and even more than men were burdened with under the law?"

Our last quotation, on the duty of avowing convictions, approaches the sublime: — "To live, and to be silent, is with me impossible; the guilt of such treason against the Lord of heaven is more to be dreaded than many deaths. Let the blow therefore fall. Enough I know of the men whom I oppose, of the times on which I am thrown, and of the mysterious providence which relates to our sinful race, to expect that the stroke will, ere long, descend. But my purpose is unalterable. I wait its coming!"

It is scarcely wonderful that a reformer who promulgated such views should be greatly distasteful to those who strongly advocate ecclesiastical establishments, or that they should speak of the merits of Wiclif as "greatly exaggerated," or of "his wild and irregular notions."* It will be gratifying, however, to many readers, to learn how an eminent man of the fourteenth century anticipated, in the darkness and gloom of so remote a period, sentiments to which the lapse of four hundred and fifty years has only added an increasing force of conviction.

Forty-three years after the death of Wiclif, the town of Lutterworth witnessed a strange and almost incredible scene. The Council of Constance, after much deliberation upon the tenets of the reformer, and after condemning forty-five of his tenets, arrived at the conclusion that the rector of that parish had lived and died an obstinate heretic. They, therefore, determined that his dead body should be treated with ignominy, and that his bones should be disinterred and thrown upon a dunghill. Thirteen years afterwards, their sentence took effect. Richard Fleming, the Bishop of Lincoln, and, as such, the diocesan of Lutterworth, sent his commis-

* Milner's Church History, III.

sary, chancellors, proctors, doctors, and their servants, to exhume Wiclif's body. The bones were burnt to ashes, and were then

LUTTERWORTH BRIDGE.
"STREAM INTO WHICH WICLIF'S BONES WERE THROWN." *

cast into the Swift, a river running close by the town. "Then the brook," says Fuller, "conveyed his ashes into Avon; Avon into Severn; Severn into the narrow seas; they into the main ocean. And thus the ashes of Wiclif are the emblem of his doctrine, which was dispersed the world over." Tradition yet marks out the spot where this poor and ineffective revenge was perpetrated.

The whole life of this celebrated reformer was devoted to the great enterprise of exposing ecclesiastical enormities, of vindicating the simplicity of gospel truth, and of resisting the inroads of ecclesiastical assumption. That such pursuits exposed him to the charge of being a sour and turbulent demagogue, — that some even of those who, like John of Gaunt, patronized him so long as he served their purpose, afterwards deserted him, and that many of his friends drew in their breath with a shudder at the boldness with which his opinions were avowed, — who can doubt? The day in which his singleness and nobility of purpose should be manifested was

* It was currently reported that miracles attended this circumstance, expressive of the displeasure of Heaven at this removal. It is not worth while to relate them in detail.

long in coming. And it can never fully come whilst any of the errors which he lived to expose survive. Yet will he appear to some "that limb of the devil, enemy of the church, deceiver of the people, idol of heretics, mirror of hypocrites, author of schisms, sower of hatred, and inventor of lies."* But, if prejudice can enact attainders, virtue and truth can reverse them; and Wiclif's name will stand an example to posterity of the moral *palingenesis* by which the apparently destroyed existence lives again from its ashes, and will supply encouragement to believe that successors may profit extensively from the very truths which now cover their propounder with ignominy and disgrace. The realms of oblivion are crowded by those who wrote or spoke in accordance only with the sentiments of their day. The renowned are mainly those who opposed the current.

The spirit of Wiclif's reformation was immensely in advance of its age. He was, indeed, to some extent, an advocate for the interference of the civil magistrate in matters of religion. But to what extent he meant this interference to reach, may be learned from the following passage:

"Let what they solicit from the magistrate be simply protection, and to meet the evils arising from the withholding of settled pastors from the established cures; and the many which must be inseparable from the appointment of improper men, let such priests as may prefer the labors of the evangelist to the more regular duties of the parochial shepherd, be allowed to act on that preference."

Wiclif's opinions on this subject are susceptible of both explanation and apology.

The history of England may be divided into two great periods, both bearing on "the constitution in church and state." The former was one in which our ancestors sought to ally the spiritual with the civil power, that they might ward off the encroachments of a secular hierarchy; — the latter, one in which dire experience caused them to retrace their steps, and to seek relief from the

* If Wiclif was occasionally somewhat coarse, Walsingham, the papal advocate, and the author of the above sentence, is more than his peer.

injuries which this ecclesiastico-political system had engendered. We shall have many occasions to refer to the latter class of opinions. At present we may mainly dwell on the former. A conviction seized the most far-seeing men, during the period of the Anglo-Norman rule, that the power of spiritual despotism, then represented by the court of Rome, "had increased, was increasing, and ought to be diminished;" and to accomplish the latter purpose was a leading object with princes or people, as the case might be, down to the time of Henry VIII. The reformation was caused by that monarch's sensual desires, only as it is the last drop which causes the cup to overflow. William I. was, it is well known, encouraged by Pope Alexander III. to undertake the conquest of the kingdom of Edward the Confessor, that by such means Rome might obtain an increased power. But that iron-willed despot, when his victory was achieved, was so far from yielding the all-submissive compliance expected of him, that not even the menaces of Hildebrand himself could exact from him the homage required by the Roman see; and he strictly forbade all relations between his subjects and the pope not sanctioned by himself. The selfishness and rapacity of his successor, Rufus, were great reductions, for the time, on the power of the clergy, who long remembered them. Under Henry the First arose the dispute respecting investitures: * Hildebrand demanded the abolition of the ceremony by the king; but whilst the monarch altered the ceremony he still retained the right of appointment, and thus substantially obtained the victory. The daring resistance of Thomas à Beckett to Henry II., who claimed the right of punishing felonious offences committed by ecclesiastics, led to the enactments of "The Constitutions of Clarendon," which, though issuing in the great and protracted troubles consequent on that archbishop's murder, drew a stricter limit around the usurpations of the papal prerogative.

* Investiture was the act by which the feudal lord placed his vassal in actual possession of his fief. In ecclesiastical preferments, it was originally effected by the sovereign delivering to the newly-appointed bishop his ring and crosier.

John attempted a still further limitation, though his shallow and reckless scheming ended only in his own debasement. Under the weak-minded Henry III., the claims prepared by the pope to appoint to vacant benefices, whilst thus trampling on the rights of patrons, caused great disaffection even among the clergy themselves, and this dissatisfaction was still further increased by the immense sums received by foreigners bearing the titles of English ecclesiastics, for services which they performed only by proxy. In this contest respecting "provisors," as they were termed, Grossteste, the Bishop of Lincoln,* eminently distinguished himself as an opponent of the pope, by his refusal to induct an Italian boy into a vacant benefice. Nor must we be unmindful of two other most signal events in British history, — the efforts made by Cardinal Langton to gain the great charter, or the contention till death of Simon de Montfort in behalf of a parliamentary representation, — both of which occurrences greatly contracted the circle of ecclesiastical sovereignty. Edward I., in defiance of the bull of Boniface VIII., and of the excommunication which it threatened against those who taxed the clergy against his authority, had recourse to the severest exactions from the ecclesiastics to support the expenses of his war against France; and, by an express act, he prohibited his clergy from sending moneys to their foreign superiors. In the following reign — in which Wiclif was born — so alive had the people become to this subject, that one of the complaints against Edward II. was that he had permitted bulls from the Roman see.

In fact, the civil power was, in those days, regarded as a harbor of refuge from the distresses consequent on hierarchical tyranny. If the convictions of our forefathers shall differ in some respects from our own, we must be content to remember that their experience was less wide and extensive than that of a later age; that learning consists greatly in un-learning; and that truths of the largest magnitude are of slow and often almost imperceptible growth. We must judge our forefathers by the light in which they lived; whilst we cannot restrain the conviction that the same

* "Terrificus Papæ redargutor," as Camden styles him.

principles, opposed to the same errors, would, under different circumstances, and conjoined with a wider experience, have landed them far beyond the point which they ultimately reached. The supremacy of God's Word, the right of private judgment, the voluntariness of true Christianity, the simplicity and energy of moral power, the self-contradiction of systems of worldly policy as means of advancing the progress of truth, — for all these doctrines were those which Wiclif maintained, — are principles which would have carried him further than he really went. The inconsistency was in the limited degree in which they were then applied; the truths are immortal and all-sufficient. We may not reduce them; we cannot exaggerate their moral power.

NOTE. — The author confesses a general obligation for the matter of the preceding chapter to Vaughan's able Life of Wycliffe.

CHAPTER II.

WRITHINGS OF THE DOWN-TRODDEN.

> "O terrible excess
> Of headstrong will! Can this be piety?" — Wordsworth.

NOTHING is proverbially more inconstant than the taste of monarchs. Of this the history of all palaces, especially the history of English palaces, affords incontestable proof. "*Varium et mutabile semper*," might be written upon each portico and pediment! Winchester, Westminster, Blackfriars, Crosby Hall, the Tower, Greenwich, Theobald's, Richmond, Hampton Court, Kensington, and others, down to Buckingham Palace, Brighton and Osborne, what "thick-coming fancies"! St. James' and Windsor alone seem permanent; yet the latter has undergone nearly as many changes as all the rest combined. If these variations afford no proof of the stability of our monarchs' tastes, they at least demonstrate that the attachment of the people to the monarchy is no fitful and uncertain thing. To appropriate structures of which the sovereign has grown weary, — though thousands, perhaps millions, of the nation's money have been profusely lavished on the magnificent decoration of them, — into hospitals for useless sinecurists, maintained at the public expense, might seem to be adding insult to injury. Yet this has been the uniform course of palace transformations! The British people are used to it. They grumble, exclaim, resist, threaten, grow furious, and — submit.

What inhabitant of the metropolis is ignorant of the pleasures of an excursion to Hampton Court? Choose a sunny day,— a small and well-assorted party,— take a return ticket by the railway, and you have within your reach as many materials for enjoyment as can be derived from fresh air, rich scenery, horticultural rarities, the wonders of ancient and modern art,— the Cartoons of Raphael included,— and abundant historical associations. You can people the scene, if you please, with the successive courts of British monarchs, from Henry VIII. down to George II.; and, should you be well versed in the history of female costume, you can vary the dress into the fashion of each age as it passes: the cap-like head attire of the court of Henry VIII.; the ruff and farthingale of Elizabeth; the thin curls of the date of Charles I.; the hood and close kerchief of the time of Cromwell; the negligent nakedness of the court of Charles II.; the ring-fence, called a hoop, of the period of Queen Anne. If your tastes be architectural, it is probable, indeed, that you will receive a smart shock as you see Wolsey's noble Tudor Gothic side by side with Grecian pillars and porticos, and you may think, somewhat emphatically, of Horace's emblem, which represents the horse's head conjoined with the fish's tail. It may possibly surprise you to learn that Sir Christopher Wren himself, no inferior man, is responsible for these incongruities. But *he,* too, could plead precedents; and Inigo Jones had marshalled the way to false taste before him. Besides, when royalty commanded, Wren had been more than once made to sacrifice — as in the re-building of St. Paul's — his own tastes and convictions. Yet, notwithstanding every apology, it must be acknowledged that Wren did not excel in alterations. With him, indeed, they were never restorations. Lincoln and Westminster Abbey cry shame; and the visitant to Hampton Court deplores the incestuous union which he there witnesses! "Most lame and impotent conclusion!" But when even "the good Homer" is allowed his occasional nod, we must be patient if Sir Christopher should sometimes betray a similar infirmity.

HAMPTON COURT.

A noble place is Hampton Court in which to study modern English history! We suggest this hint to parents, and advise them now and then to abandon the labored volumes over which their children are poring, and to give their lessons in some place like this — *vivâ voce.* The course of the projector of this pile is in itself a high moral. How industry and learning can lift a man from littleness; how sensuality, luxury and pride, can thrust him down from greatness; how insecure is the tenure of the mightiest possessions; how the pomp of the world is like the *fata morgana* — dazzling, indeed, but airy and unsubstantial; how the man who rises suddenly by ambition may fall like lightning down; how adversity often brings out of the humble all the good that was ever in them; how the possessions of the mind transcend and outlast the acquisitions of the powerful; and how a conscience-stricken death-bed is the saddest scene on this side of the infinite; — all these lessons, and many more, are suggested by the name and by the

4*

ancient palace of Cardinal Wolsey. Every court and ornament recalls some passage of his history. Imposingly went forth from under these arches the train of the last of English cardinals,— the last, at least, before Pio Nono imparted new life to a defunct title, — with its array of pursuivants, esquires, retainers, and even nobles; of cross and basin and chalice; whilst in the midst of all rode forth the reverend priest, his sumptuous array of blazing scarlet relieved only by golden stirrup and ermined fur; himself the personification of grandeur, as his mule was meant to be of humility; uniting thus the opposite emblems of godliness with worldly pride. Sad scene! sadder even in its triumphs than in its catastrophe! We turn from the bloated rich man with disgust; but when we hear the humbled poor man ejaculating, "Vain pomp and glory of the world, I hate ye!" we feel that the moralities of the tragedy are satisfied. About this spot moved, as long as he could move,— after Wolsey had resigned Hampton Court to his imperious master, — Henry VIII.; passing here through his successive phases of gayety, gallantry, extravagance, selfish hard-heartedness, imperious self-will, cruelty, wholesale oppression, bloated animalism, ulcerated death by inches! Here, by the strong will which beat down More, Wolsey, the pope, his successive wives, the great monastic establishments, and which only failed before Luther, he formed, to the extensive injury of his neighbors, and in imitation of the Anglo-Norman sovereigns, an enormous park, which was mercifully de-chased by his successor. Whatever our sympathy with Wolsey may be, who can have any with the brutal tyrant who called himself his lord?

The title of "Head of the Church" was in his case a monstrous anomaly; the Church of England was not wont to set a layman at its head. "The limits of the authority which he possessed as such were not traced, and indeed have never been traced, with precision. The laws which declared him supreme in ecclesiastical matters were drawn rudely, and in general terms. If, for the purpose of ascertaining the sense of those laws, we examine the books and lives of those who founded the English church, our perplexity will be increased. For the founders of the English church wrote and acted in an age of violent intellectual fermentation, and of constant action and reäction. They, therefore, often contradicted each other, and sometimes contradicted themselves. That the king was, under Christ, sole head of the church, was a doctrine which they all with one voice affirmed; but those words had very different signification in different mouths, and in the same mouth at different conjunctures. Sometimes an authority which would have satisfied Hildebrand was ascribed to the sovereign; then it dwindled down to an authority little more than that which had been claimed by many ancient English princes, who had been in constant communication with the Church of Rome. What Henry and his favorite counsellors meant at one time by the supremacy, was certainly nothing less than the whole power of the keys. The king was to be the pope of his kingdom, the vicar of God, the expositor of catholic verity, the channel of sacramental grace. He arrogated to himself the right of deciding dogmatically what was orthodox doctrine and what was heresy, of drawing up and imposing confessions of faith, and of giving religious instruction to his people. He proclaimed that all jurisdiction, spiritual as well as temporal, was derived from him alone, and that it was in his power to confer episcopal authority and to take it away. He actually ordered his seal to be put to commissions by which bishops were appointed, who were to exercise their functions as his deputies and during his pleasure. According to this system, as expounded by Cranmer, the king was the spiritual as well as the temporal chief of the nation. In both capacities his highness must have lieutenants. As he appointed civil officers to keep his seal, to collect his revenues, and to dispense justice in his name, so he appointed divines, of various ranks, to preach the gospel and to administer the sacraments. It was unnecessary that there should be any imposition of hands. The king — such was the opinion of Cranmer, given in the plainest words — might, in virtue of authority derived from God, make a priest; and the priest so made needed no ordination whatever. These opinions, Cranmer, in spite of the opposition of less courtly divines, followed out to every legitimate consequence. He held that his own spiritual functions, like the secular functions of the chancellor and treasurers, were at once determined by a demise of the crown. When it was objected that a power to bind and to loose, altogether distinct from temporal power, had been given by our Lord to his apostles, some theologians replied that the powers to bind and to loose had descended, not to the clergy, but to the whole body of Christian men, and ought to be exercised by the chief magistrate, as the representative of the society. When it was objected that St. Paul had spoken of certain persons whom the Holy Ghost had made overseers and shepherds of the faithful, it was answered that King Henry was the very overseer, the very shepherd, whom the Holy Ghost had appointed, and to whom the expressions of St. Paul applied." *

Like Napoleon with his iron crown, the king put the super-episcopal diadem upon his own head; and he knew well how to give effect to the motto, "*Gâre qui la touche!*" What schemes connected with his headship may have been projected and matured within these walls, who can tell? The mode by which Henry forced his clergy into the acknowledgment of this title is well known. As Wolsey had been appointed legate by bulls from the pope,—an illegal act,—the king proceeded against the ecclesiastics for the crime of acknowledging that authority, and obtained judgment against them under the statute of præmunire, which declared their possessions forfeited. Under this judgment, he extorted from them, in addition to the sum of one hundred and eighteen thousand pounds, their admission of the coveted title. This designation was afterwards confirmed by parliament, and set forth the astounding proposition, "that our sovereign lord, his heirs and successors, kings of this realm, shall have full power and authority to visit, repress, redress, reform, order, correct, restrain and amend, all such errors, heresies, abuses, contempts and enormities, whatsoever they be, which by any manner of spiritual

* Macaulay's Hist. of England, vol. I., pp. 54—56.

authority or jurisdiction ought or may be lawfully reformed, repressed, ordered, redressed, corrected or amended, most to the pleasure of Almighty God, and increase of virtue in Christ's religion, and for the conservation of peace, unity, and tranquillity of this realm, any usage, custom, foreign authority, prescription, or any other thing or things to the contrary, notwithstanding."

The execution of the maid of Kent, and of Sir Thomas More and Bishop Fisher, who sympathized with her hysterical ravings, but who were guilty of the much higher offence of denying the king's new-made authority, followed rapidly in the wake of this enactment.

Hampton Court witnessed, soon after this period, another scene forming a consequence of this new assertion of ecclesiastical authority. The snake of popish intolerance — "scotched, not killed,"— had, during the latter years of Henry's life, recovered not a little of its former influence. Disgusted with his new wife, Anne of Cleves, the king had conceived a hatred against the minister who had advised the marriage. A suspicion, too, that he was secretly opposed to the *six articles*, recently passed by parliament, had rendered Cromwell increasingly obnoxious to the papists. These articles asserted that the sacrament was the real body and blood of Christ; that the communion in one kind was sufficient; that priests should not marry; that vows of chastity were binding; that private masses were desirable, and that auricular confession was necessary. To these suspicions Cromwell fell a sacrifice. Other victims followed, and with one of these this palace is associated.

Dr. Barnes, a man of distinguished learning and piety, was prior of the Augustine monastery at Cambridge. He greatly reformed the studies of that university, and took occasion to expound in public the apostolical epistles, and to inveigh against the vices of the clergy. He had learned from Bilney the true doctrine of salvation, which he hesitated not to proclaim; and for this offence had been brought, at a previous period, before Wolsey, at Westminster. "What! Mr. Doctor," said that prelate, "had you not a sufficient scope in the Scriptures to teach the people, but that my golden shoes, my pollaxes, my pillars, my golden cushions, my crosses, did so sore offend you that you must make us *ridiculum caput* amongst the people, who that day laughed us to scorn?" Barnes replied that he had preached the truth out of the Scriptures, according to "his conscience and the old doctors." He was, however, committed to the custody of the sergeant-at-arms, and was on the Saturday following brought up before the bishops. The prospect of martyrdom so terrified the poor man that he was induced in their presence to abjure his heresies; was compelled in St. Paul's church to ask forgiveness of "God and the Catholic church, and the cardinal's grace;" and was, with others holding sentiments similar to his own, marched three times about a fire kindled at the outer gate of the church, and declared to be received once more into the body of the faithful. Yet these men were, notwithstanding, recommitted to prison. Barnes, by some means, made his escape to Antwerp, where he enjoyed the friendship of Luther, Melancthon, and other distinguished reformers. The King of Denmark sent him as his ambassador to England, where his person was respected, though Sir T. More, at that time lord chancellor, and in violation of the toleration which he had advocated in his Utopia, desired his apprehension on the old charge. When his mission was fulfilled, Barnes returned to the continent, and afterwards revisited London. Ann Boleyn protected and promoted him. Afterwards, whilst the marriage with Anne of Cleves was in progress, Henry sent him ambassador to the Duke of Cleves, and expressed his satisfaction at the manner in which Barnes had discharged that office.

But Gardiner, who, after being the friend of Wolsey, had sided with the king in the matter of the divorce, and had recently written his treatise "*De verâ obedientiâ,*" in favor of the supremacy, was now lord of the ascendant, and complained to the king of Barnes and two of his friends, Thomas Garret and William Jerome. In consequence, they were brought before Henry at Hampton Court. The particulars of the interview are not recorded. But the result was that the king, who cherished some favor for Barnes, permitted him to go home with the bishop for the purpose of private conference. The result may be anticipated. Barnes and his companions were attainted of heresy, and sentenced to be burned. Their end was worthy of the doctrines they had proclaimed. When brought to Smithfield, Barnes asked for the sheriff: "Have ye any articles against me for which I am condemned?" "No." "Is there any man else that knoweth wherefor I die, or that by my preaching hath taken any error? Let them now speak, and I will answer." He proceeded to add, "If Dr. Stephen, Bishop of Winchester, have sought or wrought this my death, either by word or deed, I pray God to forgive him as heartily, as freely, as charitably, and as sincerely, as Christ forgave them that put him to death. And if any of the council, or any other, have sought or wrought it through malice or ignorance, I pray God forgive their ignorance, and illuminate their eyes that they may see and find mercy for it."

"He then," says Fox, "begged all men to forgive him; to bear witness that he detested and abhorred all evil opinions and doctrines against the Word of God, and that he died in the faith of Jesus Christ, by whom he doubted not to be saved. With these words he desired all the spectators to pray for him, and then he prepared himself to suffer."

Garret and Jerome addressed the people in a similar manner; the latter concluding his address with the following words:

"And thus do I now yield my soul up unto Almighty God, trusting and believing that he, of his infinite mercy, according to the promise made in the blood of his Son Jesus Christ, will take it, and pardon all my sins, of which I ask him mercy, and desire you all to pray with and for me, that I may patiently suffer this pain, and die in true faith, hope and charity."

The three then took an affectionate embrace of each other, were fastened to the stake, and bore witness in their death to the faith of Christ and to the energy of protestant supremacy.*

* Fox's Acts and Monuments.

Bishop Burnet, summing up the various persecutions of this ill-starred reign, says, "So there were many brought into the bishop's courts, some for teaching their children the Lord's prayer in English, some for reading the forbidden books, some for harboring the preachers, some for speaking against pilgrimages, or the worshipping and adorning of images, some for not observing the church fasts, some for not coming to confession and the sacrament, and some for speaking against the vices of the clergy."* The catalogue is sufficiently large. Thomas Bernard and James Merton, *burned.* Pearson, Testwood and Filmer, *burned.* Adam Damlip, *burned.* Kirby and Clarke, *burned.* Anne Askew, Nicholas Belenian, John Adams, John Lacells, *burned.* Hinton, *burned.* Hugh Latimer, *imprisoned.* Thomas Bilney, *burned.* Byfield and others, *burned.* Frith, *burned.* John Lambert, *burned.* Bent and Trapnel, *burned.* Thomas Benet, *burned.* Launcelot, John and Giles German, *burned.* Style, *burned.* John Brown, *burned.*

Such were the first fruits of the English state-church! In what respects did it differ from the ecclesiastical tyranny which it had superseded?

Edward VI. was frequently a resident in the palace of Hampton Court, and his diary contains the following entry descriptive of the palace at this period:

"Monsieur le mareschal came to me at Hampton Court at nine of the clock, being met by the Duke of Somerset at the Wall End, and so conveyed first to me; when, after his master's recommendations and letters, he went to his chamber on the queen's side, all hanged with cloth of arras, and so was the hall, and all my lodging."

This is not the place in which to enter upon the ecclesiastical proceedings of this memorable reign. It may be enough to observe, that the progress of the reformation exhibited the strongest contrast to the principles which could alone have justified it. The Princess Mary might justly complain of persecution. Ana-

* Burnet's Reformation, Book III.

baptists, who are reported to have been very numerous, were proscribed, and many of them burnt in various parts of the kingdom. George Van Parre, a Dutchman, was consigned to the flames for denial of the divinity of Christ; Hooper was committed to the Fleet for not wearing, as Bishop of Gloucester, the episcopal vestments; and a commission was issued empowering Cranmer and others to correct and *punish* * those who would not conform. The reluctance of the young king to sign the sentence against Joan of Kent is well known. She was, however, burnt at the stake!

In the year 1558 Hampton Court exhibited an unusual scene of splendor and revelry, in connection with a Christmas visit of Philip and Mary. The Princess Elizabeth, who was invited to attend, seems on this occasion to have manifested no dislike to the rites of the Catholic worship. She heard matins in the queen's closet on St. Stephen's day. How many of the barbarities and horrors which desolated the land, and poured a crimson flood through its borders, were discussed and planned in this palace, is unknown. But it is obvious to remark, that, however essentially intolerant and persecuting the spirit of popery may be, it perpetrated its fierce deeds, during this reign, as during others, by means of the mechanism of an ecclesiastical establishment. And, though we do not confound the *animus* of the papal with that of any protestant system, it must still be remembered that even popery itself would be comparatively harmless but for the secular power which obeys its dictates. Had the church been, as the principles of the reformation demanded, dissevered from the state, into what comparatively small dimensions would the "acts and monuments of British martyrs" have been reduced! Papal, episcopal, puritan, — the degrees of intolerance may vary, but the fact of persecution under any state-church is invariable.

The reconciliation of England with the church of Rome was the signal for a storm of vengeance. The alliance of the queen with

* Hallam infers, from the word *puniendus*, that the penalty intended was death; but Sir J. Mackintosh urges sufficient reasons to avoid this conclusion, Hist. Eng., vol. II., p. 318.

Charles V., her marriage with Philip of Spain, the history of her mother's divorce, the movement by which Lady Jane Grey had so nearly possessed the throne, the instigations of Gardiner and Bonner, were all electric elements in the deep thunder-cloud which now hung over the ecclesiastical horizon. The queen's headship was nominally foregone; but, as the pope's supremacy was not acknowledged, it was really exercised. The old statutes for burning heretics were revived. Rogers, Hooper, Taylor, were put to death by Gardiner, to try the example of severity in terrifying the rest. On its failure, Bonner took up the work in a spirit akin to the blood-thirstiness of a famished tiger. Bradford, Ridley, Latimer and Cranmer, are the world-wide names of some who followed. "Turn or burn" became the prevailing motto! Tomkins, a weaver, whose hand Bonner held in the flame of a candle till the skin burst, and the blood flew out in the face of the bystanders; companies of martyrs consigned to a common and miscellaneous death; women in travail executed, and their just born infants committed to the flames; children pitilessly destroyed; Christian men driven in all directions into foreign countries; one martyr forbidden to say farewell to his wife and children, come out to take their final leave of him on his way to execution; another denied fire enough to put an end to the inexpressible torture of his death; horrible severities in prison, where multitudes perished by famine and wretchedness; — these, and many similar details, from the memory of which humanity shrinks appalled, testify the demoniacal spirit of this persecution. Many of the exiles formed themselves at Frankfort into a congregational church. They disputed respecting the liturgy; those who opposed it joined the Presbyterian discipline at Geneva; those who admitted it, after many debates among themselves, became the harbingers of English puritanism.

It is computed that in this reign four hundred persons were publicly executed for their religion.

Again Hampton Court experiences a change. Elizabeth has succeeded to the throne, and holds her occasional residences here.

According to the testimony of an eye-witness, the palace in this reign exhibits much of regal magnificence. The canopy is still embroidered with the name of Henry VIII.; the tapestry is superb;. one of the cabinets is called Paradise; the gardens are "most pleasant;" the chapel is "most splendid;" "in the centre of the area, which is paved with white stone," is "a fountain that throws up water, covered with a gilt crown, on the top of which is a statue of JUSTICE." The reader of history asks in vain for the counterpart of the allegory!

A protestant sovereign now stood in the place of the pope, and became the polar star of hope. The more pious among her clergy believed that she would not fail to remove some of those minor ceremonies which, while they fretted men's consciences, were by no means essential to the protestant establishment. The mitigation of the censures against uniformity in worship, the change of habits during divine service, the abolition of some minor festivals, the sign of the cross in baptism, the use of the ring in marriage, liberty not to kneel at the Lord's supper, — these, and others like them, were the points on which the early puritans sought relief. Moderns can scarcely sympathize with all these difficulties; but, because they were points of conscientious conviction, they were momentous to our forefathers; and all that they asked was, with due allowance for the opinions of others who differed from them, that these points should not be rigidly, pertinaciously and authoritatively enforced.

But the queen had all the blood of Henry VIII. in her, and was, like him, only opposed to popery because it limited her prerogative. The most careless visitant to Hampton Court, who wanders through the "Queen's Gallery" and studies the pictures of the father and daughter by Holbein, will instinctively feel how dangerous it might be to trifle with either the one or the other. Elizabeth was resolute in maintaining the Act of Uniformity; and, though even men like Walsingham, Burleigh, Sir R. Bacon, Leicester, Sir F. Knollys, and many other noblemen, knelt at her feet on behalf of the persecuted puritans, she was still inexorable.

The natural consequence was, that these people began to form separate congregations. They were immediately brought to trial, and imprisoned. But law could not stop the schism which had begun, though it severely punished all aiders and abettors, by suspension, deprivation, imprisonment, and banishment. The issue of these proceedings was, that from some counties all the most faithful ministers were exterminated, whilst the services of the church were administered by men of inferior ability or of tarnished character. Even the parliament ventured in defence of the oppressed, and two bills for the redress of these severities were introduced; but a peremptory message from the queen commanded the Commons to abandon their proceedings, to withdraw their bills, and to introduce no more measures bearing relation to religion. The condemnation of Udal, and his death in prison; the hanging, after imprisonment, of two ministers and a layman, for distributing Brownist tracts; the trial and death of Greenwood and Barrow, for adopting the same sentiments; as also of Penry, who was cruelly and disgracefully executed, demonstrate that, how glorious soever the days "of good Queen Bess" might be so far as the national character was maintained among foreign potentates, much of its domestic administration was intolerable. In the severity of her laws the queen exceeded every predecessor.

Great were the hopes entertained by the puritan party at the time of the accession of James I. Were not monarchs' opinions something like lovers' promises, we might have expected this monarch to bear some favor towards puritanism. In the Advocates' Library, Edinburgh, is still preserved a document entitled "The Confession of Faith," in reality the first Scottish Covenant, A. D. 1580; and the first name appended to it, at an imposing distance from all others, is

Twenty-three years, however, had passed since the king's signature had been affixed to that document, and James I. was not the only one, as we shall observe hereafter, who forgot his covenanted engagements. The same city preserves another instance of a similar kind, in a copy of the Solemn League and Covenant, many of the signatures of which are written in blood, whilst all are preceded by one name of celebrity, though not of consistency — MONTROSE. Not to do James injustice, we readily avow that we have not the strongest conviction of the voluntary agency granted to sovereigns and nobles on occasions of such national signature. But let that pass. Perhaps James might recollect certain passages in his early life, — the raid of Ruthven, for instance, — which struck uncomfortably on his notions of royal prerogative; whilst the puritan speech, — "It is better that bairns should greet than gray-headed men," together with the appellation of "God's silly vassal," bestowed on him by Andrew Melville, were not likely to be soon forgiven. There were, besides, many other causes at work to produce this altered issue. The instructions of Buchanan had contributed to make James a learned man; but not a fifty-Buchanan power could have made him a wise one.* James' learning, indeed, only manifested his real weakness. The man who, monarch though he was, could employ his mind in comparing tobacco to the fires of everlasting punishment, — who could send forth a production like that of "Dæmonology," and who was to be found on the bench whenever a trial took place for witchcraft in any of the courts of Scotland, and who could himself direct the application of the torture to the wretched victims, — might be capable of acquiring learning, but could scarcely be of improving it. Self-important, flippant, conceited; continually leaning on favorites who wore him as an appendage to their state; his constitutional firmness lessened by at least occasional intemperance;† dis-

* When asked why he had made James a pedant, Buchanan answered, "I was happy to be able to accomplish even that!" — *D'Israeli's Curiosities of Literature.*

† He divided his time between his standish, his bottle, and his hunting. — WELWOOD.

trusted by the Scottish religionists as hollow, though he had praised their kirk as "the sincerest kirk in the world;" * convicted repeatedly of falsehood and treachery to every holy cause; — such was the man whom the death of Queen Elizabeth promoted to the throne of Great Britain!

James had sent a remonstrance to Elizabeth, imploring her that "the puritans might be relieved of their present strait." During his progress from Scotland to London, at the rate of fifteen miles a day, he had, however, given utterance to sentiments by no means favorable to the religious party. He had said that there was more pride under the cap of Diogenes, or of a puritan, than under a king's crown. He acknowledged that he had read more papists' books than protestants'; though this reading, he declared, had only confirmed him in the protestant religion. He had avowed, moreover, that he would not admit a conference between twelve papists and twelve protestants, "because he might lose more that would not be satisfied, than he could win, although the papists' side were convicted." On his journey, he had received the petition of nearly a thousand ministers — hence called the millenary petition — praying for relief of their grievances. As an answer to this, he called a conference, to be held in Hampton Court palace, on Thursday, January 12, 1603.

The visitant to the palace who shall endeavor to ascertain the precise room in which this conference was held will be disappointed. It was probably a chamber communicating with the exquisitely adorned room which stands at the end of the great banqueting-hall, and was termed at that day "the interior privy chamber." † The courts of the palace presented, on the 14th of January, — which was the real date of the conference, — a somewhat unusual appearance. Rochets, lawn, and square caps, designated the numerous ecclesiastical party, on the one hand; whilst to encounter them, on the other, were only four plainly-attired

* Sully also mentions the distrust with which he always regarded James. — Book XIV.

† Neal calls it the drawing-room.

puritans, — men, however, of the highest standing. The king was to decide between them. Some of these divines deserve a passing comment. There was Whitgift, the primate, the strong-hold of the anti-puritan party, — a passionate and vigorous partisan, not without fits of moderation, but a restrainer of the liberty of the press, and a determined persecutor. By his side was Bancroft, Bishop of London, whose preferment was obtained by a sermon, preached at Paul's Cross, against the puritans; the dictator to the archbishop, and the manager of his ecclesiastical affairs, — a man bitter, resolute, unsparing, well described by Bishop Kennet as "a sturdy piece," who proceeded with rigor, severity, and wrath. There was also Bilson, who had written a celebrated defence of episcopacy; with others, whose names are less known to posterity. On the other side were Dr. Rainolds, reputed the most learned man of his times, the vigorous opponent of Bellarmine, the answerer of Bancroft, and the refuser, from conscientious scruples, of a bishopric, offered by Elizabeth; Dr. Sparke, the defender of puritanism against Whitgift, in public conference, at Lambeth, — a divine of great learning, and exemplary life; Dr. Chadderton, also an eminent scholar, and master of Emmanuel College, Cambridge, tutor of Bishop Bedell, and one of the translators of King James' Bible; and Mr. Knewstubs, formerly fellow of St. John's, Cambridge, but now under suspension, in consequence of his refusal to sign "Whitgift's Three Articles."

Dr. Barlow, Dean of Chester, who has given an account of these proceedings, at which he was present, with the suppressions of a partisan, tells us that, as "the deans and doctors attended my lords the bishops into the presence-chamber, there we found, sitting *upon a form*, the agents for the millenary plaintiffs." Here they were left, whilst the ecclesiastics, attended by the lords of the privy-council, were summoned to the king's chamber, and the door was shut.

Small, indeed, had been the probability, from the very terms in which this convocation was announced, that any important concessions would be made. The king's proclamation had already stated that he was "determined to preserve the ecclesiastical state in such form as he found it established by law, only to reform such abuses as he should find apparently proved." The misgivings of Whitgift, respecting the anti-episcopal influence of "the Scotch mist," were entirely superfluous!

The entrance of his majesty constituted the assembly. "He sat down in his chair, removed forward from the cloth of state a 'pretty distance.'" "His summoning the assembly together was," he said, "no novel device, but according to the example of Christian princes," instancing Henry VIII., Edward VI., and last, "the queen of famous memory." As yet he saw no cause to alter anything done by his predecessors; but thanked God — at which words he put off his hat — "for bringing him into the promised land," &c. Yet, as corruptions might creep into the best-ordered community, his purpose was to inquire into them, and cure them, if scandalous; but, if frivolous, "to cast a sop into Cerberus' mouth, that he may never bark again."

To follow the debate, if such it can be termed, through the whole of the questions, would occupy more space than would be interesting to the reader. Let it suffice to make a few extracts from the strange admixture.

The first day was principally occupied by objections taken by the king himself to various parts of the church ritual. Galloway, who was present at some subsequent parts of the conference, declares that the bishops, on their knees, entreated his majesty not to consent to any alteration, lest it should be regarded as affixing a stigma on their past treatment of the puritans. Bishop Andrewes, clerk of the closet, declares that the king did on that day wonderfully play the puritan. It is difficult to reconcile this with Barlow's statement, who, after speaking with unbounded admiration of James' "understanding, speech and judgment," attributes to him this sentence, "that, since he was the age of his son — ten years old — he ever disliked their (the puritans') opinions: as the Saviour of the world said, though he lived among them, he was not of them." But the king was a bundle of incongruities, and the divines who represented the Church of England were equally notorious for flattery of the monarch, and for misrepresentation of such portions of the conference as did not coincide with their views.*

On the second day, nearly the same party was again assembled, the king being, however, accompanied by his son, Prince Henry. After an introduction, as before, Dr. Rainolds, on the part of the puritans, opened his case. Taking exception to certain parts of the doctrine of the church, especially a portion of the sixteenth article, he was interrupted by Bancroft, who besought the king to remember the ancient canon, "that schismatics should not be heard against bishops." Bancroft proceeded to complain of the inconsistency of men who had once subscribed the articles now speaking against them; and complained that the objectors were wanting in due regard to the orders of the church, in that they came attired in Turkey gowns instead of their proper college uniforms. (It will be remembered that one prominent puritan objection arose out of ecclesiastical habiliments.) But the king ruled that Bancroft was out of order, though Rainolds had offensively trespassed in traducing the church. Among other topics, Rainolds urged the importance of a new translation of the Scriptures. Bancroft testily replied, that if every man's humor should be followed there would be no end of translation.† But the king favored the request, providing the new translation were without marginal notes, saying that he had found some of them in a Geneva translation, which taught disobedience to kings. The suppression of popish books was next urged. On which it pleased his majesty to tell Dr. Rainolds "he was a better collegeman than statesman," and that the permission of such books was by warrant, to keep up the schism between the seculars and Jesuits. Rainolds

* Barlow has certainly reported the conference in an extremely *ex parte* manner. He has suppressed all the king's objections to the Church of England. Neal tells us, on the authority of Dr. Jackson, that Barlow, on his death-bed, repented of the injustice his narrative had done to the adverse party.

† Barlow.

again desired that every parish might be provided with a learned minister. The king declared that there were more learned men already than maintenance for them; and Bancroft besought his majesty to let them rather have a praying ministry; for that there was too much of preaching, and too little of praying, already.* James, well pleased, assented to these observations.

When the Bishop of London petitioned "that pulpits might not be made pasquils, wherein every humorous or discontented fellow might traduce his superiors," the king threatened "that if he should but hear such an one in a pulpit, he would make him an example; concluding with a sage admonition to his opponents, that every man should solicit and draw his friends to make peace; and if anything were amiss in the church officers, not to make the pulpit the place of personal reproof, but to let his majesty hear of it — *yet by degrees!*"

The next point was a sore one, and related to subscription. Rainolds said that there was no objection to subscribe to the articles, and to *the king's supremacy;* but that there were other points to which serious objections were felt; among others, to the books called apocryphal. The bishops were here somewhat at a loss; till the monarch himself, with a vast display of useless and impertinent learning, came in to their rescue, concluding with the observation, as he turned to the lords, "What, trow ye, make these men so angry with Ecclesiasticus? By my soul, I think he was a bishop, or else they would never use him so."

Certain other of the puritan objections were afterwards raised *seriatim.* The day was now closing, and the patience of the king was ebbing fast. When, therefore, Rainolds proceeded to ask for "liberty of prophesying," James broke out into a flame. "I will have one doctrine, one discipline, one religion in substance and ceremony. Never speak more to that point, how far you are bound to obey!"

After other observations of the same kind, he asked if they had

* Elizabeth was accustomed to say that two or three preachers in a county were enough.

anything more to say. Upon their answering in the negative, he ended the conference, declaring, "If this be all, I shall make them conform themselves, or I will harry them out of this land, or do worse!"

The utter indecency of the king's conduct was only to be surpassed by that of the bishops. Bancroft declared "he was fully persuaded that his majesty spoke by the instinct of the Spirit of God!" Lord Cecil declared that they were much bound to God, who had given to the king an understanding heart. And the lord chancellor added, that he had never understood the conjunction of the monarch and the priest till that day.* Barlow adds that the king was "a living library and a walking study." Comment is utterly superfluous!

The third day's conference was worthy of its precursors. During a considerable period the puritans were kept waiting in the outer chamber, whilst the divines of the church were endeavoring within to satisfy the king — no difficult matter — respecting some points of his prerogative relating to the church, especially the High Commission Court and the *ex-officio* oaths.

The king said that he regarded subscription as wise and requisite. "If any, after things are well ordered, will not be quiet and show his obedience, the church is better without him, and he is worthy to be hanged. Better that one perish, than the whole body."

He then described the *ex-officio* oath, "in such a compendious but absolute order, that all the lords and the rest of the present auditors stood amazed at it." †

Whitgift: "Undoubtedly his majesty speaks by the special assistance of God's spirit."

Bancroft, on his knees: "I protest that my heart melts within me with joy that Almighty God has given us such a king, as, since Christ's time, the like hath not been."

* Barlow. Warburton observes, in his notes on Neal, "Sancho Panza never made a better speech, nor more to the purpose, during his government."

† Barlow.

This sentiment was unanimously applauded!

After the discussion of questions regarding the high commission, and plans for instituting schools and appointing ministers in Ireland and the border, the puritan ministers were called in for the last time, but it was now only to receive the royal pleasure touching the points in issue. The king announced to them the parsimonious alterations agreed on in their absence; gave them a special exhortation to unity — that is, to uniformity; — and, in answer to requests for indulgences to weak consciences, said, among other matters:

"This is just the Scottish argument; for when anything is there concluded which dislikes some humors, the only reason why they will not obey is, that it stands not with their credit to yield, having so long time been of the contrary opinion. I will none of that; and, therefore, either let them conform themselves, and that shortly, or they shall hear of it!"

And thus ended the Hampton Court Conference.

Contemporary accounts agree in their description of the insulting nature of this whole council. One of the number said that he now saw that "a puritan was a protestant frightened out of his wits." The king, writing to Scotland, says that "he had soundly peppered off the puritans;" and, moreover, "They fled me so from argument to argument, without ever answering me directly, that I was forced to tell them that, if any of them, when boys, had disputed thus in the college, the moderator would have fetched them up and applied the rod." Sir J. Harington said, "The king talked much Latin, and disputed much with Dr. Rainolds, telling the petitioners that they wanted to strip Christ again, and bade them get away with their snivelling." The puritans were evidently borne down and confounded; no one point was thoroughly debated; the prelates interposed the most unbecoming interruptions; the king was witness, advocate, judge and jury, by turns; and the whole debate, if such it could be termed, was a mockery of the ends for which it had been professedly summoned. "This great mountain," says, Heylin, too truly, "which had excited so much expectation, was delivered only of a mouse. The millenary plaintiffs have gained nothing by their fruitless travail, but the expounding of the word *absolution* by *remission of sins*, the qualifying of the rubric about private baptism, the adding of some thanksgivings at the end of the litany, and of some questions and answers at the close of the catechism." "In the accounts that we read of this meeting," says Hallam, "we are alternately struck with wonder at the indecent and partial behavior of the king. It was easy for a monarch and eighteen churchmen to claim the victory, be the merits of their dispute what they might, over four abashed and timid adversaries." Let it be also observed that these men were not selected by the puritan party, and that the four were not even agreed among themselves as to the points at issue. Well might their brethren say, "Therefore the puritan ministers offer — if his majesty will give them leave — in one week's space to deliver his majesty, in writing, a full answer to any argument or assertion propounded in that conference by any prelate; and in the mean time they do avow them to be most vain and frivolous!"

The preconcerted scheme of which this conference was only the exponent was soon made apparent by a royal proclamation, March 5, 1603. The king declared that, after listening to "the exceptions of the nonconformists, which he had found very slender," and after yielding some explanations for their "satisfaction," "he now requires and enjoins all his subjects to conform to the liturgy, as the only public form established in this realm; and admonishes them not to expect any further alterations, for that his resolutions were absolutely settled." The Book of Canons was immediately adopted by the convocation, in which it was set forth that those denying the royal supremacy, or the orthodoxy of the English church, or the congruity of the public service to the Word of God, or asserting the erroneousness of the Articles, the ceremonies of the church, or administration of its prelacy, or maintaining the legitimacy of ministers not established by law, or favoring conventicles, or holding other anabaptist errors, should be excom-

6

municated, and only restored by an archbishop after due and public recantation.

The effect of these enactments was subsequently aggravated by the publication of the "Book of Sports," which allowed, after divine service, "all lawful recreations," but prohibited all puritans and recusants from the indulgence.

Under these canons, it was computed that fifteen hundred ministers were suspended.

In relating this conference, mention has been made of the names of four ministers of reputation, though they were not actually leaders among the puritan party. This is, perhaps, the proper place to add the names of a few others, who, in or before the reign of James, were conspicuous for similar opinions. That the party was very considerable is obvious, if from nothing else, yet, at least, from the number of names attached to the "millenary petition;" that it comprehended men of the highest position, both in church and state, has been already shown. Detesting popery, because it obscured the gospel, because of its essential intolerance, and because it repressed liberty of thought and progress, it had been the design of the early puritans to substitute a spiritual religion in its stead. They were not precisely agreed how far it might be desirable to go; but all were of opinion that they might advance far beyond the point reached already, without hazard. They had therefore witnessed, with surprise and alarm, the sudden check given, by Cranmer's means, to the progress of the reformation. They exclaimed against the arbitrariness of so sudden a pause in reform, and urged upon the higher powers points in which it appeared to them that further amendment was indispensable. Could the stream have rolled onward, the muddy waters would soon have wrought themselves clear, and the reformers would have seen wherein the channel was defective. But as yet they had never recognized the alliance between the ecclesiastical and civil powers as the great instrument of their sorrow; and by admitting it they involved themselves in endless contradictions, and knotted the whip which lacerated their own flesh. The error mainly consisted in setting up the model of the Jewish polity as the law of the Christian church. Lacking a special revelation to point out who were the peculiar people, and what, to its very letter, was the belief they should hold, the notion was a mere dream, a phantom, an "airy nothing." It seemed clear to them that *they* held the truth, and should, therefore, be protected, whilst others were in error, and their opinions should be extirpated. But they forgot that there is more self-delusion in the world than absolute hypocrisy; and that the same doctrine was preached on the opposite side against them. The distinction was not only unfair, but such as it would prove impossible for any civil power to make. Protestantism destroying puritanism was to them murder; protestantism destroying anabaptism, or popery, or Arianism, was no murder at all. The only defence which can be offered for this is, that it was the error of the times. The apology will avail as well for the persecutor as the persecuted. It is not without some force as applied to men; but incorrect principles deserve no favor, and indulgence to them is high treason to truth.

Yet the position in which the puritans stood had much which rendered it unutterably galling and intolerable. Not knowing, as yet, by long experience, the anomalous influence of civil power over spiritual men, they might well wonder how those who, from their very position, ought to be seeking the same great objects as themselves, should — only because the puritans were in earnest — first forsake, and then trample them down. War between reformers and Roman Catholics they could understand; but this was more than a civil war — it was fratricidal. The wounds were the cruel infliction of a brother; the puritan thus was struck by the very hand which he prayed for. A few of the leaders of this party may be briefly distinguished.

At the foot of the old London-bridge formerly stood a church, destroyed by the great fire of London, but long since rebuilt, bearing the name of St. Magnus. Here, during two years, preached a poor and infirm old man, who had acted a conspicuous part in the great movements of his day; but now, battered and worn, had become an object of contempt to the high persecuting powers. He was called Father Coverdale. He was one of the first preachers of protestantism, when Henry VIII. renounced the authority of the pope. In conjunction with William Tindal, — afterwards burnt for heresy at Wilford, near Brussels, — he had translated and printed, for the first time, the Bible in the English language, — A. D. 1535. A second edition was published in 1537. When Cromwell procured liberty from Henry VIII. to print the English Bible, Coverdale was engaged to superintend it at Paris, where he narrowly escaped the tortures of the inquisition. Persecuted by the bishops in England, he was compelled to retire to Germany, where Lord Cromwell maintained him. Under Edward VI., he was made Bishop of Exeter, and was associated with Cranmer, Latimer and Parker, in a commission for punishing the anabaptists. During the reign of Mary, he was compelled again to retire to Germany, where, with several of his brethren, among whom Knox was included, he issued the Geneva Bible, with marginal notes. On the accession of Queen Elizabeth, he returned home, refusing to be reïnducted into his former bishopric, because of his objection to the vestments, and assisted at the consecration of Archbishop Parker, dressed in a plain black gown. Grindal, Bishop of London, gave him the living of St. Magnus; but his obnoxious principles forced him, after a brief ministry, to relinquish it under the Act of Uniformity; and, though he still preached, it was in secret and in terror. He died almost broken-hearted, and was buried in St. Bartholomew's church; great crowds, to show their respect for his useful and exemplary life, attending at his funeral. This was in the year 1568.

The University of Cambridge was not a little distinguished, at this period, for the number of those who, educated within its halls and colleges, had imbibed the new principles. That they were exposed to considerable privations we learn from a sermon preached before Henry VIII., by Thomas Lever, B. D., master of St. John's, in which he complains that ecclesiastics and courtiers had stripped the university of its aids and preferments. "A small number of poore godly dylygent students, now remaynynge only in colleges, be not able to tary, and contynue their studye in the universitye for lack of exhibition and helpe. There be dyverse ther which ryse dayly, betwixt foure and fyve of the clocke in the mornynge, and from fyve till syxe of the clocke use common prayer, wyth an exhortation of God's worde in a common chappell; and from sixe unto ten of the clocke, use ever either private study or common lectures. At tenne of the clocke, they go to dinner, where, as they be contente wyth a penye piece of biefe among foure, having a fewe porage made of the broth of the same byefe, wythe salte and otemel, and nothynge els. After this slender dinner, they be either teachinge or learnynge untyll fyve of the clocke in the evening, whereas they have a supper not much better than theyr diner. Immedyatelye after the wyche, they go eyther to reasonynge in problems, or unto some other studye, untyl it be nyne or tenne of the clocke; and there beynge wythout fyre, are fain to walke or runne up and downe halfe an houre, to gette a heate on their feete, when they go to bed."* This was, truly, "the pursuit of knowledge under difficulties;" but under such hard regimen piety flourished, and conscience asserted itself.

Special prominence is, however, due among these men to Thomas Cartwright, fellow of John's and afterwards of Trinity College, — a man of extraordinary acquisition and piety, said by Beza to be the most learned man under the sun; and the opponent against whom Hooker argued in his "Ecclesiastical Polity." So popular was he as a preacher, that when he occupied the pulpit at the University church, it was necessary to remove the glass from the windows, that the crowd without might hear his voice. When Queen Elizabeth visited Cambridge, Cartwright was selected as one of the public disputants, and received her majesty's high encomium. He was appointed Margaret Professor of Divinity, in which capacity he lectured on the Acts of the Apostles, and asserted, "with all possible caution and modesty," that the Church of England had

*Baber's MSS. Collection, vol. I., pp. 147, 148.

6*

declined from its primitive model, and ought to be purified. He was, moreover, accused of objecting to the names of archbishops and archdeacons, of desiring that each minister should be capable of preaching and be chosen by the people, of opposing the observance of Lent and the transaction of business on the Lord's day, and of objecting to the phrase "Receive the Holy Ghost," in the ordination service. Dire offences, especially at a time when reformation was supposed to be in progress! Yet, for these crimes, he was expelled the University by Whitgift, the vice-chancellor, and forbidden to preach within its jurisdiction. Whilst thus deprived, his persecutor accused him of idleness, and of living at other people's expense!! After spending five years abroad, he returned to England. At this time was published "The book of Discipline," which obtained much celebrity as an exposition of puritan principles. Its authors were Field and Wilcox, who underwent a long imprisonment because of its publication. Cartwright published a supplementary volume, which was replied to by Whitgift, and to which he rejoined with great moderation; but he was a mark to many archers, and, after much hunting, was compelled to withdraw from the country once more. He appeared again in England, and was cast into prison at the suit of Bishop Aylmer; but on this occasion — marvellous to relate! — Whitgift interposed, and set him free. At this juncture he was patronized by one who, though from motives of worldly ambition he often advocated the puritan cause, was destitute of a single virtue which could have entitled him to that honor. The Earl of Leicester gave him the mastership of his hospital, at Warwick.*

* This hospital was originally a monastery, which, despoiled at the Reformation, was conveyed, either by descent or purchase, to "Lord Robert Dudley, Earl of Leycester," who obtained its constitution as a collegiate body. It is an interesting relic of the times. The gate-posts are entwined with texts from the Bible. Each brother occupies separate apartments, with the use of a common kitchen, and is allowed eighty pounds per annum. The brethren wear the cognizance of the Earl of Leicester — a silver badge, with a bear and a ragged staff — suspended from their left sleeve. Cartwright resided in the master's lodge.

Here, accordingly, Cartwright resided; and, though unable to obtain a preaching license, was sometimes surreptitiously listened to in the neighboring church of St. Mary's.

LEICESTER'S HOSPITAL, WARWICK.

The death of Leicester immediately afterwards was the occasion for a new attack upon Cartwright; and, after many torturing cross-examinations before the Court of Star Chamber, he, together with others, was committed to prison, where, notwithstanding the interposition of James VI. of Scotland, Lord Burleigh and others, they remained two years. Cartwright never recovered the shock which damp prisons and numerous privations inflicted on his constitution.

It is certain that Whitgift entertained no small regard for his former adversary; but the queen again pursued him, and drove him, in old age, from his native land. He returned, however, to Warwick, and died in great peace and religious enjoyment, the lustre of his last days displaying the radiance of the jewel which intolerance had trampled in the dust. His death took place at the time when the writs for the Hampton Court Conference were issued, and he was interred in the hospital at Warwick.

Oxford produced at this time some men not less memorable. For a period after Elizabeth's accession, only three preachers were to be found in the university, — Dr. Humphrey, Dr. Sampson, and Mr. Kingsmill. In an address presented by them, explanatory of their reasons for wearing the "popish habits," we find the following sentence: "Because these things do not seem so to you, you are not to be condemned by us; and because they do seem so to us, we ought not to be condemned by you." To these names may be added that of Bernard Gilpin, the apostle of the north; of Walter Travers, who was member of the first Presbyterian church established at Wandsworth, part of whose library is incorporated in Zion's College, London; and of Henry Jacob, who formed the first independent church in England, and afterwards emigrated to Virginia. We have not hitherto mentioned John Robinson, justly regarded as the founder of the English Independents. He had been originally settled as a clergyman near Yarmouth, in the midst of a knot of persecuted puritans; but after citations and legal harassments, till he and his friends were almost ruined by ecclesiastical proceedings, he had taken refuge in the south of Lincolnshire, where he became the pastor of a small and persecuted flock, with whom he migrated to Holland. The narrative of the difficulties encountered by this little band is extremely interesting, and is related in the first number of the "British Quarterly Review." Robinson formed in Leyden an independent church, and there he died. He was a man of singular wisdom, piety, and ability. The archives of St. Peter's church, in Leyden, preserve a note of his burial: "1626, 10 March. — Open and hire for John Robens, English preacher, 9 florins."*

The effect of the vigorous measures taken by the prelatical party, immediately after the Hampton Court Conference, was to scatter the puritans in every direction. Hundreds of them fled to Holland, then the asylum of the persecuted. But that country was in many respects unsuitable for a permanent residence. It was at best but a lodging, and the emigrants longed for a home. They were, moreover, imperfect in the language, and they disliked the low and humid climate. Bred — most of them — to agricul-

* Cheever's Pilgrim Fathers, p. 157.

ture, they pined in the close but necessary confinement of mechanical occupations. With the natural longings of the human heart, — and who shall censure the impulse out of which the advance of mankind has grown? — they sighed for family establishment, for lineage, for a government adapted to their wants, and for a position which might enable them to become free members of society, and important workers in the business of the world. The accounts which they had recently received respecting the territories of the western continent excited and allured them, superadding to their other desires a noble missionary feeling, — an impulse to spread the gospel in the regions of Virginia, the name which the queen had affixed to the greater portion of these transatlantic domains. Long and anxious were their debates respecting this project. The timid shrunk back; the aged recommended caution; the ardent overleaped the apparent difficulties, and bounded with hope. After much prayer, the exiled church at Leyden came to the conclusion that they would bend their course to the Western World. They began negotiations with one of the Virginia companies, — at that time there were two, — and endeavored, though fruitlessly, to gain the sanction of King James. They resolved to sail for New England. It was with them no mercantile adventure; it was strictly an ecclesiastical movement, in which the whole church under Robinson's pastoral care, now amounting to three hundred members, were interested. It had been originally designed that the pastor himself, and the greater part of his flock, should remove to Virginia, and set up a new church there; but unexpected difficulties intervened, and, in the issue, Robinson, with the majority of his members, was reluctantly compelled to remain. Yet did he not the less encourage his followers in the enterprise which he might not join; whilst his holy character, his judicious discrimination, and his weighty counsel, were of unspeakable service to them in their proceedings. Two vessels were hired to convey the emigrants, under the direction of Brewster, an elder of the church: the *Speedwell* of sixty and the *Mayflower* of one hundred and eighty tons. Larger means of transport they could not obtain.

And now the *Speedwell* is anchored in Delft Haven, whilst the *Mayflower* waits in London to convey the greater part of the passengers across the Atlantic. It is a time of activity and solicitude, but yet of hope, — moistened eyes and brightening ones alternate. In preparation for their voyage, the pastor had proclaimed a fast, and called a solemn assembly; had set before them noble motives, and warned them against probable dangers. "Brethren," said the holy man of God, "we are now quickly to part from one another, and whether I may ever live to see your face on earth any more, the God of heaven only knows" — such, at this moment, was, however, his earnest hope; — "but whether the Lord has appointed that or no, I charge you before God and the blessed angels, that you follow me no further than you have seen me follow the Lord Jesus Christ." He knew their unbounded regard for him, and feared lest truth might be sacrificed to that affection. "If God reveal anything to you by any other instrument of his, be as ready to receive it as ever you were to receive any truth by my ministry; for I am verily persuaded the Lord has more truth yet to break forth out of his holy Word."* The times of primitive Christianity were almost come again, when these emigrants, attended by the mass of Robinson's congregation, by hoary men, tender women and weeping children, were accompanied from Leyden to Delft Haven, seventy-four miles. All were strangers, in a strange land; all were now especially dear to each other, because they could interpret each other's beating hearts and bleeding sympathies. In the affecting language of Bradford, "they knew that they were pilgrims, and lifted up their eyes to heaven,

* The text from which Robinson preached was Ezra 8: 21. And it is evident from its context what were the sentiments then present to his mind: "For I was ashamed to require of the king a band of soldiers, and horsemen to help us against the enemy in the way; because we had spoken unto the king, saying, The hand of our God is upon all them for good that seek him; but his power, his wrath, is against all them that forsake him."

their dearest country, and quieted their spirits. That night was spent with little sleep by the most." The next day they went on board. The parting was unspeakably sad, especially for those who were left behind; and uncertainty spread its impenetrable shadow over those about to embark. Who could tell what perils they might encounter on their passage, or what dangers might meet them on the distant strand to which the eye of their hope was looking? But faith in God, for which they had sacrificed so much, imparted a solemn grandeur to the affecting scene. Tears, sobs and mutual prayers, impressive even to the Dutch strangers, mark their final leave-taking. The pastor falls on his knees, his departing children all around him, and, with "watery cheeks," commends them, in a last most fervent supplication, to the God of the winds and the waves, and the Lord of the ends of the earth. It was a chapter in the history of time! They are gone, and Robinson's best hopes on this side the grave are gone with them. This was the 20th of July, 1620. * * * *

It was the middle of November in the same year, the commencement of a stern season, though somewhat less inclement than usual. The *Mayflower*, with its passengers, is now on the other side of the Atlantic. Perplexities and disasters have accompanied the pilgrim fathers on their way, and they are now a diminished band. Many were the delays before they could set sail from England. They had not proceeded far before the *Speedwell* was declared, truly or falsely, unfit for her passage. They returned to Dartmouth, repaired her, and again set sail. A hundred leagues of their passage were traversed, when Reynolds, master of the *Speedwell*, declared his ship in imminent danger of foundering. Again they returned, depositing "the feeble and faint-hearted" on their native shores, and the *Mayflower* pursued her voyage alone. For a time the winds were favorable; then a succession of storms invaded them. Their vessel is shattered, cracked, and during many days incapable of bearing a sail. Treachery, too, had *brought them to a part of the coast very different from the banks of the Hudson, which had been intended for their future home.*

To land upon the shore they had now reached, was to forfeit the conditions of their charter; yet, worn by perils and exhausted by privation, they regarded any land as welcome. As with prayer they had left the Old World, so with devotion and thanksgiving they planted themselves upon the New. Providence had opened for them an unexpected home. The season was bitter — the land unknown. They were feeble in body, sickly in health, unhoused, unwelcomed, unblessed, except by Him whose eye was upon them for good. They found cleared land, springs of water, and a good harbor. They formed themselves into a body politic, as loyal subjects of King James; chose John Carver for their governor, and began to take measures for their future security. They had left Europe in search of liberty, and they found it in a desert. On the 9th of December they kept their first Sabbath on shore. On the 10th they removed their goods and chattels to the spot now occupied by the flourishing wharves and mercantile riches of the modern town of Plymouth. In commemoration of this event, sacred services still mark the return of "Forefathers' Day," and the rock on which the pilgrim fathers set foot is enclosed and enshrined as an enduring monument of the ancestors of the now great North American community.

Such were some of the hardships of the days of King James, — such the firmness of noble-minded Christians, and such the manner in which Providence transformed many of their evils into blessings! Whilst we may not suppose that all, or even many of the puritans, held clear views respecting that domination of the civil power in religious matters from which their sufferings had sprung, they were rapidly advancing towards the attainment of more correct principles. We admire their fortitude, and love their memory; we must estimate their opinions by a clearer light than their own.

CHAPTER III.

CONTESTS WITH DESPOTISM.

"I know how to add, Sovereign to the King's person, but not to his power."
— P[illegible].

Few ancient cities have undergone such changes as London. The continental traveller delights to observe how quaint and abnormal structures of the olden times solicit the eye at every turn, and their recurrence gives to foreign cities no inconsiderable amount of their strangeness. In Rome, in Paris, in Brussels, in Antwerp, in Cologne, in Mayence, in Frankfort, he who penetrates into the crowded mass of houses which usually bears the name of the old town becomes surrounded by the vestiges of other days, and delights to hang historical associations on each projecting frieze, or overhanging balcony, or grotesque ornament. But London is, with few exceptions, a city of very modern growth. Much of this is doubtless attributable to the great fire, which nearly destroyed the old metropolis, in 1666; but even had this desolation never occurred, the busy enterprise, the increasing commerce, the readiness to adopt recent improvements, the love of cleanliness and care of health, which distinguished the English people, would probably have led to nearly the same results.

How few of the countless multitudes who daily press along that crowded thoroughfare, the Strand, which runs between Temple-bar and Charing-cross, think, or care to think, of the successive changes which have passed over the spots around them! Yet there was a time when that causeway had no crowd! St. Clement Danes, Somerset House, and their environs, were not always what they now are. Time was when no public carriages rattled along those streets; when no crowd hastened to share in the excitements of Exeter Hall; when no Waterloo-bridge invited architectural admiration, and when even Charing-cross presented no statue of Charles the First! In Saxon times, Westminster — the name distinguished it from the East Minster of St. Paul's — was little better than a reclaimed morass, just redeemed from insignificance by the erection of a cathedral, by Edward the Confessor. Yet even this was not the first church which stood upon the spot. An earlier one had been built between 604 and 606; and, if we give heed to tradition, St. Peter himself had set up an oratory upon the same site. During the Saxon monarchy, and under the reign of the Anglo-Normans, Westminster was the seat of royalty, and the place of the inauguration of the successive monarchs. Rufus built the hall as a banquet-room. It was afterwards rebuilt or restored by Richard II., and the monastic church, as it now exists, was added in the reign of Henry III. Henry VII. built the gorgeous edifice which bears his name, in the place of the "Ladye-chapel," which he removed. At a much later period, the western towers were erected, after the designs of Sir Christopher Wren.

In early days, Westminster was a suburban village, important from its cathedral and palace, and connected with London by a highway, which ran along the side of the river, and passed through the village of Charing. Even so lately as the reign of Elizabeth, the Strand was mainly occupied by the houses and gardens of the nobility. In the time of James I., part of it had become the favorite resort of fishmongers. These traders increased so much, that they at length became a nuisance, and were in the year 1630 dispossessed of the positions they had before occupied in the middle of the street. It may be not uninteresting to ask the reader to accompany us on an imaginary journey from Temple-bar to Westminster, during the reign of Charles I., a period which gives its date to the ensuing chapter.

Passing from the clumsy wooden building which stretched itself across the street, where now the insignificant erection of Wren, called Temple-bar, stands in commencing ruin, we notice, on the left, a building called, successively, Exeter House, as being the "inn" of the Bishops of Exeter; then Paget House, because occupied by Lord Paget; afterwards Leicester House, as having been enlarged, and in part rebuilt, by Dudley, the favorite of Elizabeth, and at this time Essex House, till lately the residence of the earl of that name, for whom the maiden queen entertained so strong an affection. The son of that great man was now residing in this building, — a building well known heretofore to Spenser, — nursing the sense of injured justice which afterwards made him an active, though not fortunate general, in the parliamentary campaigns. We next pass Arundel, afterwards Norfolk House, in which died the Countess of Nottingham, who withheld Essex's ring from Elizabeth. Afterwards comes within view Somerset House, built by the protector of that name, in the year 1549, successively inhabited by Queen Elizabeth and Ann of Denmark, the wife of James I., now by Henrietta Maria, — whom Charles, despising the omen, resolutely called Mary, — a palace the intrigues of which occupy a prominent position in the history of the times. From this house Charles had just sent away the French household, which he said "have so dallied with my patience, and so highly affronted me, as I cannot and will not longer endure it." Within this building the queen had fitted up a splendid catholic chapel, served by a host of capuchins. Here the body of King James had lain in state, and hereafter it furnished other state beds for the dead body of the Protector, and subsequently for that of Monk. We next pass the Savoy, formerly the residence of John of Gaunt, burned by the populace during the insurrection of Wat Tyler, now converted into a hospital for the poor. Beyond this is Bedford House, built by Sir Robert Cecil, but now in the possession of the family of Russell; and next to it, on the other side of the spot where Ivy-bridge once stood, the magnificent palace of the Duke of Buckingham, now recently erected, of which the fine water-gate by Inigo Jones is all which is destined to be known to posterity. Northumberland House, occupying the site of the hospital of St. Mary, — dissolved at the Reformation, — is one of the lordly structures of the last reign which was destined hereafter to be the sole survivor of a line of stately residences.

We have now arrived at Charing, where once stood a cross erected by Edward I. in memory of his deceased queen, — *Chère Reyne*, — but now a place for the pillory. In its immediate vicinity is Whitehall, which we must pause a little to describe.

A mass of buildings, courts and gardens, extending from St. James' Park to the river, in breadth, and from Scotland-yard, along the side of the Thames, nearly to Westminster-bridge, in length, formed at this time the precincts of the royal palace. Here, in the days of his grandeur, Wolsey held state, and displayed the profuse magnificence which made him popular with those of the king's subjects who fed themselves from his prodigalities; and here, it is conjectured, he built the palace then called York Place, but subsequently Whitehall, from the whiteness of its stone in comparison with the surrounding buildings. The former name, however, ceased at the period when the possessions of the cardinal passed away under the statute of *præmunire*.

> ——————— "Sir, you
> Must no more call it York Place — that is past;
> For since the cardinal fell, that title 's lost:
> 'Tis now the king's, and called Whitehall."—SHAKSPEARE.

Here Henry married Anne Boleyn, and here he died of "an inveterate ulcer in the thigh," which, says Hollinshed, "added to the irascibility of his temper," an addition which will generally be admitted to have been quite unnecessary.

Passing over the period during which Edward VI. and Mary held court here, we dwell with no small interest upon the next name, alike memorable for good and for evil, — Elizabeth. She held her court alternately at Greenwich and at Whitehall. Resolute despotism was the law of her reign. Whether she were in any great degree susceptible of the softer passions may be doubted; the only strong demonstration of such a weakness — the case of

Essex — is of somewhat doubtful authenticity, and is besides equivocal in its amount of proof. That she had no hesitation in overstepping law, when it suited her purpose, is evident from her whole history, and from nothing more than from the manner in which she acted — then fortunately — during the terror of the Spanish Armada. If religion had been a dogma held carelessly and doubtingly, — an affair of interest or an opinion of a political party, — she would have extinguished its light, when with flashing eye she trampled it in the dust. But, as an eternal verity, it was beyond her power. She, who was flattered by her courtiers for personal charms she had long ceased to possess, — if, indeed, she had ever possessed them at all, — till she believed herself a Diana, became, when her spiritual supremacy was in question, so instinct with wrath as to be almost a demon.

Rightly to understand the history of this period, let us take the reader a little further into the liberties of the ancient city of Westminster. We walk under the gloomy but majestic Gate-house, designed by Holbein, — in a style not altogether unlike the front of the present St. James', — then stretching itself across the road, and forming the southern precinct of the palace; and passing by the side of Privy Gardens, then really the private gardens which the name imported, and bestowing a thought on the pulpit erected there by Edward VI. for Latimer, we pass on to Old Palace-yard, which derived its name from having been an adjunct to the ancient residence of the English kings. Two remarkable buildings there meet our eye.

The first of them is the Star Chamber Court.

The second of them is the Gate-house.

Stow, who published his "Survay of London" in the year 1603, thus describes the Star Chamber, which during his day existed in all its dread authority:

"Then there is also the Star Chamber, where in the term-time every week, once at the least, which is commonly on Fridays and Wednesdays, and on the next day after the term endeth, the lord chancellor, and the lords, and other of the privy council and the chief justices of England, from nine of the clock till it be eleven, do sit. This place is called the Star Chamber, because the roof

COURT OF STAR CHAMBER.

thereof is decked with the likenesses of stars gilt; there be plaints heard of riots, routs, and other misdemeanors; which if they be found by the king's council, the party offender shall be censured by these persons, which speak one after the other, and he shall be both fined and commanded to prison."

It appears that so early as the reign of Edward III. this court was protested against by the commons, as interfering with the course of common law. Henry VII. revived or reconstituted it, and appointed it to try, *inter alia*, cases of unlawful assembling, together with all kinds of irregularity and disorder, not coming under the cognizance of the more ordinary courts. That it had some points of utility may be inferred from Lord Bacon's approval of its constitution. But when, in the reign of Elizabeth, it developed its full powers, it became a tremendous instrument of despotism. It possessed the power of fining, imprisoning, banishing, mutilating, inflicting corporal punishment; and as it had authority to proceed on confession, every kind of examination, not excepting that by torture, was within the range of its jurisdiction. It was, moreover, administered by judges whose appointment and removal were entirely within the power of the crown. Hume says, "I question whether any of the absolute monarchies of Europe contain at present so illegal and despotic a tribunal."

"It was also usual for the judges of assize, previously to their circuits, to repair to the Star Chamber, and there to receive from the court directions respecting the enforcement or restraint of penal statutes. Numerous instances of this unwarrantable interference with the administration of the criminal law occur, with reference to the statutes against recusants in the reigns of Elizabeth and James I."

Second only to the persecutions of Laud, of which we shall hereafter speak, were those instigated by Archbishop Whitgift, under the powers of this court.

Conjointly with the Star Chamber, Elizabeth established another court, termed "the Court of High Commission," the proceedings of which, being often not very clearly distinguishable from that of the Star Chamber, may without injury be associated with it. The authority of this court embraced offences against the canons, and it exercised a jurisdiction greatly resembling that of the inquisition in other countries. The rack, torture and imprisonment, were means it was authorized to employ. It watched over the enforcement of the oath of supremacy, writing or preaching against which was punishable, for the first offence, with forfeiture of goods, and a year's imprisonment; for the second, with the pains of *præmunire;* and for the third, with proceedings as against high treason. It was entitled to administer the oath called the *ex-officio* oath, which demanded that the prisoner should answer all questions put to him; if he did, he was convicted on his own confession, and if he did not, he was imprisoned for contempt of court. This tribunal was established in December, 1583, at the special instance of Archbishop Whitgift. It was not the first of its kind, though its powers were more extensive than those of its predecessors. It was presided over by forty-four commissioners, twelve of whom were bishops.

The Gate-house, of which mention has been made, is thus described by Stow, in his "Survay":

"The Gate-house is so called of two gates, the one out of the college court towards the north, on the east side whereof was the Bishop of London's prison for clerks convict; and the other gate adjoining to the first, but toward the west, is a gaol or prison for offenders hither committed. Walter Warfield, cellarer to the monastery, caused both these gates, with the appurtenances, to be built in the reign of Edward III."

In this prison was confined John Udal, accused of having signed "the Book of Discipline," — a treatise drawn up by Travers, and sanctioned by Cartwright, explanatory of puritan opinions. Here he was kept most strictly, being denied the use of pen, ink, paper, books, and all communication with his friends. With fetters on his legs, he was afterwards tried at Croydon on written depositions, without being allowed to confront the accusing witnesses, and so to cross-examine them, or to produce any evidence in his own exculpation; he was denied even to be heard by counsel. Though no legal evidence proved Udal to be the author of the book, he was condemned as a felon. When he heard the sentence of death pronounced upon him, his exclamation was, "God's will be done!" He died in the Marshalsea prison, worn out and broken-hearted. It is said that when James I. came to England, the first person he inquired after was Mr. Udal; and that, when informed of his end, he said, "By my soul, then, the greatest scholar in Europe is dead!"

In the same prison was confined Robert Johnson, domestic chaplain to lord keeper Bacon, for refusing subscription, baptizing without the cross, and marrying without the ring. From this prison he wrote to the bishop, his accuser: "If to imprison and famish men be the proper way to instruct the ignorant and reduce the obstinate, where is the office and work of a shepherd, to seek that which was lost and bring home that which went astray? * *

I pray you let us feel some of your charitable relief, to preserve us from death under this hard usage; especially as you have been the chief cause of my trouble, I desire you to be some part of my comfort. Let pity requite spite, and mercy recompense malice." Another petition was presented on his behalf to Whitgift, informing him that the prisoner "was sick and ready to die, unless he might enjoy more air." But the intercessions were vain,—Johnson died a prisoner in the Gate-house.

Here, too, was confined Giles Wigginton, vicar of Sedberg, in Yorkshire, where, for refusing to take the oath to furnish evidence against himself, he was treated with the utmost barbarity, being so imperfectly supplied with food, and so heavily loaded with irons, as to be nearly dead. "My old adversary, the archbishop," he complained, "hath treated me more like a Turk or a dog than a man, or a minister of Jesus Christ." This suffering divine was unjustly accused of treasonable practices against the government of his day.

The heart sickens at the recital of atrocities like these. One or two others must, however, be mentioned as having occurred within the jurisdiction of the Star Chamber, or its blood-relation, the High Commission Court:

Francis Johnson had embraced the principles of the Brownists, and whilst assembled with a congregation in Islington was apprehended, with fifty-five others. A somewhat similar apprehension had occurred at the same place in the reign of Mary. These criminals, as they were called, were dispersed among the various prisons of London. A petition presented by them to the privy council sets forth the hardships which ecclesiastical offenders at that time endured. Some, they said, were overladen with irons; many, and among them aged women and young maidens, had died; in certain cases prisoners had been beaten with cudgels, and in case of death under such treatment no inquest was held; while the houses of those suspected of puritanism were liable to be broken into and rifled at any hour of the night. Such were some of the outrages against which they petitioned. Johnson, when examined, though he refused the *ex-officio* oath, made a candid statement of his principles and practices, but expressed his wonder that he should be treated in a manner which could only make men hypocrites. The commissioner's reply is thorough-going; and, as an exponent of the whole system of ecclesiastical compulsion, is worthy of being commemorated,—"*Come to the church and obey the queen's laws; and be a dissembler, be a hypocrite, or a devil, if thou wilt!*" Johnson was consigned to perpetual banishment.

What nonconformist is not familiar with the names of John Greenwood, co-minister with the last sufferer, and Henry Barrow, a lawyer and a Brownist? Accused with others of publishing seditious writings, these men were separately brought to trial. Greenwood was examined at great length, in the hope that he would accuse himself. "The inquisitors of Rome," said Lord Burleigh of similar proceedings, "use not so many questions to trap their prey." Among other points was the following:

Whitgift. What say you of the prince's supremacy? Is her majesty supreme head of the church, in all causes, as well ecclesiastical as civil?

Greenwood. She is supreme magistrate over all persons, to punish the evil, and defend the good.

W. Is she over *all causes?*

G. No: Christ is the only head of his church, and his laws may no man alter.

W. What say you of the oath of supremacy? Do you approve of it?

G. If these ecclesiastical orders mean such as are agreeable to the Scriptures, I do. For I deny all foreign power.

W. It means the order and government, with all the laws of the church, as now established.

G. Then I will not answer to approve of it.

The result of their several examinations was, that these men were sentenced to die. They were brought to the gallows to try their firmness, and afterwards reprieved. But, at length, they were carried to Tyburn a second time, and there executed!

Nor these alone. Penry, whose Welsh blood rendered him somewhat vehement against ecclesiastical abuses, was apprehended as an enemy of the state, arrested and condemned. Whilst lying under sentence of death he addressed a most affecting letter to his fellow-Christians:

"I humbly beseech you, not in any outward regard, as I shall answer before my God, that you would take my poor and desolate widow, and my mess of fatherless and friendless orphans," — he had four, the eldest only four years old, — "with you into exile, whithersoever you go; and you shall find, I doubt not, that the blessed promises of my God, made to me and mine, will accompany them."

He was executed in an unexpected moment to himself, and in secret!

The inveteracy of Whitgift against anabaptism was especially vehement. "Anabaptism," said he, "which usually followeth the preaching of the gospel, is greatly to be feared in the Church of England." Multitudes were, therefore, persecuted; two, John Wielmaker and Hendrick Terwood, were burned at Smithfield. The latter fact is memorable, as having called forth a remonstrance to Queen Elizabeth from John Fox, the martyrologist.

The death of Elizabeth — had remorse, for her part in these barbarities, any share in embittering her last hours? — abated little of the severities practised in these terrible courts. James I. received and transmitted them as a part of the heirloom of the British monarchy. During the transactions related in the preceding chapter, the Star Chamber and the Gate-house, as well as the Clink, Newgate, the Marshalsea, overflowed with victims. The king was intent on maintaining his own saying in the *Basilicon Doron:* "That puritans were the very pest of the church and commonwealth; whom no deserts can oblige, neither oaths nor promises bind; breathing nothing but seditions and calumnies; aspiring without measure, railing without reason, and making their own imaginations the square of their consciences;" and he declared "before the great God that he should never find in any Highlander baser thieves, greater ingratitude, and more lies and vile perjuries, than among those fanatical spirits he should meet withal." Such is the testimony which Heylin, the vindicator of the high church party, quotes with approbation.*

Whilst at Westminster we cannot forget an event which in its day shook all Europe, and went deep into the hearts and memories of puritans, — the gunpowder plot. Those who know not how, in royal hunts, game is planted within the reach of royal huntsmen, that they may have the credit of superior skill, may give to James, and not to Cecil, the credit of really discovering the bloody conspiracy.† It was evident that the plot was not undertaken from any deep dislike, on the part of the catholics engaged in it, of James himself. So to believe would be too great a compliment to the monarch; and it would be at variance with his repeated declarations, and with his conduct in the matter of Spain and the Palatinate, to regard him as bearing any decided hostility to popery. In a curious volume, entitled "King James, his Apopthegmes, or Table-talk as they were by him delivered occasionally, and by the publisher — his *quondam* servant — carefully received, by B. A., Gent., London, 1643," we have several proofs of the royal sentiments on this subject. He declares that he himself would not condemn anything for heresy that had been anciently confirmed by a universal consent. He says, moreover, that if there were no quarrel between papists and protestants but the number of sacraments, he would himself be a papist; and then tells a story of two persons, a papist and a protestant, who fought together fatally to them both: and adds, "Before I would have lost my life in this quarrel, I would have divided the seven into three and a half." But, though James was in the eyes of catholic conspirators scarcely regarded as an enemy, or at all events a dangerous one, the plot stood out portentously before thinking religious men of that day, and inexpressibly deepened their detestation of and their panic at

* Heylin's Aërius Redivivus, lib. x.

† It is not certain if it belong to either. A passage in Lodge's Portraits may seem to destroy the claims of both. See Mackintosh's England, vol. IV., p. 187.

the errors of popery. They saw in Romanism a system of huge ecclesiastical domination, which claimed the homage of the body, and would fain extinguish the soul. They saw that in proportion as their own rulers advanced towards it they became insolent, imperious and persecuting, and they suspected that all this arose, as in some degree it did, from the essential nature and genius of catholicism itself. But they overlooked the fact that whenever any system of religion holds the civil sword, it becomes an oppressor, and in its measure a tyrant. Yet the crisis was certainly a fearful one, and puritans might well fear that their whole reformation was at stake.

The plot might have read men a higher lesson. It might have told them that physical force, as a means of maintaining religion, was an implement which could be wielded by enemies, as well as by friends. But men's eyes were as yet only half open, and they derived from this monstrous combination only a small fraction of the lessons it really conveyed. When, five years after, Henry IV. of France was assassinated in the streets of Paris by the Jesuits, the dire result led to a sad confirmation to the worst fears of good men; especially when James, released by that event from all protestant leagues, approximated to Romanism as closely as he could without actual contact.

In the mean time, but less vigorously after the death of Bancroft, the severities against the puritans continued. Heylin declares that if James had done his duty he might have extirpated the system altogether: a thing easier to speak of now than to execute at that time. Certainly, Bancroft, though a right man for that purpose, could not accomplish this villany; and Abbot, his semi-puritan successor, would not. Lacking the power to exterminate, which alone could have been successful, the court took to tormenting, to which it was more competent; and no inquisitor showed more alacrity for the task. Touched by a feeling of sympathy for the sufferings of the puritans, a lady of piety had bequeathed five thousand pounds to be distributed among the sufferers. The money was seized and distributed among conformists. Bartholomew Leggatt was cited for denying the divinity of Christ. The king held a conference with him till his royal patience was exhausted. Then, rising from his chair and dealing a kick to the heretic, he said, "Away, base fellow! it shall never be said that one stayeth in my presence that hath never prayed to our Saviour for seven years." He was burnt at Smithfield. Another, named Whiteman, convicted of "unheard-of opinions," was similarly executed; and a third, ordered to the fire, to which he was not brought, because of the sympathy feared from the spectators, died miserably in Newgate.

Before we leave the Star Chamber we must make room for "a sermon" preached by James in that court. He took his text from Psalm 72: 1,—"Give the king thy judgments, O God." After dividing and subdividing, and giving the literal and mystical sense of the text, he applied it to the judges and courts of judicature, telling them "that the king sitting in the throne of God, all judgments centre in him; and therefore, for inferior courts to determine difficult questions without consulting him, is to encroach upon his prerogative, and to limit his power; which it is not lawful for the tongue of a lawyer nor any subject to dispute. As it is atheism and blasphemy to dispute what God can do, so it is presumption and high contempt to dispute what kings can do or say; it is to take away that mystical reverence that belongs to them who sit in the throne of God."*

Well might some of the courtiers speak of King Elizabeth and Queen James!

But there were materials in the adjacency of the king's state which were festering already into a mortal gangrene. A proof of this was soon afforded. Roused by James' supineness in defending the protestant interests of his son-in-law, the elector palatine, and also by his desire that Prince Charles should contract a Spanish, and, therefore, catholic alliance, the commons prepared a remonstrance. His majesty threatened; they drew up another paper, which they sent to the king, then at Newmarket, by a

* Neal's Puritans.

committee of twelve. The king ordered twelve chairs to be brought, "for there were so many kings a coming." He browbeat. They resisted; and passed the spirited resolution, "that the liberties, franchises, privileges, and jurisdictions of parliament, are the ancient and undoubted birthright and inheritance of the subjects of England." The king tore the protest from the book, dissolved the houses, and committed several leading members of the commons to prison. Among these were Sir Edward Coke, Selden, and Prynne. Prince Charles learnt from his father's example, and practised the trick once too often!

The last considerable act of James' reign was the publication of "The Book of Sports." The purport of this enactment may be learned from the following extract:

"That, for his good people's recreation, his majesty's pleasure was, that they should not be disturbed, letted or discouraged, from any such harmless recreations on the Lord's-day, — such as dancing, either of men or women, archery for men, leaping or vaulting, or any such harmless recreations; nor having of May-poles, or other sports therewith, so as the same may be had in due and convenient time, without impediment or let of divine service." * * But "no recusant (papist) was to have the benefit of this declaration; nor such as were not present at the whole divine service; nor such as did not keep their own parish churches." This was designed as a blow for the puritans; but its effects reached far beyond them, and prepared the way in no inconsiderable degree for the tumults and disasters of the following reign. "The Book of Sports" was ordered to be read in churches, and refusal exposed the offender to all the penalties of the high commission. Yet, said the king, in 1620, "I mean not to compel any man's conscience: for I ever protested against it." Under this enactment, many were imprisoned, or ruined by heavy costs. Fresh gloom and terror gathered on good men's minds. But the death of James suspended operations for a moment, though only for a moment.

Of Whitehall, as it appeared a century ago, and much nearer to the time of James, the following engraving is a representation :

WHITEHALL, AS IT EXISTED IN 1746.

Nothing could be more heterogeneous and confused than the mass of buildings which, under the general name of Whitehall, met the eye at this period. They were all in great ruin, and extremely ill-assorted. The only nucleus of order was in the banqueting-house, designed by Inigo Jones, and still remaining, as a proof of the graceful conceptions and exquisite taste which that great architect could exhibit in erections of the Grecian order. The palace planned by him, of which this is the only executed portion, was of the most extensive and magnificent description, intended to look out on St. James' Park, and the banqueting-house was meant to be the ornament of its principal court. By the side of this great design most modern palaces look extremely contracted. But other things, in addition to an appropriate design, are requisite for the construction of a splendid palace ; and it so happened that in these other things — in cash, for instance — James and his successor proved dismally deficient. As it turned out, the father, in providing for that building, was only preparing his son's grave.

We have now to imagine, occupying Whitehall, the staid, sober, and generally decorous court of Charles I. Not, however, that we must suppose that nothing was heard or seen about Charles I. which would prove incongruous to our modern sense of propriety; for we are told that Charles II., when once reproved for swearing, replied, — not very gracefully, — "Oaths! why, your martyr was a greater swearer than I am." But Charles I. was haughty, ceremonious and unbending, exhibiting the not uncommon paradox of much obstinacy with little firmness, a scholar, a gentleman, — in its popular sense, — capable of warm affections and distinguished by fine tastes, but uniting with these an ungracious manner, a preposterous notion of the royal prerogative, a contempt for the people, and an overweening estimate of himself. His person was imposing, but somewhat crooked in the lower extremities; he stammered in his talk; he avowed himself no orator, but declared to his second parliament that he desired to be known by his actions — a wish which has certainly been amply fulfilled. Large sums were, in the commencement of his reign, expended on the diversions of the court. The monarch boasted that he possessed "four-and-twenty palaces, all of them elegantly and completely furnished." His collection of pictures was unrivalled.

The features of Henrietta, his queen, are good-looking, but shrewish; her countenance, distinguished by the thin curls of the period, is probably known to every reader. She was a haughty coquette, full of vivacity and fond of intrigue, proud of being the daughter of Henri Quatre, and capable of an activity to which her intellect bore no proportion.

Some of the earlier portions of this reign exhibit no little irritation of feeling between the king and his spouse.

"The king and queen, dining together in the presence, Mr. Hacket, being then to say grace, the confessor would have prevented him, but that Hacket shoved him away; whereupon the confessor went to the queen's side, and was about to say grace again, but that the king, pulling the dishes unto him, and the carvers falling to their business, hindered. When dinner was done, the confessor thought, standing by the queen, to have been before Mr. Hacket, but Mr. Hacket again got the start. The confessor, nevertheless, begins his grace as loud as Mr. Hacket, with such a confusion, that the king in great passion instantly rose from the table, and taking the queen by the hand, retired into the bed-chamber."*

Amidst the elements of Charles' reign there was one hostile force, however, on which the king had little calculated, and which he was little prepared to meet; which had acquired prodigious strength during the folly and imbecility of the last reign, and which, when tortured into madness by Charles himself, proved a Hercules by whose strength the monarchy was strangled. It was PUBLIC OPINION.

What scenes — scenes now faded from men's eyes into the obscurity of oblivion — did Whitehall witness in those days! There might be seen, immediately after Charles' accession, the new court going forth from the palace with its huge array of attendants and purveyance, to seek a refuge in the country, because the knell of the plague-bell was sounding in its ears! There, in the next year, the plague being now abated, might be witnessed the great ceremonial attending the coronation, in which the queen, from catholic scruples, refused to bear a part, — which gave rise to the prejudice that she was no queen at all, — the king, clothed in white, going by water from Whitehall, whilst Buckingham, though nominally the dependent, took the right hand of the king, and, by advice of Laud, a ceremonial was administered in which occurred some singular interpolations assertive of ecclesiastical power; whilst men might note with what singular coldness and silence the new monarch was received by his already suspicious people. There might be heard the whispers of the day respecting the feud now commencing between Charles and his parliament, —

* D'Israeli's Curiosities of Literature.

the criminations heaped on the head of Buckingham on the one hand, and the spirited defence made by the king on the other. There was witnessed the crowd of the commons, as, in obedience to the monarch's summons, they thronged to meet him at his palace, and as they received the following *dictum* at their dismissal: "Remember that parliaments are altogether in my power for their calling, sitting, or dissolution; therefore, as I find the fruits of them good or evil, they are to continue or not to be." Courtiers burn with indignation as they learn that, nothing daunted by such reprehensions, the commons complain of grievances, and in the end proceed to the impeachment of the great duke himself; and the names of Digges, Selden, Whitelock, Pym and Elliott, are handed about, in detestation or in scorn. Of these courtiers, how many afterwards moistened the earth with their blood in the king's cause! There, too, might be seen, on the day after the imprisonment of Digges and Elliott in the Tower, the king in earnest conversation with the duke in the royal bed-chamber, whilst Charles was overheard to pronounce the words: "What can I do more? I have engaged mine honor to mine uncle of Denmark, and other princes. I have in a manner lost the love of my subjects. What wouldst thou have me to do?" Was the duke urging the king to a dissolution, and was Charles' firmness beginning to give way already? At length the king rescued his favorite by dissolving the parliament.

How the king after this dissolution embarked upon his new career of forced loans; how the Gate-house and other prisons were crowded with the victims of his oppression; how the orthodox clergy sanctioned his proceedings and preached up the doctrine of divine right; how, whenever his majesty appeared in public, whether at Whitehall or in Westminster, he was greeted by the cries of "a parliament!" how, after much hesitation, Charles was compelled at length, by the strong pressure of his own necessities, to give way; how the commons, thus brought together, framed with much stormy debate the celebrated petition of right; how the king gave his assent to it; how, after parliament had been prorogued, this petition of right, though purchased with the people's subsidies, was faithlessly and shamelessly broken, and even the copy of it ordered to be printed garbled or suppressed; how Wentworth deserted to the court; how the Duke of Buckingham was suddenly and cruelly assassinated; how his murderer was executed at Tyburn, and afterwards hung in chains at Portsmouth; — such are the matters now notorious to the world, but then matters of surmise, or whisper, or doubt, of conversation, concern or horror, to the circle about Whitehall. The contest between the king and his people had begun!

Charles' prime favorite at this time was one whose name is bound up with the tragical history of his times, William Laud. He was the son of a clothier in Reading. His education was gained at Oxford, where, in some of his chapel-exercises, he had defended the side of the Church of Rome. In taking his degree of B. D., he maintained two points, — the necessity of baptism to salvation, and that there could be no true church without diocesan bishops. Such principles smoothed his way to the court, though Abbott, Archbishop of Canterbury, threw constant obstacles in his path. He became successively Prebendary of Lincoln and Archdeacon of Huntingdon. He accompanied King James in his visit to Scotland in 1617, and on his return became Prebendary of Westminster. He next became Bishop of St. David's. Laud took a large share in the correspondence relative to the marriage of Charles I. with Henrietta Maria, and, soon after the new reign had begun, delivered to the king, by royal command, a list of the clergy in the kingdom, or at least of the principal of them, distinguishing them by O. for Orthodox, and P. for Puritan, as the case might be. After holding for a short time the bishopric of Bath and Wells, he was translated to that of London. It is at this period we find him at court; in person a short, ruddy, self-satisfied-looking man; in disposition active, bustling, but not a little choleric withal; a conscientious persecutor, who transacts his greatest barbarities upon his knees; a meddling, officious person, as obstinate as rash; in short, one of that tribe apparently born to do mischief, and to take credit in doing it. This man, the right hand of Buckingham whilst that duke was living, is now highest in the king's confidence; suspected already of being the author of those speeches of Charles in which he abuses members of the commons; asserts that he does not deign to threaten them because they are not his equals; and declares his own prerogative in almost every sentence. In addition to these reasons of dislike, Laud is known to be an Arminian, and suspected of being a Romanist in disguise.

Nor were similar apprehensions frivolous. Under Henry VIII. the crown had been the dominant influence, and the church had taken life from it. But now the bishops began to declare that they did not hold the jurisdiction of their spiritual courts from the king. Religion, armed with civil power, was aiming at the pre-eminence, as in the worst days of Romish despotism. The affairs of chancery were very extensively conducted by arbitrary courts, altogether beyond the reach of law. It behoved men to be awake and in earnest. Had they not been so, all that Britons most prize would have been speedily and irretrievably lost.

Charles' third parliament was full of action. It was not noisy, but it was resolute. There was a general understanding that Laud suggested the moves which the king was making. In the midst of encounters, therefore, respecting "tonnage and poundage," the commons take up religion. The subject was promising, it was very sincerely entered upon; but it proved the fly in the pot of ointment. The course taken undid Laud, which was one object; but it also undid in the issue religion itself, which was grievous to all concerned. If parliament, according to Pym's doctrine, must settle religion, it must needs establish, at that time, presbyterian worship. Pym might not object to the conclusion, but it was Pym's boast that they were legislating for posterity; and there were those who, both now and hereafter, would dispute the legislative right. How little advance had been made in the understanding of true religious liberty by this parliament, may be learned from one of the protests voted by the commons at the time when the king attempted violently to stop their proceedings: — "Whoever shall bring in innovation in religion, or by favor seek to extend or introduce popery or Arminianism, or other opinions disagreeing from a true and orthodox church, shall be reputed a capital enemy to this kingdom and commonwealth." On the same day, the king, without summoning the commons, dissolved the parliament —1629.

Charles seemed now to have nailed his colors to the mast. He resolved to rely no more on parliaments, but to govern by his own sole authority, and believed that in this effort at despotism he would be successful. Canute might as well command the roaring waves to retire. In this expedition the king was sustained by two advisers, Strafford and Laud.

The Star Chamber and High Commission Court now asserted all their terrors. Laud republished "The Book of Sports," and suspended, deprived, expelled, without justice or mercy, those who opposed its introduction, or who resisted, or were even suspected of resisting, the royal prerogative. Let one or two scenes exhibit to the reader the tender mercies of these tribunals!

It is the 26th of November, — cold and piercing weather. A multitude is assembled at Westminster, to witness the punishment of one of Laud's victims. Surrounded by a host of constables and truculent attendants, is seen a man of fair complexion and low stature, with light hair and high forehead, between forty and fifty years of age; evidently a man of thought and mental vigor. He is mounted on a stage, probably in Palace-yard. First, with a sharp knife, one of his ears is sliced off; then, with the same instrument, one side of his nose is cut open; the attendants then bring a red-hot iron, which with hissing sound imprints on one of his cheeks the letters S. S. (sower of sedition), amidst the prisoner's yell of agony. Then, maimed, bleeding, frantic with pain, he is left amidst the murmurs and execrations of the mob, — not on him, but on his persecutors, — to stand for two hours in the severity of the weather. This done, the poor victim is tied to a post; whipped with a triple cord, whilst each stripe tears away the flesh from his lacerated back; he is denied to be carried back to his prison in a coach which had been provided for him, but instead of this is compelled, with those bleeding wounds, to go by water in an open boat! And this is only the half of his sentence. For, seven days after, he undergoes in Cheapside the cutting off of another ear, the branding with a red-hot iron of another cheek; a similar whipping; after which, he is kept in the Fleet prison for a fortnight, in an apartment exposed to the snow and cold. Such is the treatment of a scholar and a divine — of the father of the future Archbishop of Dumblane! His crime was, that, maddened by oppression and outrage, he had been guilty of denouncing his persecutors. And when this terrible sentence was pronounced upon him, Laud had taken off his hat and given God thanks! And this by way of promoting — according to Laud's views — true religion! Was it wonderful that when the petition of this sufferer, Dr. Leighton, was read to the Long Parliament, the House interrupted the reading of it with floods of tears? Or that, when by the interposition of that parliament he was set free, being then scarcely able to walk, or see, or hear, men should have execrated the author of such barbarities?

Not less memorable were the sentences passed upon Burton, Bastwick and Prynne.

The first of these men was minister of Friday-street, London. He had been clerk of the closet to Prince Henry, and after his death to Prince Charles, — with whom, after the latter came to the throne, he had remonstrated on the popery of some of its favorites, especially of Laud, whose very religion is intolerance. He had been cited, tormented, imprisoned; but all efforts had failed to subdue the spirit with which he inveighed against papistry. He had still complained, to Laud's great annoyance, of tables turned into altars, the worship of the crucifix, and the suppression of Sunday-afternoon services. He had refused to condemn himself on the *ex-officio* oath, and did not appear when cited before the High Commission Court. For these offences he had been apprehended.

The second of these victims had published reflections on the proceedings of the bishops.

The third had written against plays and players, as tending to the corruption of public morality; and because the queen, some six weeks after its publication, had performed a part in a *pastorale* at Somerset-house, he had been represented by Laud as directing his attacks against her; and in consequence he had been brought into the Star Chamber.* These three were sentenced by this court to be fined five thousand pounds each, and to have their ears cut off; and, as Prynne had already lost his ears by a sentence of the court in 1633 (his wife had them caught in her lap, and had sewn them on again), the remainder of the stumps were ordered to be cut off, and the letters S. L. (seditious libeller) branded on both cheeks. They were condemned, moreover, to suffer separate imprisonment in three of the most distant prisons; namely, Burton in Lancaster Castle, Prynne in Carnarvon, and Bastwick in Launceston. In vain did Burton's parishioners numerously petition on his behalf. The two individuals who presented the memorial were themselves imprisoned, and the sentence was executed!

When it was passed, Laud, after a speech to the judges, declaratory of the rectitude of his intentions, and the singleness of his heart, said, "I humbly give you all hearty thanks for your just and honorable censure upon these men, and your unanimous dislike of them!"

Burton came to the scaffold in the spirit of a martyr. "Shall I be ashamed," said he, "of a pillory for Christ, who was not ashamed of a cross for me?" "I never was in such a pulpit before." "The truth which I have preached I am ready to seal

* "On the restoration of Charles II., some one asked the king what must be done with Prynne to make him quiet. 'Why,' said his majesty, 'let him amuse himself with writing against the catholics, and in poring over the records of the Tower.' To enable him to do the latter, Charles made him keeper of the records of the Tower, with a salary of five hundred pounds per annum." — Wood's *Athen. Oxon*, vol. II., pp. 311—317.

with my own blood, and this is my crown both here and hereafter." So mercilessly was the sentence executed, that the temporal artery was cut, and the blood streamed in torrents, amidst the cries of an excited multitude, who treasured up the bloody rags as relics.

Prynne's ears were almost sawn off. " Cut me, tear me," said the fiery and intrepid man. " I fear thee not. I fear the fire of hell, not thee ! "

When these men were taken out of the city to be forwarded to their respective places of confinement, the concourse of spectators was very great. Burton's wife had large sums of money thrown into her coach, and Prynne, on his way to Carnarvon, stopped at Coventry, where many persons visited him, and contributed towards the furniture of his prison. At this sympathy Laud was furious. In a letter to the Earl of Strafford, he expresses the most lively indignation. Those who had aided Prynne were apprehended, fined, and compelled to make a public acknowledgment of their guilt. Prynne's portrait had been taken and copied. The painter was prosecuted, the pictures destroyed and publicly burnt. Prynne's servant was proceeded against because he had refused to give evidence against his master. Not content with this, the archbishop procured an order to be sent after the prisoners, increasing the severity of their imprisonment. No letters were allowed ; not even the wives of the two who were married were permitted to see their husbands, and they were commanded to be separated from all intercourse, except with their jailors. Burton was afterwards removed from Lancaster, contrary to his sentence, to Guernsey, where he was confined in a dungeon of the most narrow dimensions; Bastwick was transported to the Scilly Islands, and Prynne to the Isle of Jersey. There these afflicted men remained till 1640. Charles I. somewhat mitigated Prynne's sentence. But Laud, enraged, sent for Hungerford, who had obtained the relaxation, and afterwards summoned him before the council.

At the same time, a Mr. Hayden, for "venturing to preach

occasionally without being restored, was apprehended again, and sent to the Gate-house by Archbishop Laud, and from thence to Bridewell, where he was whipt, and kept to hard labor. Here he was confined in a cold, dark dungeon, during a whole winter, being chained to a post in the middle of a room, with irons on his hands and feet, having no other food but bread and water, and a pad of straw to lie upon." *

Great numbers of persons were expatriated to Holland and New England, from fear of the consequences to which their nonconformity would expose them. One of these persons — Mr. Cotton — applied to the Earl of Dorset to shield him from the anger of the archbishop, and received for reply: "If you had been guilty of drunkenness, uncleanness, or any such fault, I could have got your pardon; but the sin of puritanism and nonconformity is unpardonable, and therefore you must fly for your safety." Informers abounded in every direction; no man was safe, either in public or in private; and, to stop the tide of emigration, all persons, except for specified purposes, were forbidden to leave the kingdom without the king's license.†

These events added other items to the catalogue of crimes subsequently to be remembered by an indignant parliament.

Well might Prynne afterwards enumerate Laud's offences with indignation, and speak of his "violent acts and tyrannous proceedings," — "by war, by bloodshed, rather than fail in his designs; by cutting off ministers', lawyers', physicians', and mechanics' ears; searing their cheeks; slitting their noses; whipping them openly through the streets at carts' tails; banishing them their country; shutting them up close prisoners in remote lands, where neither their kindred, friends, wives nor children, must have any access to them, — no, nor yet once set footing in those lands to inquire how their husbands did, under pain of like imprisonment. Nor have they pen, ink or paper, once allowed to them, to write to their

* Neal, vol. II., p. 224.

† Clergymen were required to swear that they would never consent to alter the existing form of prelatical government. — NEAL, vol. II.

friends for necessaries; and by a bloody, cruel war between England and Scotland, which Bishop Pierce truly termed *Bellum Episcopale*, — 'the bishops' war.' " All this can be strictly verified by contemporaneous history. Some were prosecuted for the violation of the canon-law; some for reprehending the practice of bowing at the name of Jesus; some for declaring against popish saints' days; some for omitting the cross in baptism; one for preaching more than an hour on Sunday afternoon. Another was suspended without any exhibited charge. Pierce, the Bishop of Bath and Wells; Wren, Bishop of Norwich; the Bishop of Chester, and others, seconded the efforts of Laud, with their whole power and influence. The case became fearful. Thousands emigrated to Holland, or to New England. So distasteful was this self-expatriation to the court, that the king issued a proclamation, declaring that none should be allowed to depart without testimonials of conformity. The infection of puritanism, nevertheless, spread extensively. Every measure adopted heightened the spirit of resistance to such monstrous oppression. The materials which had been long gathering into one huge volume of combustible matter were fired, at length, by the insanity of the king; and Laud, Strafford, prelacy, lords, and the king himself, perished in the tremendous explosion.

Never was there a more memorable series of events than that which led to this dire conclusion! It was truly a momentous conflict. Every high interest, as men understood the matter then, was involved. Right, liberty, religion, — that is, religion according to the Jewish polity, which was nearly as far as that age could go, — were dependent on the issue. Men had greatly outgrown their governments. The feudal system was blown out, even to its last spark. There was a deep conviction of right, and that always makes men strong. A growing notion of a noble name, and of a self-perpetuating power, loomed before their eyes. That name and power are now embodied in the phrase, "the British people." But Charles I. little thought of this. He sought to be all that his predecessors had ever been. He dreamed not of progress. He endeavored to back the fiery steed; but that task surpassed his powers. Irritated by the opposition, he had recourse to violence. He thought that *will* could do it! Blow succeeded to blow, and goad to goad, yet without effect. Therefore, with Laud and Strafford at his side, he had recourse to greater violence. The whip was more vigorously applied, the rowel went deeper, till the noble steed rose with one furious effort, threw off, by a sudden plunge, its mad rider, and left him dead! This is but metaphorically the course pursued by "the royal martyr" towards his people. "The advocates of Charles," says Macaulay, in that brilliant article which first gave him fame, "like the advocates of other malefactors against whom overwhelming evidence is produced, generally decline all controversy about the facts, and content themselves with calling testimony to character. He had so many private virtues! And had James II. no private virtues? Was even Oliver Cromwell, his bitterest enemies themselves being judges, destitute of private virtues? And what, after all, are the virtues ascribed to Charles? A religious zeal, not more sincere than that of his son, and fully as weak and narrow-minded, and a few of the ordinary household decencies which half the tombstones in England claim for those who lie beneath them. A good father! A good husband! Ample apologies, indeed, for fifteen years of persecution, tyranny, and falsehood! We charge him with having broken his coronation oath; we are told that he kept his marriage vow! We accuse him of having given up his people to the merciless inflictions of the most hot-headed and hard-hearted of prelates; and the defence is, that he took his little son on his knee, and kissed him! We censure him for having violated the articles of the Petition of Right, after having, for good and valuable consideration, promised to observe them; and we are informed that he was accustomed to hear prayers at six o'clock in the morning! It is to such considerations as these, together with his Vandyke dress, his handsome face, and his peaked beard, that he owes, we verily believe, most of his popularity with the present generation.

CHAPTER IV.

PIONEERS OF LIBERTY.

"An honest soul is like a ship at sea,
That sleeps at anchor when the occasion 's calm,
But when it rages, and the wind blows high,
She cuts her way with skill and majesty."

HE who has never visited the Chiltern-hills is ignorant of one of the most agreeable varieties of English scenery. The ever-varying undulations of rapid hill and dale, the thick woods of beech, now hanging over the steep declivities and now distributing themselves over the rich meadows, the frequent abrupt turns which present points of scenery altogether unexpected, the pellucid springs, the steep ravines, and the richness of the long-extended vale of Aylesbury, which stretches itself out in a long channel of luxuriance, render this vicinity, though not often visited, one of special interest to every lover of nature in its undress. Not many miles distant from High Wycombe, in Buckinghamshire, and perfectly shut in amidst these lovely accompaniments, is an old ancestral mansion, connected in its history with one of the noblest biographies, that of John Hampden. The name is of itself an Englishman's inheritance. In these deep seclusions the patriot lived; here he nursed his soul for great actions; to this delicious spot his mind, jaded by public cares, often turned with fond longings; and here in death he has found, by the side of his cherished wife, a grave. What spot can furnish môre attractive materials for a passing visit?

The family of Hampden was of great antiquity, coëval with the earliest periods of authentic history. The name occurs in Domesday book, written Hādenā (Hamdenam). It is related that in the fourteenth century the family was one of the wealthiest in England. It is, moreover, told how one of the ancestors of Hampden, having quarrelled with the Black Prince in a game at tennis, struck his royal antagonist with the racquet with which he was playing. The offence was grave; the punishment was the loss of a hand. To avoid so serious a penalty, the offender gave to the prince in compensation three of his best manors, which gave occasion to the traditionary distich:

> "Tring, Wing and Ivinghoe,* did go
> For striking the Black Prince a blow;"

and the memory of the rhyme furnished a title for one of Scott's most popular productions. By the last of these villages the Northwestern railway passes, immediately before reaching the Tring station, which itself stands in one of the manors so forfeited.

The family mansion of the Hampdens is of great antiquity. It has been altered many times. One of its chambers is still called King John's bedroom; not that it preserves any appearance of so ancient a time, but that it, or some part of it, once received that monarch during a visit to the spot. On one of the hills in the immediate neighborhood has been cut a white cross, which may be seen to a great distance, and bears the name of the White Leaf Cross, supposed to have been left as a memorial of the last battle of Hengist and Horsa with the Britons, when the Saxons planted their standard upon this eminence. The house itself, though bearing some marks of a later date, is of the age of Elizabeth, who directed one of her royal progresses hither; on which occasion the mansion was almost rebuilt, and its stately and extensive avenues planted. One of these, visible from the surrounding neighborhood, still bears the name of the Queen's-gap. The edifice is not large, nor perhaps convenient; but it has suffered no very exten-

* Scott's memory failed him in the spelling.

sive alterations, and is a striking specimen, though in great dilapidation, of the architecture of the sixteenth century. The house is not seen till the traveller is just upon the spot, nor is its first view very imposing or even antique, its principal front having been repaired during the time probably of the earlier Georges, in the tamest style possible. But when it is approached on the side nearest to the little church which adjoins it, it is discovered to be a castellated mansion, adorned with grotesque and arabesque ornaments, and topped by tall and clustered chimneys, whilst noble cedars of Lebanon, of a great age, spread out their branches by its side, and trees of large dimensions throw their protecting shadows over its vicinity. One large forest tree is especially remarkable, — a huge elm, — under the shadow of which a small army might repose, — more like an Indian banyan-tree than one of the vegetable productions of these degenerate latitudes, — full of verdure and vigor, and likely enough yet to last for centuries.

The inside of the house more than redeems the promise of its outside. A large hall, now called the billiard-room, has a carved balustrade running round, and forming a gallery which at once admits to the sleeping apartments, and which heretofore accommodated the members of the family, when they assembled as spectators of mimes or pageants below. The principal entrance exhibits a groined and coved ceiling, somewhat in the style of a crypt, but bearing traces of ancient splendor. The India room is fitted up with a superfluity of arabesque ornament, and is extremely beautiful, though very ancient. The richly-carved mantel-piece, the pendent chandelier of colored glass, cut into forms of fruit and foliage, the cabinets and appendages, all belong to the days of the Virgin Queen; whilst the windows open out upon a large and extensive avenue, diminishing to a narrow point in the distance, formed in honor of that great monarch's visit. Beyond the India room is the queen's state bed-room, preserved in all the fashion of 1550, though the silk window-hangings and the coverlid of the sleeping-couch are now faded and tattered with age. The cabinet still holds the innumerable receptacles for the toilet conveniences of that day, and before it that ancient lady "tricked her beams," spread out her farthingale, and meditated, perchance, some of her many schemes of regal flirtation. The very washing-basin is preserved, and also a huge pair of carved bellows; the attendant naïvely saying, as she exhibited the latter, that she did not know whether Queen Elizabeth herself had used them or not. In the library is preserved a volume, exhibited as a great curiosity, — a family Bible belonging to the Cromwell family, in which the name of Oliver Cromwell occurs, written, our attendant assures us, by the protector himself. A moment's examination convinced us that this could not be; it was the property, evidently, of one of Oliver's uncles, a brother of the protector's father, who was, it may be remembered, brother of Hampden's mother, and the writing was a record of his children, one of whom bore the name of the protector, or rather of the protector's uncle, Sir Oliver. But as the visitor ascends the massively-balustraded staircase, a portrait of the real Oliver presents itself, exhibiting a well-made and not inelegant figure, clad in the half armor of the time; and, though not very finely painted nor well preserved, it is probably a veritable likeness. Extending along the top of the house is a large though not lofty library, its chair and tables evidently of a remote date; commanding a magnificent view of the park and of its grand avenue, and, among other interesting recollections, exhibiting a portrait of John Hampden as a child in a go-cart! Full as one is of lofty and solemn musings, as one traverses a house associated with the memory of so great a name, the unexpected occurrence is almost ludicrous, — a step from the sublime to the ridiculous! Yet "the child is father of the man;" and a careful observer could have doubtless detected, even at that age, the traits which gave to Hampden his future greatness; the kindliness, urbanity, self-sacrifice and integrity, which made so noble a man!

John Hampden was not born in the mansion of his family. Where the place actually was will, perhaps, never be discovered. Probably it was in London. Nor is the year precisely known;

probably it was 1594. His mother was a daughter of Sir Henry Cromwell, of Hinchinbrook (of which place we shall write in the next chapter), aunt, as we have said, of the great protector. She appears to have sympathized but little with the politics of her son; on the contrary, she was aspiring and ambitious. At his father's death, John Hampden was a minor. He received his education at Oxford, where he was coëval with Laud, by one of those singular juxtapositions which sometimes occur in history, reminding one of a house to be seen in Derbyshire, which transmits every shower that falls upon it into two different oceans, one east, the other west. Laud and Hampden were associated as authors of the Oxford congratulations on the marriage of the Elector Palatine with the Princess Elizabeth, — a union which afterwards called forth the bitterest hostility of the prelate, whilst in a conflict with their son Hampden received his death-blow.

The youth of the patriot was probably much spent in the hunting diversions of his native residence. He is traditionally reported to have been extremely fond of the chase, in which amusement he became an expert horseman; and the knowledge he gained of all the passes of the country proved of signal service to him in his future military career. His early life is reported by Clarendon to have been characterized by "great pleasure and license," — a stigma anxiously affixed by the royalists on those who were subsequently distinguished by puritan propensities. But he married very early a lady in every way worthy of his future character, — a daughter of Edmund Symeon, Esq., of Pyrton, in Oxfordshire. The next year he entered the House of Commons, as member from Grampound (1620).

What hopes his mother formed of the young senator, may be learned from an extant letter in the British Museum: "If ever my sonn will seek for his honor, tell him nowe to come; for heare is multitudes of lords a making — Vicount Mandvile, lo. Threasorer, &c., &c. I am ambitious of my sonn's honor, which I wish were nowe conferred upon hime, that he might not come after so many new creations." But it was not by dangling at the court of

James that Hampden "achieved greatness." He took his stand, from the first, by the side of freedom. It was then no gaining cause, and he did not live to witness its victory.

Here, amidst these woods, and in these foliaged recesses, as often as time and space during a most busy life would allow, was Hampden found. Devotedly attached to domestic life, he might seem to have full materials of the purest enjoyment placed within his reach. He was beloving and beloved; he was far beyond the reach of want; he had learned to regard religion as the food and medicine of his soul. It was about this period that his cousin Oliver Cromwell underwent that change of sentiment regarding religion, which, it is likely, awoke in his bosom sympathetic and corresponding emotions. But there was rising up before his view in England's history a future over which every dark cloud seemed to concentrate its shadow; and Hampden's mind could not rest in peace when such disturbed elements were around him. The name of Buckingham was getting famous, or rather infamous, and that of Laud was becoming notorious with it. Hampden felt that, when evil was so dominant, he too had a work to do, and that the senate was the appropriate sphere for executing it. Much of his time was spent at this period in those heavy but important studies of parliamentary papers and similar documents, without which no senator can be pronounced accomplished, or even qualified for his position. Lord Nugent tells us that there is abundant evidence of the labor bestowed at this period by the young member on questions of precedent and privilege.

Such stormy times as those of which we write demanded also much counsel and compact. Many were the conferences held at the various houses of the leading patriots. One may seem yet to see among these Hampden glades, or in those wildernesses, grouped in a mass, or distributed into earnest parties of two or three, such men as Pym and Sir John Eliot, Hampden's friends; Cromwell his cousin, Lord Manchester his neighbor, the witty Lord Warwick, the stern Lord Say, the pious Lord Brooke. What discussions have not been held in that library! what letters have not been written on those venerable tables! A house adjoining, built in a style not altogether unlike that of Hampden itself, and bearing the name of the Checquers, is reported to have been a frequent place of such meetings.

In a dressing-room of Hampden-house, distinguished by the beauty of the painted window which opens towards the ancient church, is preserved a small row or two of those "dumpy quartos" which swarmed like flies in autumn at the period of the commonwealth. The visitor turns them over with uncommon interest, and longs to be able to sit down and peruse them at his leisure. Many of them relate to the questions of royal prerogative then agitated. The part taken in this matter by Hampden forms the "stand-point" in his history.

When Charles dissolved his second parliament for impeaching the Duke of Buckingham, and for insisting on a redress of grievances, he, by advice of Laud, had recourse to forced loans for the supply of his wants. Hampden resolved to resist the arbitrary demand. It was at no slight expense that he did so. None can look round on his lovely and sequestered residence, in every respect so congenial with his literary* and domestic tastes, without feeling that, to expose himself to the risk of losing by a forward movement quiet, property, rank, liberty, peace and fame, was the highest sacrifice which patriotism could demand. But he resolutely made it. When questioned on what ground he refused to lend money to the king, his reply was, "that he could be content to lend as well as others, but feared to draw upon himself that curse in Magna Charta, which should be read twice a year against those who infringe it." The result was, that Hampden was torn away from his home, and shut up in the Gate-house, as were also Sir John Eliot and many others. After some imprisonment, the question whether he would pay was repeated, and, on his renewed refusal, he was imprisoned in Hampshire.

When Charles resolved upon calling the parliament of 1628,

* Hampden's literary attainments may be inferred from the fact that it was once in contemplation to appoint him tutor to the Prince of Wales.

Hampden was, as a matter of conciliation, set at liberty. It was not easy, however, to banish from his mind the hardships he had personally undergone, or those others with which his imprisonment in the Gate-house must necessarily have made him familiar.

Not very far from Hampden, nestling in a quiet nook of the surrounding hills, and still bearing upon its aspect the traces of considerable antiquity, stands the little pleasant town of Wendover. About the time of which we speak, this little borough had recovered, in spite of King James, its franchise, which by the reform bill it has since lost. This was the borough which Hampden represented several times in the legislature. He became a prominent man on *all* questions involving *either liberty* or *religion.* Among other subjects on which he was engaged, one was "for the better continuance of peace and unity in the church and commonwealth." Another, "on acts against scandalous and unworthy ministers;" another, "on redressing the neglect of preaching and catechising;" another, "to examine into the legality of the imprisonment of Williams, Bishop of Lincoln, by Laud;" another, "to inquire into the proceedings of the Star Chamber;" and another, "for giving increased liberty to hear the Word of God." From this it will appear that on the many questions of civil and religious liberty agitated at that period, Hampden was a most distinguished advocate of sacred franchises. No man was more deeply concerned than himself in the preparation of the "Petition of Right," the king's signature to which the parliament purchased for five subsidies. But, purchased though that celebrated petition was, it was violated even before the parliament which had passed it was dissolved. The king, in opposition to its provisions, continued to raise taxes under the name of "tonnage and poundage," without consent of parliament. The commons protested, exclaimed, grew inflamed, and the impetuous Eliot led the way against the king, who for a moment quailed before the storm. A fierce onslaught on the encouragement which had been given to Arminianism, was the signal for a vigorous attack on Laud; and the result was, that a vote was entered upon the journals that "the commons of England claimed, professed and avowed for truth, that sense of the articles of religion which were established in parliament in the thirteenth year of Queen Elizabeth, which, by the public acts of the Church of England, and by the general and current exposition of the writers of that church, had been declared unto them; and that they rejected the sense of the Jesuits, Arminians, and of all others wherein they differed from it." Simultaneously with this movement Eliot drew up a most vigorous protest, declaring that he who should attempt to bring in popery, or who should counsel the king to levy tonnage and poundage, should be reputed a capital enemy to the king and commonwealth; and that any person paying the subsidies without consent of parliament should be reputed "a betrayer of the liberty of England, and an enemy to the same." When this resolution was submitted to the house, on the last day of Sir John Eliot's senatorial career, the following scene occurred: After a powerful speech, "Eliot concluded, as if by a forecast of the future, with these memorable words,—'I protest, as I am a gentleman, if my fortune be ever again to meet in this honorable assembly, where I now leave, I will begin again.' Advancing to the speaker, Sir John Eliot then produced his remonstrance, and desired that he would read it. The speaker refused. He presented it to the clerk at the table. The clerk also refused. With fearless determination, Eliot now read the remonstrance himself, and demanded of the speaker, as a right, that he should put it to the vote. Again the speaker refused. 'He was commanded otherwise by the king.' A severe reprimand followed from Selden, and the speaker rose to quit the chair. Denzil Holles and Valentine dragged him back. Sir Thomas Edmonds, and other privy councillors, made an attempt to rescue him, but 'with a strong hand' he was held down in the chair, and Hollis swore he should sit still till it pleased them to rise. The house was now in open and violent disorder. The speaker weepingly implored them to let him go; and Sir Peter Hayman, in reply, renounced him for his kinsman, as the disgrace of his country, the blot of a noble family, and a man whom posterity would remember with scorn and disdain. Every moment increased the disorder, till at last it threatened the most serious consequences. Some members involuntarily placed their hands upon their swords. Above the throng was again heard the voice of the steady and undaunted Eliot: 'I shall then express by my tongue what that paper should have done.' He flung it down upon the floor, and placed the protestations in the hands of Hollis. 'It *shall* be declared by us,' he exclaimed, 'that all that we suffer is the effect of new counsels, to the ruin of the government of the state. Let us make a protestation against those men, whether greater or subordinate, that may hereafter persuade the king to take tonnage and poundage without grant of parliament. We declare them capital enemies to the king and the kingdom! If any merchants shall willingly pay those duties, without consent of parliament, they are declared accessaries to the rest!' Hollis instantly read Eliot's paper, put it to the house in the character of speaker, and was answered by tremendous acclamations. During this, the king had sent the serjeant, to bring away the mace; but he could not obtain admission, and the usher of the black rod had followed with the same ill success. In an extremity of rage, Charles then sent for the captain of his guard to force an entrance. But a later and yet more disastrous day was reserved for that outrage; for, meanwhile, Eliot's resolutions having been passed, the doors were thrown open, and the members rushed out in a body, carrying a king's officer that was standing at the entrance 'away before them in the crowd.' Such was the scene of Monday, the 2nd of March, 1629, 'the most gloomy and portentous day for England that had happened for five hundred years.' The king instantly went down to the House of Lords, called the leaders of the commons 'vipers,' who should have their rewards, and dissolved the parliament."*

Several of the leading patriots were imprisoned, amongst whom was Eliot, who died before he recovered his liberty.

Hampden was now again at his country seat; but his heart was

* Forster's Life of Sir J. Eliot.

with his captive friend, with whom he kept up a regular correspondence, and whose sons were intrusted to Hampden's charge. The following letter, which has been exhibited this year (1851) in the British Museum, will afford a beautiful illustration of the nature of this correspondence:

"NOBLE SIR: 'T is well for me that letters cannot blush, else you would easily read me guilty. I am ashamed of so long a silence, and know not how to excuse it; for as nothing but businesse can speake for mee, of wch kind I have many advocates, so can I not tell how to call any businesse greater than holding an affectionate correspondence with so excellent a friend. My only confidence is, I pleade at a barr of love, where absolutions are much more frequent than censures. Sure I am that conscience of neglect doth not accuse me; though evidence of fact doth. I would add more, but ye entertainment of a stranger friend calls upon me, and one other inevitable occasion; hold mee excused, therefore, deare friend; and if you vouchsafe mee a letter, lett mee beg of you to teach mee some thrift of time; that I may imploy more in your service, who will ever be

"Your faithful servant and affectionate friend,

"JO. HAMPDEN.

"Commend my service to ye soldier, if not gone to his colors.*

"*Hampden, March* 21."

About this time an event occurred which doubtless modified to a considerable extent the subsequent career of this admirable man. We have seen how open his whole nature was to the delights of domestic privacy; and it seems almost directly providential, that at the moment when his country demanded him, the closest of all those ties which interfered with that paramount claim was suddenly dissolved. When Hampden was already beginning to admit the thought of the terrible national crisis which was approaching, and was intent on the study of Davila's "History of the Civil Wars

* One of Eliot's sons, then on a visit to his father in the Tower.

of France," his beloved wife sickened and died. The depth and fervor of Hampden's affection for her may be conjectured from the annexed epitaph, placed by her desolate husband in the church which immediately adjoins his mansion.

To the eternal memory
OF THE TRUELY
VERTUOUS AND PIOUS
ELIZABETH HAMPDEN WIFE OF JOHN
HAMPDEN OF GREAT HAMPDEN ESQUIER
SOLE DAUGHTER & HEIRE OF EDMUND
SYMEON OF PYRTON IN THE COUNTY OF
OXON ESQ. THE TENDER MOTHER
OF A HAPPY OFSPRING IN 9
HOPEFUL CHILDREN
In her pilgrimage
THE STAIE & COMFORT OF HER NEIGHBOURS
THE JOIE & GLORY OF A WELL ORDERED FAMILY
THE DELIGHT & HAPPINESS OF TENDER PARENTS
BUT A CROWNE OF BLESSINGS TO A HUSBAND
In a Wife
TO ALL AN ETERNALL PATERNE OF GOODNES
AND CAUSE OF JOIE WHILE SHE WAS.
In her Dissolution
A LOSSE UNVALUABLE TO EACH YET HERSELFE
BLEST AND THEY FULLY RECUMPENED IN HER
TRANSLATION FROM A TABERNACLE OF CLAYE
AND FELLOWSHIP W[TH] MORTALS TO A CELESTIALL
MANSION & COMMUNION W[TH] A DEITY THE
20th day of August 1634.
JOHN HAMPDEN HER SORROWFUL
HUSBAND IN PERPETUALL TESTIMONY
OF HIS CONIUGALL LOVE HATH
DEDICATED THIS
Monument.

Those only who have experienced the loss of so dear a relative can understand the sensations with which this generous and ardent spirit would retire from the church in which he had just deposited the remains of her he had loved so well. How sad and solitary was now that widowed heart! How often would he visit the spot become so sacred, or trace the memory of his cherished companion in the scenes and seclusions they had so often visited together!

Nothing can be more beautiful than is the position of the little ecclesiastical structure which holds the remains cf Hampden's wife. It stands in the midst of the park, within a very few steps of the mansion, and is overhung by beech-trees of the largest size. Its interior is mainly such as it must have been in the time of Hampden himself. Its carved oaken pews have a massiveness extremely unlike the present style of church erection. Beneath its chancel many of Hampden's ancestors lie; and the foot of the visitor, as he paces the aisle, treads upon the monumental brasses which mark their last resting-place. Hampden's monument to his wife is a simple slab of Derbyshire marble, originally without decoration of any kind, though modern hands have attempted to add some slight adornments; in bad taste, however; for it seems as if he who placed it there had disdained the artificial, and had been anxious for no paraded display of his real grief. Within that pew, — now renovated and curtained round, — his manly countenance clouded by inexpressible grief, would sit Hampden, surrounded by his tenantry, to hear from some puritan minister of the day the lessons read to the living by voiceless death; he, perhaps, taking a review of the excellences of the departed lady, and offering to the afflicted husband such consolations as evangelical religion offers to the mourner. Nine years after, the husband was himself laid by the side of his lamented companion!

But sterner duties now awaited the patriot. In 1635 Charles issued his writs of ship-money; * and, amongst other places, they

* Clarendon tells us that the king had gained two hundred thousand pounds in ten years by the ship-money project. But only a fraction of that sum found its way to the royal exchequer.

reached the parish of Great Kimble, at the base of the Chiltern Hills, not far from Great Hampden, and on the estate which belonged to Hampden's ancestral residence. Instead of payment, the constables and assessors returned a protest; and foremost among the names is that of John Hampden, who was amerced in the sum of twenty shillings, — "as a passport," says Lord Nugent, "for the rest to an honorable memory so long as the love of liberty shall retain a place in the hearts of the British nation."

The well-known case was brought before the courts of law with much preparation on both sides; and, after a display of the highest style of legal pleading by St. John, till then almost unknown, the judges pronounced in favor of ship-money, by a majority of seven out of twelve. The victory was, however, in fact, a defeat; and though the king's messengers continued to levy the hateful tax, they enforced it upon a people now thoroughly aroused and indignant. Clarendon tells us that "the judgment proved of more advantage and credit to the gentlemen condemned than to the king's service." It was a grand era in the history of a great nation's liberties!

Hampden, soon after this period, was returned, for the county of Buckingham, to Charles' next parliament, and left the Chiltern Hills, as a residence, forever. They had probably become distasteful to him since the death of his wife; and the large amount of public business now pressing on his attention rendered a residence in town indispensable. He took lodgings in Gray's Inn-lane, and afterwards in Old Palace-yard, Westminster, near to Pym, now the leader — though Hampden was scarcely second — of the liberal party in the House of Commons. What kind of a speaker he was, we learn from Lord Clarendon, who describes him as "not a man of many words, who rarely begun the discourse, or made the first entrance upon any business that was assumed, but a very weighty speaker; and, after he had heard a full debate, and observed how the House was like to be inclined, took up the argument, and shortly, and clearly, and craftily so stated it, that he commonly conducted it to the conclusion he desired; and if he found he could not do that, he never was without the dexterity to divert the debate to another time, and to prevent the determining anything in the negative which might prove inconvenient in the future." The same thing may be inferred from an examination of Hampden's letters, in which courtesy and kindness, always predominant, are often made the agreeable vehicle of conveying truths otherwise likely to prove salutary, but unpalatable. He had evidently great power over the minds of others; and, as a natural correlative, large control over his own. The amount of business which he transacted during this parliament was extraordinary. In the course of six weeks we find him thus engaged: on a committee respecting the bill against spiritual pluralities; assisting in managing matters relative to the Earl of Strafford; on a committee respecting the seduction of the king's army; on a committee respecting the queen-mother and the tumults in London; on a committee respecting the affairs of the kingdom; on a committee respecting the affairs of Jersey and Guernsey; on committee respecting patent of wines; on committee respecting tonnage and poundage; on committee respecting melting the plate of the kingdom; on committees respecting removing bishops from temporal concerns; on the impeachment of Laud; on disbanding the armies; on the abolition of the Star Chamber; on danger from popish recusants; on danger of popish vestments; concerning a branch of a statute in things ecclesiastical; for giving thanks to the lord admiral and Lord Essex; and on a deputation for waiting on Lord Northumberland. This is but a fraction of a list of parliamentary engagements which extended over a considerable period.

It will have been observed by the reader that many of these questions on which Hampden exercised his high talents were ecclesiastical ones. It will also have been observed with regret that Hampden did not extend to the papists the liberty which he claimed as a puritan. Still, regarded on the large scale, the course taken by Hampden and Pym was equally creditable to their heart and their head; and, with a full margin allowed for their errors, it must be allowed that they were greatly in advance of their age.

In Pym's speech before this parliament, on the redress of grievances, he says:

"The greatest liberty of the kingdom is religion, whereby we are free from spiritual evils; and no impositions are so grievous as those that are laid upon the soul." Again — the admission was a large one for the age: — "I do not desire any new laws against popery, or any rigorous course in the execution of those already in force; I am far from seeking the ruin of their persons or estates; only I wish they may be kept in such a condition as may restrain them from doing hurt." But he complained of the license given to popish books and ceremonies, and that thereby "a shape and face of poperie" had been given to the churches. After complaining of the court of Star Chamber as "an instrument of erecting and defending monopolies and other grievances," he goes on to say, "Although he was come as high as he could on earth, yet the presumption of evil men did lead him one step higher — even as high as heaven, as high as the throne of God! It is now grown common for ambitious and corrupt men of the clergy to abuse the truth of God and the bond of conscience, * * pretending divine authority for an absolute power in the king to do what he will with our persons and goods. This hath been so often published in sermons and printed books, that it is now the highway to preferment." The effect of this most vigorous and able speech was so strong as to lead the king to dissolve the parliament.

Great was the consternation with which the news of this dissolution was received by the nation at large. But some of the more long-sighted leaders saw in the arbitrary act an omen for good. Oliver St. John especially told Hyde — afterwards Lord Clarendon — that "all was well, and that it must be worse before it could be better."

Pym and Hampden now took a more decided course against the royal tyranny. They made common cause with the army of Scotland, then advancing beyond the border. The king's army refused to fight against them; and Charles was compelled, after much hesitation, to summon another parliament. He could never dissolve that parliament again!

In this Long Parliament, which comprised men of such abilities as had never been gathered into an English senate before, Pym and Hampden were the avowed leaders, — the former being the most forward, the latter the most trusted man. "I am persuaded," says Clarendon, writing of Hampden, "that his power and interest at that time were greater to do good and hurt than any man's in the kingdom, or than any man of his rank hath had in any time; for his reputation of honesty was universal, and his affections seemed so publicly guided that no corrupt or private ends could bias them. * * He was, indeed, a very wise man, and of great parts; and possessed with the most absolute spirit of popularity, and the most absolute faculties to govern the people, of any man I ever knew." It was now no carpet warfare. Pym is known to have said to Hyde, "that they must now be of another temper than they were the last parliament;" "that they must now not only sweep the house clean below, but must pull down all the cobwebs which hung in the tops and corners, that they might not breed dust, and so make a foul house hereafter: that they had now an opportunity to make their country happy, by removing all grievances, and pulling up the causes of them by the roots, if all men would do their duties." The conflict had begun in earnest. The Earl of Strafford was the first against whom the hostilities were directed. Men felt that they had a great work to do, and they did it thoroughly. Strafford was impeached; monopolies were denounced; ship-money was proclaimed a subversion of law; Laud's recent canons were declared hostile to the liberties of the subject; and a petition, signed by fifteen thousand citizens of London, which prayed that episcopal government might be abolished, with all its dependencies, called from its nature "the root and branch petition," was brought into the houses. This was met by a counter-petition in favor of the hierarchy, in which the petitioners declare "that since the reformation the times have been very peaceable, happy, and glorious," and that "so much care is taken that no man should be offended in the least ceremony." In a similar strain we find Lord Clarendon saying, "Now, after this, I must be so just as to say, that from the dissolution of parliament, in the fourth year of the king, to the beginning of the Long Parliament, which was about twelve years, this kingdom and all his majesty's dominions enjoyed the greatest calm and the fullest measure of felicity that any people, in any age, for so long time together, have been blessed with, to the wonder and envy of all parts of Christendom." * * "Charles might have said that which Pericles was proud of upon his death-bed concerning his citizens — that no Englishman had worn a mourning gown through his occasion. In a word, many wise men thought it a time wherein those two adjuncts, *imperium* and *libertas*, were as well reconciled as possible." Such is the spirit and truth of party! Prelates were now censured or impeached; the secretary and lord keeper fled to Holland; and the lord chief justice was publicly arrested in the court in which he was sitting, and consigned to prison. "The civility of our law tells us," said Pym, "that the king can do no wrong; but then only is the state secure when judges, their ministers, dare do none. Since our times have found the want of such examples, 't is fit we leave some to posterity." "The power of future preservation," said Pym, "is now in us. *Et qui non servat patriam cum potest, idem tradit destruenti patriam.* What though we cannot restore the damage of the commonwealth, we may yet repair the breaches in the bounds of monarchy: though it be with our loss and charge, we shall so leave our children's children fenced as with a wall of safety, by the restoration of our laws to their ancient vigor and lustre." "When religion is innovated, our liberties violated, our fundamental laws abrogated, our modern laws already obsoleted, the property of our states alienated, nothing left us we can call our own but our misery and our patience, —if ever any nation might justifiably, we certainly may now, most properly, most seasonably, cry out, and cry aloud, '*Vel sacra regnet justitia, vel ruat cœlum!*'"

"Shall it be treason," again Pym says, "to embase the king's coin, though it be but a piece of twelve-pence or six-pence? and must it not needs be the effect of a greater treason to embase the spirit of his subjects, and to set up a stamp and character of servitude on them, whereby they shall be disabled to do anything for the service of the king and commonwealth?"

The reader must look elsewhere for the details of the trial and death of Strafford, — that "bold, bad man," — accused of designing, under the watchwords of *Thorough* and *Thorough-out*, to subvert and abolish the essential liberties of the English nation. Of all the scenes which Westminster Hall has ever exhibited during successive periods, none has been more memorable than the trial of the lord-deputy. The dauntless courage with which Pym advanced, in the name of truth and justice, to the attack; the contrary emotions excited, on the one hand, by the sight of the prisoner loaded with torturing infirmities, and, on the other, by the recollection of his crimes; the display of his heroic firmness set in opposition to the proofs of an unsparing resolution to beat down all resistance to his course; the overpowering eloquence of the accused, standing, though he did, against a world in arms; the effect of his sudden glance on Pym himself, recalling, as that glance did, years of ancient friendship and intercourse, so that even Pym for a moment forgot himself; the promises made by the king to save the servant who had imperilled all in the royal causes; the manner in which those pledges, like all which Charles had ever made, were violated under the strong pressure of the serious emergency; the clamors of the people for the death of the traitor to their rights; the calm composure with which Strafford appeared on the scaffold and underwent his sentence, — form together a picture full of materials for the pencil of art, and instructive in the highest degree alike to the statesman and the moralist.

Admirably has Macaulay painted a companion portrait: that of Laud, whose name has often occurred in these pages, and who suffered, about this time, a similar fate: —

"The mean forehead, the pinched features, the peering eyes, of the prelate, suit admirably with his disposition. They mark him out as a lower kind of Saint Dominic, differing from the fierce and gloomy enthusiast who founded the inquisition as we might imagine the familiar imp of a spiteful witch to differ from an archangel of darkness. When we read his grace's judgment,— when we read the report which he drew up setting forth that he had sent some separatists to prison, and imploring the royal aid against others, — we feel a movement of indignation. We turn to his diary, and we are at once as cool as contempt can make us. There we learn how his picture fell down, and how fearful he was lest the fall should be an omen; how he dreamed that the Duke of Buckingham came to bed to him; that King James walked past him; that he saw Thomas Flaxney in green garments, and the Bishop of Worcester with his shoulders wrapped in linen. In the early part of 1627, the sleep of this great ornament of the church seems to have been much disturbed. On the fifth of January, he saw a merry old man with a wrinkled countenance, named Grove, lying on the ground. On the 14th of the same memorable month, he saw the Bishop of Lincoln jump on a horse, and ride away. A day or two after this, he dreamed that he gave the king drink in a silver cup, and that the king refused it, and called for glass. Then he dreamed that he had turned papist; of all his dreams the only one, we suspect, which came through the gate of horn. But of these visions our favorite is that which, as he has recorded, he enjoyed on the night of Friday, the 19th of February, 1627. 'I dreamed,' says he, 'that I had the scurvy, and that forthwith all my teeth became loose. There was one especially in my lower jaw, which I could scarcely keep in with my finger, till I had called for help.' Yet this was the man who claimed to have the superintendence of the opinions of a great nation!"*

In the impeachment of this despicable man — whose name, though of late years it has become almost fashionable to canonize it, is worthy only of the emphasis of scorn — Pym also took, as is well known, a distinguished part.

"My lords," said he, "there is an expression in the Scripture

* Macaulay's Critical and Historical Essays, I., p. 450.

which I will not presume either to understand or to interpret; yet to a vulgar eye it seems to have an aspect something suitable to the person and cause before you. It is a description of the evil spirits, wherein they are said to be 'spiritual wickednesses in high places.' Crimes acted by the spiritual faculties of the soul — the will and the understanding — exercised about spiritual matters, concerning God's worship and the salvation of man, seconded with power, authority, learning, and many other advantages, to make the party who commits them very suitable to that description, — 'SPIRITUAL WICKEDNESSES IN HIGH PLACES!'" * * * "Herein your lordships may observe that those who labor, in civil matters, to set up the king above the laws of the kingdom, do yet, in ecclesiastical matters, endeavor to set up themselves above the king." * * * "You have the king's loyal subjects banished out of the kingdom, not as Elimelech, to seek for bread in foreign countries, by reason of the great scarcity which was in Israel, but travelling abroad for the bread of life, because they could not have it at home by reason of the spiritual famine of God's Word, caused by this man and his partakers; and by this means you have had the trade, the manufactory, the industry, of many thousands of his majesty's subjects, carried out of the land. It is a miserable abuse of the spiritual keys to shut up the doors of heaven, and to open the doors of hell; to let in profaneness, ignorance, superstition, and error. I shall need say no more. These things are evident, and abundantly known to all."

The hour of Laud's retribution had arrived. He, before whom an insulted nation had trembled, now felt the weight of a people's indignation, and found it terrible. Reparation was required of him and others for the sentences passed in the Star Chamber, especially on Burton, Bastwick, and Prynne; he was fined twenty thousand pounds, was removed from the chancellorship of Oxford, his jurisdiction was put into trust, and it was enacted that he should give no presentation to benefices without the previously-obtained consent of the House. His arms were removed; the rents of his archbishopric sequestrated; his house plundered, whilst for the outrage he could obtain no restitution; his goods and books sold, after his papers had been searched, in no very forbearing spirit, by the earless and now remorseless Prynne. It is impossible to give a detailed account of his trial and sentence. The last was what sentences passed in the passion of a moment which puts revenge within a people's power are apt to be. And it was at last forced upon the commons, mainly by the popular cry for his blood. No act which emanated from the Long Parliament is more open to censure than the proceedings against Laud, considered as a legal sentence. No act was at the time felt to have been more richly deserved by a long and cold-blooded course of persecution. Subsequently, Laud, like Strafford, was beheaded, and met his death with a stubborn fortitude.

Coincidently with these transactions, bills were introduced and passed abolishing the courts of Star Chamber and High Commission, with other parts of the despotic apparatus of Laud and Strafford. The king was, with great difficulty, persuaded to sign these bills. The conduct of the monarch on this occasion revived the question of the root and branch petition. The Long Parliament now began a serious and most comprehensive attack on prelacy. As a vindicator of this course of procedure, Hampden must be regarded as favorable to stronger anti-episcopal measures than Pym. Both, however, are described by Hyde, afterwards Lord Clarendon, as inviting to their table at Westminster "those of whose conversion they had any hope," and, among the rest, Mr. Hyde himself. This clearly proves that, in Clarendon's opinion, at least, there was an agreement between the two on the general question then agitated. Yet Clarendon, in another place, seems to contradict himself. Thus much is certain: that when the bill came into a committee of the whole house, Hyde was himself placed in the chair, and that he boasted, in the first volume of his "History of the Rebellion," "how he had perplexed them very much;" how, "when they were in the heat and passion of the debate, he often ensnared them in a question;" and how, "after nearly twenty days spent in that manner, they found themselves very little advanced towards a conclusion." One of the foremost speakers upon this root and branch question was Sir Harry Vane, jr.; one of the strongest defenders of episcopacy was Lord Falkland. We shall have occasion elsewhere to review the proceedings of the Long Parliament in relation to prelacy. It will be sufficient, at present, to observe the two resolutions of the commons which followed this debate: — "That the legislative and judicial power of bishops in the House of Peers is a great hindrance to the discharge of their spiritual function, prejudicial to the commonwealth, and fit to be taken away by bill, and that a bill be drawn up to this purpose." March 11, it was resolved further, "That for bishops or any other clergymen to be in the commission of the peace, or to have any judicial power in the Star Chamber, or in any civil court, is a great hindrance to their spiritual function, and fit to be taken away by bill." And, not many days after, it was resolved that they should not be privy-councillors, or in any temporal offices. This took place in 1640. Prynne the next year took courage and published his celebrated book, entitled "The Antipathie of the English Lordly Prelacie both to Regall Monarchy and Civill Unity; or, An Historical Collection of the several Execrable Treasons, Conspiracies, Rebellions, Seditions, State-schisms, Contumacies, Oppressions, and Anti-Monarchical Practices of our English, British, French, Scottish and Irish Lordly Prelates, against our Kings, Kingdomes, Laws, Liberties; and of the severall Warres and Civill Dissentions occasioned by them in or against our Realm, in Former and Later Ages, &c., &c. By Wm. Prynne, late (and now again) an utter Barrister of Lincolne's Inn." Bastwick also signalized himself on the occasion, by publishing a pamphlet entitled "Lord Bishops none of the Lord's Bishops: a short Discourse, 1640." We will by no means undertake to justify all the contents of these pamphlets: they both contain, however, many important facts. The consent of the king was with difficulty obtained to the bill for abolishing prelacy, and he only yielded on the understanding that, by yielding, his queen should not be molested in going abroad, a movement now essential to him.

About this time, the king having determined to pay a visit to Scotland, the parliament, having become extremely suspicious of all his movements, commissioned Hampden, as part of a deputation, to follow and observe him. What intrigues were carried on by Charles at this time against the cause of liberty in general, and against the popular leaders in particular, are made most apparent by the correspondence of Evelyn; and we must refer the reader, for an account of them, to Forster's able life of John Pym. By means of Lady Carlisle, who, though about the court, was in Pym's interest, the popular leaders were fully instructed in the dangers of their position. An attempt was made to assassinate Pym; but the blow fell upon another man, mistaken for the statesman. The Irish Rebellion, in which the queen and the king were suspected of bearing a part, and the occurrence known by the name of the "incident,"— of which all that has transpired is, that Montrose proposed to the king a system of assassination, and that Charles continued him in his service and confidence, — rendered the puritan party still more suspicious than before, and induced them to bring in the measure to which they attached the most emphatic importance, "The Grand Remonstrance." Some of those who had been advocates on the side of liberty in the commons were now beginning to grow exhausted and cold. The nation was weary of tumult and contention. Charles' most pernicious favorites had been extirpated, and a feeling of sympathy was arising for the misfortunes of the king himself. But the multitude was, as usual, very imperfectly informed on the subject, and did not see through the intrigues of the court; though, had Charles' wisdom been equal to the demands of his position, he might at this time have re-settled himself upon his throne. His wife's folly, however, and his own fatuity, destroyed him, and saved the liberties of his country. In this divided state of opinions, it was a great question whether the Remonstrance would pass. The debate was long and angry. The "Grand Remonstrance" was carried by a majority of nine. Carlyle calls the Irish Rebellion, which gave rise to it, "An Irish Catholic imitation of the late Scotch Presbyterian achievements in the way of religious liberty."* Many of the puritan leaders, and Cromwell among them, are said to have declared their resolution, had the Remonstrance been lost, to leave the kingdom. Such a statement, perhaps, constitutes the only ground for the tradition that Hampden and Cromwell had, at a former period, actually prepared to embark, and had been stopped by the king's order.

Roused by this "Grand Remonstrance," Charles now performed the crowning act of his own infatuation. He resolved to impeach the leading members of the two houses of high treason. This he did, not by the ordinary legal processes, but by sending the attorney-general to the House of Lords to accuse them in the king's name. The lords instantly sent a message to the commons, stating to them the fact, and informing them that pursuivants were already employed in sealing the trunks and papers of the accused members. Immediately the commons sent a speaker's warrant to remove the seals. In the mean time the sergeant-at-arms demanded, by a message from the king to the speaker, Pym, Hampden, Hollis, Hazlerigg and Strode. The house replied that the matter was too serious to be decided without consideration, but that the accused members would be ready to answer any legal charge. Pym and Hampden were then present in the house. The next morning, amidst the intense silence which frequently accompanies great events, the five members rose in their places, each to refute in his turn the charges which the king's attorney-general had brought against them. The house had retired for its usual dinner-interval, and resumed its sitting, when, by means of a letter from Lady Carlisle, who had overheard in the palace the queen's† premature

* Carlyle's Cromwell, vol. I., p. 166.

† The queen had spirited the king to this attack. When Charles left her to seize the members, he said to his wife, "If you find one hour elapse without hearing ill news from me, you will see me, when I return, the master of my kingdom." The queen waited, her eyes fixed on her watch. At last she said to Lady Carlisle, "Rejoice with me, for at this hour the king is, as I have reason to hope, master of his realm; for Pym and his confederates are arrested

triumph at the king's act, Pym was made aware that the king was coming down to the house, and he lost no time in proclaiming it to his fellow-members. As it was felt that bloodshed would be the inevitable consequence if Charles seized them in the house, they were requested to withdraw. The commons then, arming themselves with the sternest resolution, awaited, in the silence of a gathering storm, their royal visitor.

The scene which followed, standing as it did in immediate connection with the action taken by the five members in the war against bishops, and the calling in of the Scots for the promotion of uniformity, is too characteristic of the period to be omitted. The door of the house was thrown violently open: this marked the arrival of the king, with his guard, his pensioners, and two or three hundred soldiers. Charles commanded the soldiers to remain, and sent word that he was at the door. The speaker was ordered by the house to sit still, with his mace lying before him. The king, in a state of high excitement, advanced from his retainers, checking their eagerness by commanding them on their lives not to enter. Only his nephew, the prince palatine, accompanied him; the Earl of Roxburgh standing by the door. Charles entered uncovered; the members of the house stood up uncovered to receive him. The speaker advanced to meet him: the king walked into his place, and stood upon the step. For some considerable time he stood looking inquiringly around in search of the five members. At length he spoke, stammering more than usual, in the agitation of such a moment, and declared, "I will not break your privileges, but treason has no privilege. I come for those five gentlemen, for I expected obedience yesterday, and not an answer." The king called Mr. Pym and Mr. Hollis by name, — there was no reply. In all that assembly there was probably not one who sympathized with the royal madness of that moment. The king asked the speaker if the five members were in the house,

before now." Lady Carlisle gave the alarm. Something had detained the king, and the news reached the members in time for their escape. Henrietta Maria confessed this indiscretion to her husband, who forgave her.

or where they were? Lenthall admirably said that he was only the servant of the house, and could neither see nor hear but by its order. The king replied, "I think my own eyes are as good as yours; the birds are flown; but I expect, as soon as they come to the house, you will send them to me; otherwise I must take my own course to find them." Amidst mutterings, loud enough to reach the royal ears, of "Privilege, privilege!" the king departed; and his armed retainers, who had stood at the door eagerly expecting the moment of their entrance, received him on his return with disappointment. There was no need for their cocked pistols that day, but the occasion was soon coming which should give them employment enough.*

The members sought refuge in the city. The king pursued them. The city defended and honored them. Four thousand men from Buckingham came up to the defence of Hampden. Pym was also strongly guarded. The king vainly endeavored to patch the rent his rash hand had made. The house ordered its accused members to attend in their places on the 11th January. They sailed up the Thames in gorgeous and magnificent procession, with all the defences of war, and the king retreated to Hampton Court. Pym and Hampden had now received from Charles' hostile hands an enlarged influence and a mightier impulse. The civil war began. Hampden summoned his Buckinghamshire retainers to form a militia, and was cheerfully obeyed. His purse was open at the same time to supply the wants of the parliament, and he received commission as a colonel. His subscription was two thousand pounds. His regiment was considered the best infantry among the parliamentary forces. His livery was green; his banner bore his own family motto, on this occasion most appropriate, "*Vestigia nulla retrorsum.*" Lord Clarendon, in describing Hampden's character, expresses a sentiment which is a true translation of this phrase, "When he drew the sword, he threw away the scabbard." His personal courage was conspicuous; it even approached to the rash

* A graphic account of this celebrated scene, from the pen of an eye-witness, is given in the Verney papers, recently published by the Camden Society.

imperilling of his life. The following lines are those of "a friend and fellow-soldier:"

> ——————— "I have seen
> Him in the front of 's regiment in green,
> When death about him did in ambush lye,
> And whizzing shot-like showres of arrowes flye,
> Waving his conquering steele, as if that he
> From Mars had got the sole monopolie
> Of never-failing courage."

These are not the pages in which to discuss the question of war in the general, or of the great civil war in particular. It is clear, however, that those who in this contest appealed to arms against the king were actuated by no sinister or unworthy motives. The war was distinctly a war for religion. It was a war for protestantism against Romanism; for puritanism against prelacy; but it was not, in its widest sense, a war for perfect religious liberty. Pym and Hampden appear to have been both attached to the forms and ceremonial of the Church of England, so far as that was consistent with Pym's deploring and Hampden's denouncing its hierarchy. Both felt that the liberty of the person and that of the religion were inseparably associated; at least, they felt this up to a certain point. In resisting the encroachments of Charles, they felt that they were opposing one, whose word, on what subject soever it had been pledged, was as unstable as a quicksand; who had bullied and then crouched down; had promised and recalled his promise; had put aside the most solemn charters of the land; had even trampled upon those which himself had conceded; and that from him nothing could be hoped, until, by his committing himself to their hands, he should give some security that he held good faith towards them. In thus resisting the king, the patriot party felt that they were fighting for their altars, their hearths, their liberties, and the decencies of a public morality outraged by the license of the times. Many of the contrasts between the two armies were uncommonly striking. It was not only that the flowing locks of the cavalier, who wore his love-token suspended round his neck, were most distinguishable from the close-cropped hair of the Roundhead, whose only conspicuous ornament was his military belt. It was not only that the uncouth psalms sung on the one side to the ancient tunes of "Old Windsor," or "Babylon Streams," formed a singular contrast to the songs which, shouted forth by some drunken cavalier, formed a mingled compound of wit, scandal, and licentiousness. But it was that, though the full development had not yet taken place, the leaders of the parliament army possessed the dignity, and some of them the enthusiasm, of martyrs; whilst on the other side, with some distinguished exceptions, the royalist leaders were little better than remorseless and revengeful rakes. The parliament army was more distinguished by dogmatic pertinacity of opinion than it was by vice, whilst the king's army suspected virtue itself to be disloyal. The Roundheads knew, almost to a man, the nature and dignity of their cause, and were prepared to argue as well as to fight for it; their adversaries, for the most part, cared more for the name of loyalty than for any truth embodied in it. Some of them were ignorant of the merit of the question for which they fought; others of them would have disdained to defend the conduct of the king; and the mass of their army was a rabble rout, the most debauched, the most reckless, the most irreligious, that ever trailed a pike or fired a matchlock.

In levying his army, Charles was compelled to forego all attention to religious differences. The following letter, written to the Earl of Newcastle, has perhaps, an eye towards Roman Catholics:

"NEW CASTEL,—This is to tell you that this rebellion is growen to that height, that I must not look what opinion men ar who at this time ar willing and able to serve me. Therefore, I doe not only permitt, but command you to make use of all my loving subjects' services, without examining ther contienses (more than there loyalty to me) as you shall fynde most to conduce to the uphoulding of my just royall power. So I rest,

"Your most assured faithfull frend,

"CHARLES R.*

"*Shrewsbury*, 23 *Sep*. 1642."

The command of the army of the parliament was, in the first instance, intrusted to the Earl of Essex. He had practised military tactics in the war of the palatinate, and was deeply earnest in the cause of freedom; but he possessed the fatal fault of hesitating in a crisis, and he knew not how to follow up his own advantages. Hampden was placed near him, on the principle of compensation, that he might add energy to his commander's prudence. Essex, though in the first instance satisfied that war with the king was a necessary evil, became, as the conflict proceeded, uncertain whether great triumphs on his part would be altogether salutary to the parliament itself; and this fear withheld him from striking when the blow might have been decisive. "It was believed," says Lucy Hutchinson, in her Memoirs of her Husband, Colonel Hutchinson, "that he—Essex—himself, with his commanders, rather endeavored to become arbiters of war and peace than conquerors for the parliament: for it was known that he had given out such expressions."

A civil war is a peculiar and a fearful thing! The greatest captain of our own day has said that, rather than witness it at home, he would freely lay down his own life. Such a war does not, like other wars, concentrate itself on a few principal points. It is an eruptive disease of singular malignity, which breaks out irregularly, and often simultaneously, on all parts of the body politic. Discord, revenge, want, rapine, murder, suffering, are of course its attendants; but, besides these, loyalty is made a reproach on the one hand, and liberty is ridiculed as an empty name on the other. The most sacred things are violated, and placed in juxtaposition with the most odious. The closest ties are severed and

* Ellis' Letters.

dislocated; families are ranged against each other; the chiefest friends become enemies. The soldier is often compelled to advance against the homesteads of his own kindred. The exercises of industry and piety are disturbed by the shouts of massacre, or the roaring of musketry. "Even things inanimate, which appeal to remembrance only, crowd in, with their numberless associations, to tell how unnatural a state of man is civil war. The village street barricaded; the house deserted by all its social charities, perhaps occupied as the stronghold of a foe; the church, where lie our parents' bones, become a battery for cannon, a hospital for the wounded, a stable for horses, or a keep for captives; the accustomed paths of our early youth beset with open menace or hidden danger; its fields made foul with carnage; and the imprecations of furious hate, or the supplications of mortal agony, coming to us in our own language, haply in the very dialect of our peculiar province; — these are among the familiar and frequent griefs of civil war." *

As the contest proceeded, Hampden was impatient of the delays which only protracted the nation's sufferings, and earnestly desired some more determinate measures on the part of the parliament. But his remonstrances with Essex were vain. Hampden had urged him to defend two regiments peculiarly exposed to attack. His advice was unheeded, and Prince Rupert fell upon them, and slew them to a man. Anticipating that Rupert was aiming to turn the eastern flank of the army, and aware that Chiselhampton Bridge was the only point by which he could return to his army, posted at Oxford, Hampden felt it to be his duty to attempt to intercept him, and drew up his infantry on Chalgrave-field, a plain where he had often been accustomed to exercise his militia. In leading his men to the charge, two carbine balls pierced his shoulder, and, breaking his arm, entered his body. Noble, however, relates that "a great man assured him that Hampden's death-wound proceeded from the breaking of an overcharged pistol,

* Nugent's Memoirs of Hampden.

given him by his son-in-law, Sir R. Pye, to whom, when he saw him on his death-bed, he said: "Ah, Robin, your unhappy present has been my ruin!" * But this is a mere figment.

"It is a tradition that he was seen," after his wound, "first moving towards the house of his father-in-law at Pyrton. There he had in youth married the first wife of his love,† and thither he would have gone to die. But Rupert's cavalry covered the plain between. Turning his horse, therefore, he rode back across the grounds of Hazelrig, in his way to Thame. At the brook which divides the parishes he paused a while, but, it being impossible for him, in his wounded state, to remount, if he had alighted to turn his horse over, he suddenly summoned his strength, clapped spurs, and cleared the leap. In great pain, and almost fainting, he reached Thame, and was conducted to the house of one Ezekiel Browne, where, his wounds being dressed, the surgeons would for a while have given him hopes of life; but he felt that his hurt was mortal. He was attended by Dr. Giles, the rector of Chimnor, and by Dr. Spurstowe, an independent minister, the chaplain of his regiment."‡

It appears that Hampden's death was attributable to a deserter, who gave Rupert information, and suggested the attack which ended on Chalgrave-field, and that this man pointed out to the marksmen the different commanders, crying, "That 's Hampden, that's Gunter, that 's Luke." Hampden's dying breath, like Nelson's on a similar occasion, directed the movements which he felt to be important for the security of his army and the vigorous conduct of the war. During six days, he suffered the most agonizing pain. As his dissolution drew near, he received the sacrament of the Lord's Supper, avowing "that though he could not away with the governance of the church by bishops, and did utterly

* Noble's Cromwell.

† Hampden had married a second time, about the period of his removal from his ancestral mansion. His lady long survived him, and lived to an advanced age.

‡ Nugent's Life of Hampden.

abominate the scandalous life of some clergymen, he thought its doctrines in the greater part primitive and conformable to God's Word, as in Holy Scripture revealed." Before his death he uttered a prayer in the highest degree affecting and sublime. "O Lord God of hosts," said he, "great is thy mercy, just and holy are thy dealings unto us sinful men. Save me, O Lord, if it be thy good will, from the jaws of death. Pardon my manifold transgressions. O Lord, save my bleeding country. Have these realms in thy special keeping. Confound and level in the dust those who would rob the people of their liberty and lawful prerogative. Let the king see his error, and turn the hearts of his wicked counsellors from the malice and wickedness of their designs. Lord Jesus, receive my soul!" He then mournfully uttered, "O Lord, save my country. O Lord, be merciful . . ." And here his speech failed him. He fell back in the bed, and expired. Hampden was buried in the manor which bears his name, and within the beautiful church we have already described.

HAMPDEN CHURCH, THE PLACE OF HAMPDEN'S INTERMENT.

The body was followed to the grave by many of his troops,—their arms reversed, their heads uncovered. They are related to have sung the ninetieth Psalm as they went, and the forty-third as they returned. Some verses of the former run thus:

"Thou guidest man through grief and pain
to dust, and clay, and then;
And then thou sayst; againe return
againe, ye sonnes of men.
The lasting of a thousand yeeres
what is it in thy sight:
As yesterday it doth appeare
or as a watch by night.

"So soone as thou doest scatter them
then is their life and trade,
All as a sleepe and like the grasse
whose beauty soone doth fade,
Which in the morning shines full bright,
but fadeth by and by:
And is cut downe ere it be night
all withered, dead and dry."

Not less appropriate were the lines sung by the mourners on their return:

"Judge and avenge my cause, O Lord,
from them that evill be,
From wicked and deceitful men,
O Lord deliver me.
For of my strength thou art the God,
why put'st thou me thee fro:
And why walk I so heauily
oppressed with my foe.

* * * *

"Why art thou then so sad, my soule,
and fretst thus in my brest:
Still trust in God; for him to prayse
I hold it always best.
By him I haue deliverance
against all paine and griefe:

He is my God which doth alwayes
at nede send me reliefe.'' *

Hampden's death, occurring as it did at so critical a point of the nation's history, spread dismay among the numerous party to which he had belonged. "The loss of Colonel Hampden," said the *Weekly Intelligencer*, one of the journals of the period, "goeth near the heart of every man that loves the good of his king and country, and makes some conceive little content to be at the army, now that he is gone. The memory of this deceased colonel is such; that in no age to come but it will more and more be had in honor and esteem; a man so religious, and of that prudence, judgment, temper, valor and integrity, that he hath left few his like behind."

"He had indeed left none his like behind him. There still remained, indeed, in his party, many acute intellects, many eloquent tongues, many brave and honest hearts. There still remained a rugged and clownish soldier, whose talents, discerned aright by only one penetrating eye, were equal to all the highest duties of the soldier and the prince. But in Hampden, and in Hampden alone, were united all the qualities which, at such a crisis, were necessary to save the state; — the valor and energy of Cromwell, the discernment and eloquence of Vane, the humanity and moderation of Manchester, the stern integrity of Hale, the ardent public spirit of Sydney. Others might possess the qualities which were necessary to save the popular party in the crisis of danger: he alone had both the power and the inclination to restrain its excesses in the hour of triumph. Others could conquer; he alone could reconcile." †

Some few years ago, with the view of determining where the remains of Hampden were actually buried, an exhumation was made of the body supposed to be his, from the chancel of the little church at Hampden. It was found in a state of complete preservation, wrapped in cere-cloth, and some who were present at the

* Sternhold and Hopkins. † Macaulay's Essays, vol. I., p. 489.

disinterment, which was made in the presence of the late Lord Nugent, and the present Lord Denman, thought they could distinctly trace the likeness of the features to the best existing portraits. But, when interrogated, the other day, on the subject, the sexton averred, though he very attentively examined the dead body, he could not find any trace of the wound by which the great patriot was reported to have died, and expressed a distinct conviction that the body was not that of John Hampden.

Worn out by his superhuman exertions, Pym, commonly nicknamed "King Pym," six months after followed his distinguished friend to the tomb. Though just appointed by the parliament to the distinguished office of lieutenant of the ordnance, he never lived to fulfil its duties. It is said that, whilst on his death-bed, a band of rioters, provoked by the sufferings of the times, beset the House of Commons with a petition for peace, crying out, for two hours, "Give us the traitor Pym, that we may tear him in pieces!" and were only dispersed by a troop of horse. He died at Derby House, in great calmness of spirit, declaring that it was "an indifferent thing to him whether he lived or died," and that, "if his life and death were put into a balance, he would not willingly cast in one drachm to turn the balance either way." With his last breath he prayed with energy for the king and the public weal, and having just recovered from a fainting fit, told his friends "he had looked death in the face, and knew, and therefore feared not, the worst it could do," and that "his heart was filled with more comfort and joy than he was able to utter." He died whilst a minister was offering prayer by his bedside. He was buried with great "pomp and circumstance" in Westminster Abbey, his body being borne to the grave by the ten principal gentlemen of the House of Commons, attended by both houses clad in mourning, by the assembly of divines just met, and by other gentlemen of rank. We have before us the sermon preached on this memorable occasion, by Mr. Marshall, from the text, "Woe is me, for the good man is perished out of the earth." The following is an extract from its close. Besides exhibiting a portrait of the man, it may be regarded as an exemplification of the fearlessness with which the godly preachers of that day were accustomed to address even their most distinguished auditors:

"And certainly, if God sends us to the pismire, to consider her waies, and thereby to learne wisdome, it can be no disparagement to any of you to consider *his* worth, and thereby to grow better; I shall, therefore, make bold to propound him as Bishop Montacute did Master Perkins in his funerall sermon, to be the man that taught England to serve God, and ministers to preach Jesus Christ; so Master John Pym to be the man whose example may teach all our nobles and gentlemen to be good Christians, good patriots, good parliament men. You all knew him well, and knew—

"That he was not a man, who when he was called to the publike service of his countrey, lay here to satisfie his lusts, spending his time in riot and wantonnesse, in gaming, drinking, whoring, &c. Take heed none of you be such.

"He was not a man who proved a traitour to God and his countrey, and the cause of religion, which he had solemnly protested to maintaine. Take heed none of you be such.

"Hee was not a man who (though hee appeared often in the parliament house, yet) neither promoted good causes himselfe, nor willingly permitted others to do it. Take heed there be none such among you.

"He was not a man who owned the good cause so long as it was like to thrive, and then tackt about when it seemed to decline; resolved to secure himselfe, whatever became of the publike. Beware none of you be such.

"He was not a man who would feed himselfe, or feather his own nest, or provide for his family or friends out of the publike stocke, or treasure of the kingdome. Take heed none of you be such.

"He was not a man who would favor the cause of his friend, or presse too heavily against his enemy; he was no respecter of persons in any cause or judgment. Take heed none of you doe so.

"He was not a man who would consider how far any publike service would stand with his own private designes, and promote the one no further than the other could be driven on with it. Beware this be none of your condition.

"He was not a man who for maintaining or propagating any private opinion, or way of his owne, would hazard the publike safety. Take heed none of you be such.

"He was not a man who feared to promote the reformation of religion, lest himselfe should be brought under the yoke of it. Take heed that none of you doe so.

"Not a man living (I believe) could justly taxe *him* for any of these; God grant none of you may be found guilty of any one of them in the day of your account.

"But instead of these things he was the holy man, the good man, adorned with that integrity, constancy, and unweariablenesse in doing good, which I before told you of. Goe, and doe likewise; get such an upright heart to God; lay out yourselves wholly in the publike cause; put both your hands to this worke, and the smaller your number is, be the more diligent, and fall the closer to it; set selfe and selfe respects aside; drive no designes of your owne; count it reward enough, to spend and be spent in this cause; esteeme the worke more worth than all your lives; imitate him in these things; so might you make him, as another Sampson, more advantageous to the cause of God in his death, than ever he was in his whole life." *

Baxter, in the earlier editions of the "Saint's Rest," is well known to have inserted a passage, which, in the copies published after the restoration, was unhappily and disgracefully expunged to please Dr. Jane, and to obtain a license for his book: "I think, Christian, this will be a more honorable assembly than you ever

* "*ΘΡΗΝΩΔΙΑ*. The Church's Lamentation for the Good Man his Losse, delivered in a Sermon to the Right Honorable the two Houses of Parliament, and the Reverend Assembly of Divines, &c., by Stephen Marshall, B.D., 1644." The Sermon is prefixed by "a Portrait of John Pym, Esq., late Burges for Tavistocke."

here beheld; and a more happy society than you were ever of before. Surely Brook and Pim, and Hamden, and White, &c., are now members of a more knowing, unerring, well-ordered, right ayming, self-denying, unanimous, honorable, triumphant senate, than this from whence they were taken is, or ever parliament will be. It is better to be a doorkeeper to that assembly, whither I wish we are translated, than to have continued here the moderator of this. That is the true *Parliamentum Beatum*, the blessed parliament, and that is the only church that cannot erre."

The testimony of these famous divines puts utterly to flight the vile and mad rumors which the royalists malignantly raised against the moral reputations of Hampden and Pym, especially the latter. It is incredible that men like Baxter and Marshall would have so

HAMPDEN HOUSE.—RESIDENCE OF JOHN HAMPDEN.

written or so spoken, had not such reports been empty as the wind. The accusation, commonly believed among the royalists, that Pym died of a loathsome disease, is a calumny which only party malice could have invented, and was disproved by *post-mortem* dissection.

Before we leave Hampden Manor, we may recall the fact that it was the place of Baxter's residence during the period of the great plague of London. He was then visiting his beloved friend, Mr. Richard Hampden, "the true heir of his famous father's sincerity, piety, and devotedness to God." From this place he returned to Acton, in March, 1666, to find "the church-yard like a ploughed field with graves, and many of his neighbors dead."

CHAPTER V.

AIMINGS AT THE IMPOSSIBLE.

"With many a weary step, and many a groan,
Up-hill rolls Sisyphus his huge round stone.
The huge round stone, resulting with a bound,
Thunders impetuous down, and foams along the ground."

POPE.

THE old town of Kimbolton, in the county of Huntingdon, has not much to recommend it, except to an historical antiquary. Yet it is situated in the midst of agreeable and quietly-varied scenery, stands amidst rich slopes of arable land, and is in the immediate adjacency of a ducal residence with an extensive park. The town itself is small, and its situation shows that in former times it had nestled as closely as possible to the baronial castle which stood there, for protection. To many readers the name of Kimbolton will at once recall the remembrance of an important history and a despotic tyrant; — of a faithless husband, an injured wife, and of a course of ecclesiastical oppression which has, from that day to this, been the fruitful source of misconduct and disorder. Kimbolton was the residence, after her divorce, of Katharine of Arragon, the first and not least injured wife of Henry VIII. One of Shakspeare's best scenes points hither:

"*Griff.* How does your grace?
"*Kath.* O Griffith, sick to death;
My legs, like loaden branches, bow to the earth,
Willing to leave their burden.
Now I am past all comforts here but prayers.
Remember me

In all humility unto his highness :
Say his long trouble now is passing
Out of this world ; tell him in death I blessed him,
And so I will. — Mine eyes grow dim. — Farewell,
My lord — Griffith, farewell — I must to bed ;
Call in more women. — When I am dead, good wench,
Let me be used with honor ; strew me o'er
With maiden flowers, that all the world may know
I was a chaste wife to my grave ; embalm me,
Then lay me forth ; although unqueened, yet like
A queen and daughter to a king inter me ;
I can no more.'' — SHAKSPEARE, *Henry VIII.*

At this time Kimbolton Castle is represented as being "double dyked, and the building of it metely strong;" in short, totally unlike the aspect it presents at the present day. Kimbolton Castle has for centuries belonged to the Montagus. This name was derived from a town in Normandy; and as it was convenient to write it in Latin "De Monteacuto," it was sometimes termed in English Montacute. Little of the baronial style characterizes the present residence of the Dukes of Manchester. The associations which this chapter is intended to connect with Kimbolton belonged to it when it was very different from that in which it now appears.

No man occupied a more prominent position during the early history of the Commonwealth than Edward, afterwards known by the name of the Earl of Manchester. His father was Lord Privy Seal in the reign of James, and had passed, as Clarendon tells us, "through all the eminent degrees in the law and in the state;" but, losing the favor of the court, had been left with the empty title of President of the Council, and, to make amends, had been created Viscount Mandeville, and, in James' latter days, Earl of Manchester. He died about the opening of the great civil war. His son, of whom we now principally write, had been one of Prince Charles' attendants during the expedition to Spain, but being of uncourtly principles, and being also known strongly to favor puritanism, he had become unacceptable to his royal patron. His first marriage was to a relative of the Duke of Buckingham, by whose influence he was raised to the peerage whilst his father was yet living, under the designation of Baron of Kimbolton. His first wife being dead, he married as his second wife the daughter of the Earl of Warwick. This alliance naturally tended to increase his predilections in favor of the puritans; for Warwick, though himself of facetious manners, is well known to have greatly encouraged and protected that religious party. After this marriage, Lord Mandeville gradually withdrew himself from court, and formed a strict alliance with many noblemen and gentlemen of similar views. Clarendon says, "There was a kind of fraternity of many persons of good condition, who chose to live together in one family at a gentleman's house of fair fortune." This was probably at Great Stoughton, which lies about three miles south of Kimbolton. Valentine Wauton, or Walton, its proprietor, was member for the county, and his wife was Oliver Cromwell's youngest sister. Between this family and Cromwell's there was, therefore, a strong alliance; and the reader of "Carlyle's Letters" will remember a striking communication addressed by Cromwell to his brother-in-law, announcing the death of Walton's son by a cannon-ball at Marston Moor.

Manchester's disposition was in early life frank, generous, and impulsive, and he was in the very centre of all the movements contemplated by the party in opposition, as well as a principal actor in the turbulent scenes of the time. He had the singular honor of being the only peer who was included in the list of the impeached members by the king's proscription.

When, in 1642, Charles, amidst adverse and discouraging omens, first erected his standard at Nottingham, Manchester was appointed to one of the principal posts of command. None was more earnest in the cause of the parliament, but the views of Manchester were narrow and confined; he could not step out of a prescribed circle. That "sweet, meek man," as Baillie terms him, was, in fact, ill qualified to conduct an enterprise so vast to a prosperous issue. He grew weary of his position; became disgusted with his former allies; was sneered at and scorned by Cromwell, as incapable; and ended by swearing allegiance to the monarch whose father he had unwittingly aided to dethrone.

KIMBOLTON, HUNTINGDONSHIRE. — RESIDENCE OF PHILIP NYE.

In the midst of the town of Kimbolton, and surrounded by houses, stands its parish church. It is a noble "time-honored edifice," dating from the mœso-gothic period, with castellated battlements, deep buttresses, and a spire which shoots up high in air, surmounted by the figure of a cock, the memorial of Peter's denial, and in ancient times admonitory to the clergy of the need of pastoral vigilance. Its interior is venerable, though it has become divested of many of the remnants of its earlier history. Banners telling of militia warfare are pendent from the roof of its chancel, and the death-memorials of a great family are conspicuous upon its walls. A costly monument, rich with marble, scroll-work and emblazonry, records the titles and the dignities of King James' lord treasurer, and seems to mock at mortality.

In a little enclosure, which might have been once a chapel, stand two marble tablets, recording the memories of the second and third wives of the parliamentary general:

In Memorye

OF THE RIGHT HOUNORABLE ANNE
LADY MANDEVILLE DAUGHTER TO
ROBERT EARL OF WARWICK AND
WIFE TO EDWARD LORD MANDEVILLE
NOWE EARL OF MANCHESTER.
SHEE DYED FEB. 14 ANN. DOM.
1641 & LEFT THREE CHILDREN
1 SONN & 2 DAUGHTERS.
HER HUSBAND HEE PRAYSETH HER
SAYING, MANY DAUGHTERS HAVE
DONE VIRTUOUSLY BUT THOU
EXCELLEST THEM ALL — PROVERBS 31.

In Memorye

OF ESSEX, COUNTESSE OF MANCHESTER
DAUGHTER TO SR. THOMAS CHEEKE
& WIFE TO EDWARD EARL OF
MANCHESTER.
SHE DYED THE 28 OF SEPTEMBER
ANN. DOM. 1658 AND LEFT
8 CHILDREN 6 SONNS &
2 DAUGHTERS 7 OF THEM
SHE NURSED WITH HER OWN BREASTS.

HER CHILDREN SHALL RISE UP & CALL
HER BLESSED
THE HEART OF HER HUSBAND SAFELY
TRUSTED IN HER
SHE DID HIM GOOD & NOE EVILL ALL
YE DAYES OF HER LIFE
THEREFORE HEE PRAYSETH HER AND
HER OWN WORKS PRAYSE HER IN
YE GATE — PROVERBS 31.

Beneath these tablets is the vault of the Manchester family. A visit to such sepulchres is sometimes repulsive for other reasons than the mental suggestions which belong to mortality. But this enclosure is remarkably clean and well ventilated. This is, however, the only praise that can be accorded to it; for the visitor who would read the inscription on the crimson velvet coffins of the fathers and mothers, and the remoter ancestors and ancestresses of the present family, is actually made to walk upon their surface, — an act which, to those "mindful of the honored dead," seems little less than sepulchral sacrilege. We look in vain amongst these mournful tenements for the coffin which once contained the body of Cromwell's superior. In a dark corner, bricked up from view, and consequently almost invisible, we saw two mouldered receptacles which might possibly have belonged to the parliamentary earl; but the brass plate, which had been perhaps originally on the coffin, had been altogether removed, and conjecture was useless. The attendant could supply us with no information; but, after being pressed with inquiries, produced at length from a dark corner of the mausoleum a bundle of plates, which it appeared had been detached at some time or other from the narrow homes of those whom nobility and fortune had once dignified. Amongst these we found the following:

Depositum.

NOBILLISSIMI & ILLUSTRISSIMI DOMINI, DNI
EDWARDI, COMITIS MANCHESTRIÆ
VICECOMITIS MANDEVILLÆ BARONIS DE
KIMBOLTON HOSPITII DNI REGIS CAMERARIUS
UNIVERSITATIS CANTABRIGLÆ CANCELLARIUS CAROLO
2DO REGI AUGUSTISSIMO A SECRETIORIBUS CONSILIIS
NOBILLISSIMI ORDINIS GARTERII EQUITIS
QUI APUD WHITEHALL PIISSIMÆ
IN DOMINO OBDORMIVIT VTO DIE MAII
ANNO A CHRISTO NATO MDC: LXXI.
ÆTATIS SUÆ LXIX.

If the classical reader shall happen to detect any errors in the composition of this memorial, he must blame the Latinity of 1699, or the ignorance of the engraver of the escutcheon, and not the transcriber.

Perhaps, after all, the object of great interest in Kimbolton church is its pulpit. It possesses a singular adornment in the shape of a large hammer-cloth, richly embroidered with gold lace of a gorgeous and elegant pattern, evidently of no recent date. This piece of tapestry is recorded to have been worked by one of the ancestresses of the Manchester family, who, when it was near its completion, pricked her finger with the needle she had used in executing it, and died of the wound. Till a very recent period the needle was itself preserved with religious veneration. It has now, we believe, altogether disappeared.

A great name is associated with the pulpit of Kimbolton church. It is that of Philip Nye. When the parliament of England gained the ascendency, and removed from their position many ignorant and incompetent clergymen, Nye, who had descended from a well-born family, had received his education at Oxford, and had fled to Holland from the persecution of Archbishop Laud, was appointed by the Earl of Manchester minister of the church at Kimbolton. A fire in Coleman-street, where Nye's papers were deposited, unhappily prevents us from forming an intimate acquaintance with the earlier history of this remarkable man; and very little except the fact we have just narrated is known of Philip Nye, till we arrive at the period in which was summoned the well-known Westminster Assembly.

We must beg the reader's pardon for a slight historical digression, whilst we attempt to lay before him some of the circumstances which led to this famous convocation. We return for a moment to the times of Archbishop Laud.

The evil spirit by which Charles was possessed led him, in a dark hour, even when all the elements of discord were raging and boiling around him in England, to impose upon the Scottish people the prelacy of the English establishment. No infatuation could be more perfect than that which led Charles at that moment to adopt Laud's advice. Who does not know the story of the cutty-stool, thrown at the Dean of Edinburgh, in St. Giles' church, by Jeannie Geddes, on the first reading of the English prayers in that ancient cathedral?* Who does not know, moreover, how from that moment Scottish episcopacy was rent to tatters? The whole country flew to arms. Christ's crown and covenant headed every array, or was lighted up by every watch-fire; and even Charles himself stood for a moment aghast at the consequences of his own stupendous folly. But Charles was no yielder; and there was no possibility of forcing into his mind anything like a sincere conviction that he had been in error. There was an Eve, too, standing at his ear and strengthening his will whenever it was irresolute, though in a manner altogether opposite to Pope's character of the wise wife:

"She who ne'er answers till a husband cools,
And, if she rules him, never shows she rules;"

for, when the king was somewhat undecided about seizing the five members, the papistical Henrietta Maria said to him: "Go, you poltroon, and pull these rogues out by the ears, or never see my face any more!" Whether under this influence or not, Charles determined to maintain his ground; and, having dissolved parliament and thrown its leading members into prison, obtained from convocation a large sum of money, to enable him to prosecute the war against the Scots. If anything were necessary to increase

* "For when a woman scolding mad is,
We call her daft as Jenny Geddes."

This celebrated lady was, we fear, of no unspotted fame. The first actors in reformation are usually to be distinguished from those whose principles prompt the movement. Jenny Geddes was only a forward expositor on this occasion of a popular sentiment. The stool — or what is believed to be such — is still preserved in the Museum of Antiquaries, Edinburgh. It is a light kind of camp-stool, bearing the date 1565. The prayer-book was called, in these times, "the mass;" the surplice, "the sark of God." — See *Minstrelsy of the Scottish Border*, vol. II., p. 167.

the odium of this illegal transaction, it was supplied by Laud, who instigated the convocation to publish seventeen canons, one of which required all clergymen to take an oath, which ran thus: "Nor will I ever give my consent to alter the government of this church by archbishops, bishops, deans, archdeacons, &c., as it stands now established." This pledge was called the "et-cetera oath," and was signally offensive on two grounds: first, because it demanded approval of the whole prelatical establishment; and, secondly, because it was so indefinite that no man knew precisely what he was required to swear. But for refusing to take this oath multitudes of worthy clergymen were reviled, fined, and imprisoned.

Charles now marched to Scotland, to subdue his refractory subjects. They, acting in correspondence with the patriot leaders in England, marched across the border, and took possession of Newcastle. The treaty of Ripon led to a temporary cessation of hostilities.

On the 10th September, 1642, the prelatic form of church government was, by vote of parliament, abolished. The oppressed puritans had now removed from the position of sufferers into that of law-makers. How did they comport themselves in their altered circumstances?

It is plainly impossible that the administration of religion, in an ecclesiastical system, could have fallen into the hands of more sincere or of more spiritual men. The quality of puritanical piety was pure, — much purer than that which ordinarily demands the respect of mankind. Their religion had been learned from no authority, except a divine one. Nothing resembling its tone of fervor had previously existed around them; and, in maintaining it, they had adopted no fashion of the day. Their professions had been winnowed and tested by persecution, — had been often placed in the crucible, or passed through the fire; and they possessed a vitality which had cheered their companions, and often silenced their very enemies. They had themselves suffered for heresy (as it was termed by others); it was a just inference that they would understand how to behave to those who were heretics in their own eyes. They had proved, in their own unaltered convictions, that the arm of power was too short to reach the inner man; and that a creed became suspicious just in proportion as its adoption was externally forced. They had experience (in their own persons, or in that of their forefathers) how Henry VIII. had led the nation away from popery, and would have restored it to popery (himself only wearing the tiara) again; they had bled under Mary for being protestants at all, and under Elizabeth for being protestants of any form save one; they had, under James' and Charles' rule, felt often convinced that, if the prelatical form of religion had been true, it would not have availed itself of such inconclusive arguments as physical ones to support it; and now, these men — men of an education fully equal to the mass of the clergy in any age (perhaps superior to most ages) — these men, whose deep and fervent piety thrilled through every fibre of their nature, and had been attested by sacrifices of every possible amount, — men whose heartfelt sincerity and simplicity will in all probability be felt, by means of their writings, to the end of time, — these men were permitted by Divine Providence to leap into the chariot from which the unskilful and malignant drivers had been just precipitated. And what was the course they pursued? They altered the venue, but they kept the legislation; they changed the hand, but they retained the sword; they mitigated the penalty, whilst, though the criminals were different, they yet pursued the offence. The consequence was, that they were preparing for themselves a sad and desolating reäction, — a reäction by which laws, liberties, religion, were a second time thrown down; and they added thus a new lesson to the many read before, — a lesson the more forcible because we love and venerate the men from whose mistake we have received it, — that force in religion makes slaves, and never freemen; that the noblest forms of piety do not flourish in its atmosphere; and that religion is a thing which men may embrace, but into which they will never be driven. Let us be wiser by the experience we have so disastrously gained!

It is with a sad and shuddering heart that the true lover of religious liberty follows the course of inconoclasticism pursued in those days. So far as prelacy was a tyrannical and unjust usurpation over the rights of conscience, it deserved to be exterminated. Happy had it been if the consequences had stopped at this point! Some considerable allowance might also be made, if the true protestants of that day believed that popery was not to be regarded as a spiritual system alone, but as one which aimed at an unrighteous temporal sovereignty. But the desolation went much further. It was not merely that they deprived bishops of their seats in the House of Peers, but it was that they proceeded against the persons of those who had been attached to prelacy with relentless eagerness. It was not merely that they took every precaution to screen themselves from the political rule of Romanism; nor yet was it that they removed from the army all Roman Catholics, — a measure which was undoubtedly justified by the excitement of the times. But it was that they desired to seize the lands of popish recusants, to execute bloody laws against priests, and to depress and subject to penalties all forms of religion except their own.

In the mean time, an enthusiastic but senseless rage took possession of the public mind, which led to the extensive destruction of ecclesiastical property. Organs were pulled asunder; communion-plate was melted down; prayer-books were torn in pieces; tombs were opened and despoiled; market crosses were pulled down or defaced.* The commons sent commissioners into the counties, to remove from the churches altars, images, crucifixes, and other idolatrous relics. "In diverse churches," says Baillie, "the people raised psalms to sing out the service; and in some they pulled down the railles before the altars." Doubtless these excesses of popular feeling often went beyond the intentions of the patriot leaders; but the prelatical party was reaping only the harvest which Laud and Strafford had sown, though, unquestionably,

* "Paul's and Westminster," says Baillie, "are purged of their images and organs, and all which gave offence. My Lord Manchester made two fair bonfires of such trinkets at Cambridge."

the proceedings were beneath the importance of the occasion, and provoked, at a later period, a tremendous retaliation. The true quarrel was not with the prayer-book, but with its impositions.

In order to supplement prelacy, thus abolished, the Long Parliament issued an ordinance convening an assembly of divines, for the purpose of effecting a reformation of religion. This measure was dated June 12th, 1643. After declaring the purity of religion to be one of the greatest blessings, and reciting the act passed for the abolition of the hierarchy, it convoked "all and every the persons hereafter in this ordinance named, that is to say" (here follow the names), "and such other persons as shall be nominated and appointed by both houses of parliament," &c. &c., "to meet and assemble at Westminster, in the chapel called King Henry VII.'s Chapel, on the 1st July, 1643," * * "to confer and treat among themselves of such matters and things touching the liturgy, discipline and government of the Church of England, or the vindicating and clearing of the same from all false aspersions and misconstructions, as shall be proposed to them by both or either of the said houses of parliament and no other, * * and not to divulge by printing, writing, or otherwise, without the consent of both or either house of parliament." The same warrant provided that Wm. Twisse, D. D., should occupy the chair, and that four shillings per day should be allowed to each member for his expenses.

The very constitution of the assembly proceeded upon confused and imperfect views of the duties of the civil government in matters of religion. Dr. Hetherington, the historian of the Free Church, says, deliberately, "It may be said, with the most strict propriety, that the native aim and tendency of the Westminster Assembly was to establish the presbyterian government in England, the great body of English puritans having gradually become presbyterians."* Unquestionably it was. Nor can we claim for any of the leading parties of that day the possession of a clear

* History of the Westminster Assembly, p. 136.

understanding of voluntary religion. It was deemed the duty of the state to be religious. It was, undoubtedly, the duty of every man regulating the state to be such; for that is an obligation which rests upon each member of the human family. But the essence of the state, as an organized system, is force; and force applied to religion neutralizes its whole character, which is the voluntary surrender of the soul to God. Religion is an affair of believed truths, of experimental conviction, of the practical exemplification of prescribed duties. The state has no soul to believe the truths, to experience the convictions, or to practise the duties, which religion involves. "The circumstance of a state church denies in principle, and compromises in fact, these sacred characteristics — namely, individuality and spontaneity — of every true worship; it annihilates, as far as in it lies, the religious being; it is not we, then, it is itself, which delivers to the state, under the name of a complete man, a wreck, a *caput mortuum* of the human being."*

In convening the assembly, the parliament authoritatively indicated the persons of whom it should be composed; though pains were taken to secure a comprehension of men of a few different shades of religious sentiment. Of Romanists, indeed, there were none, and it was impossible that there should be. Nor were quakers and baptists represented in the convocation. But summonses were addressed to moderate episcopalians,— that is, to those who were not prominent among the ranks of the stronger prelatists; Erastians — that is, those who believed with Erastus, that the ecclesiastical powers of a state should be altogether subordinated to its civil apparatus — were also summoned, and a few of the most eminent among the independents were nominated. But the majority of the assessors was composed of presbyterians. The lords were, — the Earls of Northumberland, Bedford, Pembroke and Montgomery, Salisbury, Holland, Manchester, Say and Sele, Conway, Wharton and Howard. Among the members of the Com-

* Vinet on Separation of Church and State, chap. x.

mons were Selden, whose book on "Tithes" — published 1618 — had shown that tithes were not the property of the clergy by divine right, but only by the law of the land, and who, for the publication of that book, had been compelled, in James' day, to make submission before the privy-council; one of Hampden's defenders in the matter of ship-money, a man of great learning, who often told the divines, "Perhaps in your pocket-books with gilt leaves the translation may be thus; but the Greek or the Hebrew signify thus and thus;" Sir H. Vane, senior, and his son, — the former had been secretary of state to Charles I., the latter had been chosen governor of New England, a man of great ability, quickness and versatility; apt to be led astray by quips and crotchets, but a sincere lover of liberty, and a man of first-rate eminence; Bulstrode Whitelocke, then member for Marlow, afterwards ambassador to the Queen of Sweden, to whose "Memorials," though tinged with party spirit, we are indebted for much information of the times; Oliver St. John, the celebrated defender of Hampden, whose wife was mother of Mrs. Lucy Hutchinson; and John Pym, who was, however, prevented by an untimely death from taking his part as an assessor.

The presbyterian divines were very numerous. Among them were Valentine, suspended for refusing to read "The Book of Sports;" Stephen Marshall, father-in-law of Nye, a man of the highest Christian eminence, a firm antagonist of the divine right of bishops, in opposition to which dogma, he had, with others, drawn up a work entitled "Smectymnuus," an anagrammatic compound of the initials of its authors, S. M. (Marshall), E. C. (Calamy), T. Y. (Young), M. N. (Newcomen), W. S. (Spurstowe); Thomas Case, who first set up the "Morning Exercises," and was afterwards imprisoned for conspiracy against the parliament; Dr. Gouge, an eminent theologian and practical writer; Dr. Reynolds, subsequently Bishop of Norwich; Dr. Love, afterwards beheaded for corresponding with Charles II.; Edward Calamy, a leading minister of London; Dr. Spurstowe, one of the chaplains of the lately-deceased Hampden, with many others.

The Erastian party comprehended Thomas Coleman, Dr. Lightfoot,—a name in the highest repute among scholars and critics,—and some others.

The independents—a portion of whom were designated, by emphasis, "the five dissenting brethren"—were principally Dr. Thomas Goodwin, of whom Owen said, "Nothing nor great, nor considerable, nor someway eminent, is by any person spoken of him, either consenting with him or differing from him," afterwards president of Magdalen College, Oxford; Sydrach Simpson, a good scholar; Jeremiah Burroughes, author of a commentary on Hosea, and remarkable for his gentle and pacific disposition; William Bridge, once minister of the parish church at St. George's Tombland, Norwich, of whom, when he fled from persecution to Holland, Laud said, "We are well rid of him!" the first pastor of a congregational church in Yarmouth; and Philip Nye, a man of remarkable learning, quickness and subtlety. "He left behind him," says Dr. Calamy, "the character of a man of uncommon depth, who was seldom, if ever, outreached." In addition to these "five," were Caryl, author of the exposition of Job, and Greenhill, who wrote the commentary on Ezekiel, and was, as evening preacher, called "the evening-star of Stepney."

The episcopal party were prohibited by the king from taking part in this assembly. Only one appeared, Dr. Featley. He was subsequently accused of revealing the secrets of the assembly to Archbishop Usher, and was expelled the convocation, and committed to prison. The places of the twenty-five who thus absented themselves were, in the end, supplied by twenty-five others. The usual attendance was between seventy and eighty. All these, however, did not take part in the debates, which were usually conducted by a few of the greatest eminence.

When the assembly met, a sermon was preached to them and to a very large congregation, in the abbey church, Westminster, by their prolocutor, Dr. Twisse. They then adjourned to Henry VII.'s Chapel. This was on Saturday, July 1st, 1643.

It is not wonderful if such a convocation drew forth expressions of very diverse opinions as to its character and value. The king, Laud (then in prison), Clarendon, Echard, all vehemently denounced it. Baxter says, "Being not worthy to be one" (of the assembly) "myself, I may the more freely speak the truth, even in the face of malice and envy; that, so far as I am able to judge by the information of all history of that kind, and by any other evidences left us, the Christian world, since the days of the apostles, had never a synod of more excellent divines than this and the synod of Dort." Milton in the first instance applauded it; but when this very assembly denounced his "Treatise on Marriage and Divorce," and caused him even to be summoned before the House of Lords, he saw reason to alter his conclusions. Hallam speaks of the assembly as "equal in learning, good sense, and other merits, to any lower house of convocation that ever made a figure in England."

Unhappily, the authorized journal of the proceedings of this assembly is irrecoverably lost. Some say that it was burnt in the fire of 1666; others, that it is still preserved in the library of Sion College, London. But there it is not to be found; and many believe it to have been destroyed by the fire which consumed the houses of parliament in 1834, having been carried there to assist the inquiries of the commissioners into the question of Scottish patronage, which was then pending. Certain it is, however, that the only sources of information open to the public are the journals of Baillie, one of the Scottish commissioners, and the other journal kept by Dr. Lightfoot, one of the assembly.

The time at which this assembly is gathered together is very critical. Essex is commander of the parliamentary forces; the Earl of Manchester having direction over the eastern counties, with Cromwell serving under him, but by no means relishing the half-measures of his superior officer. Strafford has been executed. Laud is in the Tower, whence he will remove no more alive. The battle of Newbury has been fought; but, out of the whole, it is difficult to say whether the military advantage be on the side of the king or of the parliament. Charles is at Oxford, and the

Scotch are summoning an army for a third expedition to England. In the view of the Scottish people, much depends upon this army. Independency has become, in their eyes, a very dangerous dogma; but it must be borne with, they think, till their army shall advance, and they shall be in a position to crush it. Besides, bad as independency is, "we expect," says Baillie, "no small help from them to abolish the great idol of England, the service-book." And again, "we did not much care for delays till the breath of our army might blow upon us some more favor and strength. So that the independent party were but walking over concealed ashes."

The labors of the assembly began upon the thirty-nine articles. The first fifteen occupied them ten weeks, and gave them much trouble. As this assembly had been originally called in compliance with the wishes of the Church of Scotland, one of the earliest acts of the parliament, after its sitting, was to send a deputation across the border, to solicit the presence in the convocation of Scottish commissioners. The embassy on this occasion consisted of the Earl of Rutland for the lords; Sir W. Armyn, Sir Harry Vane, jr., Mr. Hatcher and Mr. Darley, from the commons; and Mr. Marshall and Mr. Nye, from the assembly of divines. Baillie, principal of the university of Glasgow, gives us a graphic account of the whole transactions.

Nye, it appears, was very unacceptable, beforehand, to the Scottish assembly. "Mr. Marshall will be most welcome, but if Mr. Nye, the head of the independents, be his fellow, we cannot take it well."* There was considerable delay during the sittings of the assembly before the English envoys arrived. "We were ashamed with waiting." "We had our first session in a little roome of the east church," (qu. of St. Giles?) "which is very handsomelie dressed for our assemblies in all time coming." Some of the business which occupied the body is mournfully characteristic of the times. "Upon the regrate" (regret?) "of the extra-

* Baillie's Letters to Spang, July 26, 1643: and Sept. 22, 1643.

ordinar multiplying of witches, above thirtie being burnt in Fife in a few months, a committee was appointed to thinke on that sinne, the way to search and cure it."

At length the English commissioners land in a "strong vessel," appointed for the voyage, at Leith. "The lords went and convoyed them up in coatch. We were exhorted to be more grave than ordinaire; and so, indeed, all was carried to the end with much more awe and gravity than usual." These messengers brought, it appears, very urgent letters from England, which made mention of the doubtful position in which the parliament stood, and requested help from the Scotch. "The letter of the private divines was so lamentable, that it drew tears from many." "The English were for a civill league, we for a religious covenant. When they were brought to us in this (and Mr. Hendersone had given them a draught of a covenant, we were not like to agree on the frame), they were more nor we could assent to for keeping of a doore open in England to independencie. Against this we were peremptor." "In none of our brethren appears as yet the least inclination to independencie."

After much debate, the SOLEMN LEAGUE AND COVENANT, framed by Henderson, moderator of the assembly, was agreed to by the English commissioners, and passed, not without considerable misgiving, we may imagine, on the part of Philip Nye. The times were, it must be perceived, uncommonly difficult. Without the aid of the Scottish army, it was manifestly impossible that the parliament could make head against the king; and every circumstance concurs to prove that the independent party, pressed by the exigencies of the times, yielded in this affair their better judgment. As it was, an opportunity of the most extensive usefulness was lost, never to be regained; and in pledging themselves to the Scottish covenant, men were abandoning the high principles of liberty for which the war with the king had been undertaken, were weaving extensive snares for men's consciences, and were arming the civil government with a power too soon to be directed against themselves.

Something, at least, which Nye said or did on this occasion, appears to have given no little offence.

"The Sabbath before noon, in the new church, we heard Mr. Marshall preach with great contentment; but, in the afternoon, in the Grey Friars, Mr. Nye did not please. His voice was clamorous; he touched, neither in prayer or preaching, the common bussinesse." That is, he did not preach about the covenant. "He read much out of his paper book. All his sermon was on the common head of a spiritual life; wherein he ran out above all our understandings, upon a knowledge of God, as God, without the Scripture, without grace, without Christ. They say he amended it somewhat the next Sabbath."* This covenant, thus agreed upon, was sent in "a ketch" to London, where it occasioned no little difficulty. In the assembly of divines, all seemed to have approved it, except Burgess.† He, we are told, "did doubt for one night." About this time a mob besieged the House of Commons, demanding peace with the king on any terms; and some of the lords, who were adverse to the proceedings of the parliament, "stole away." "Surely," says Baillie, "it was a great act of faith in God, and huge courage, and unheard-of compassion, that moved our nation to hazard their own peace, and venture their lives and all for to save a people irrecoverablie ruined, both in their owne, and all the world's eyes."

* * * * *

The scene now changes to St. Margaret's Church, Westminster, which the reader may remember to be a parochial edifice, standing by the side of the great abbey. The whole assembly of divines, together with the House of Commons, here met with the Scottish commissioners, among their number Henderson, Lord Maitland (subsequently Lord Lauderdale), and Gillespie. To these were

* Baillie's Letter to Spang, Sept. 22, 1643.

† "A wretch," says Dr. Lightfoot, speaking of Burgess and his opposition, "that ought to be branded to all posterity, who seeks, for some devilish ends either of his own or others, or both, to hinder so great a good of the two nations.

added, at a later period, Archibald Johnston, of Warrington, a victim, in later days, of Lord Lauderdale's barbarity; Samuel Rutherford, largely known by his religious and devotional works; and Robert Baillie, afterwards Principal of Glasgow, to whose letters we are mainly indebted for our information of the period. After solemn prayer, Nye ascended the pulpit, and addressed the audience in a prolonged speech, in which he exhibited the scriptural authority for covenants, and dilated on their advantages. Henderson followed, in a shorter speech, but one described as possessing "great dignity and power." Nye then read the covenant. The document is too long to be here quoted at large, but its contents are well known. It was a pledge that those entering into it would preserve "the reformed religion in the Church of Scotland, in doctrine, worship, discipline, and government;" and would "endeavor to bring the churches of God in the three kingdoms to the nearest conjunction and uniformity in religion;" that they would "endeavor the extirpation of popery, prelacy, superstition, heresy, schism, profaneness, and whatsoever shall be found contrary to sound doctrine and the power of godliness;" that they would preserve the rights of the parliament, the liberties of the kingdom, and the king's majesty; that they would endeavor to discover malignants, and those who hindered the reformation of religion; that they would be at peace with each other; and that they would amend their lives, and give an example of real reformation. "And this covenant we make in the presence of Almighty God, the searcher of hearts, with a true intention to perform the same, as we shall answer at that great day, when the secrets of all hearts shall be disclosed," &c. &c. At the end of each clause of this covenant, the whole assembly arose and lifted up their right hand to heaven. They afterwards appended, in the chancel, their names to the oath. The covenant was afterwards taken by both houses of parliament, and by various congregations in and around London. The House of Commons ordained that it should be sworn to by all persons in England above the age of eighteen; and that those who refused to take it should be disqualified from becoming common councilmen of the city, or from voting for such officers. It was a part of the conditions necessary for ordination, and for holding any post, military or civil. The historian of the free church says that the league and covenant was too good for the age. We believe the garment to have been too small to be adapted to men whose opinions must necessarily differ. It was like a straight waistcoat upon energetic spiritual action. Men will never go to solemn leagues and covenants again. Religion proved incomprehensible by such a mould; — not worldly enough for a machine of state, and not spiritual enough for earnest and heaven-born men, it exploded in the hands of its workmen, and hundreds of them were wounded by its fragments.

The first place in which this assembly met was Henry VII.'s Chapel at Westminster. As the winter came on, they transferred their sittings to a less splendid, but more venerable and more convenient apartment.

The visitor to the abbey who stands at its western front, opposite to the two towers erected by Wren, may mark a small knot of buildings, insignificant when compared with the church itself, abutting on the south tower. One of these, the window of which is defended by wire, still bears the name of the Jerusalem chamber. It was erected in the reigns of Edward III. and Richard I. The chamber is thirty-eight feet long and nineteen broad, with a coved ceiling, and a handsome mantel-piece of cedar, erected in the reign of James I. Its side-walls exhibit some old tapestry hangings, removed from the choir of the abbey, and a curious painting of Richard II.; a colored window mitigates and tinges the light of day. The room is memorable as the death-place of Henry IV., who, when preparing for a voyage to the Holy Land, was taken sick whilst worshipping at the shrine of St. Edward. "He became so syke," says Fabian, "while he was makynge his prayers, to take there his leve, and so to spede hym upon his journeye, that such as were aboute him feryd that he would have dyed right there; wherefore they, for his comforte, bare hym into the abbot's place and lodged him in a chamber, and there, upon a pay-let, leyde him before the fyre." He asked where he was, and on being told the Jerusalem Chamber, he imagined it to be the fulfilment of a previous prophecy that he should die in Jerusalem.

> "Laud be to Heaven! — even there my life must end.
> It hath been prophesied to me many years
> I should not die but in Jerusalem,
> Which vainly I supposed the Holy Land!"
>
> SHAKSPEARE, *Henry IV., Part II.*

It was in this chamber, also, that Addison's body lay in state before his funeral in Westminster Abbey.

JERUSALEM CHAMBER.

Baillie, one of the Scottish commissioners, now arrived in London, shall himself describe the assembly as it sat in this building: "At the one end nearest the door, and along both sides, are stages of seats, as in the new assembly house at Edinburgh, but not so high; for there will be room but for five or six score. At the uppermost end there is a chair set on a frame, a foot from the earth, for the Mr. Prolocutor, Dr. Twisse. Before it, on the ground, stand two chairs for the two Mr. Assessors, Dr. Burgess and Mr. White. Before these two chairs, through the whole length of the room, stands a table, at which sit the two scribes. * * Opposite the table, upon the prolocutor's right hand, there are three or four ranks of benches. On the lowest we five do sit. Upon the other, at our backs, the members of parliament deputed to the assembly. On the benches opposite to us, on the prolocutor's left hand, going from the upper end of the house to the chimney, and at the other end of the house and back of the table, till it come about to our seats, are four or five stages of benches, upon which their divines sit as they please: albeit, commonly they keep the same place. From the chimney to the door there are no seats, but a void space for passage. The lords of the parliament use to sit on chairs, in that void, about the fire. We meet every day of the week but Saturday. We sit commonly from nine till one or two afternoon. * * No man is called up to speak; but whosoever stands up of his own accord speaks as long as he will without interruption. * * They study the questions well beforehand, and prepare their speeches; but withal the men are exceedingly prompt and well-spoken. I do marvel at the very accurate and extemporal replies that many of them usually make."

At this period the Scottish commissioners were the lions of London. They were fêted, consulted with the utmost deference, and their preaching was attended by such crowds, that many retired unable to obtain an entrance.

Soon after the assembly of divines was constituted, it, with the members of both houses of parliament, was invited to a great feast by the Lord Mayor and Sheriffs at "Taylor's Hall." This was a grand occasion. A sermon of thanksgiving was preached in the morning by Stephen Marshall. The guests then walked in procession to Taylor's Hall in the following order: first, the common council in their gowns; next, the mayor and aldermen in scarlet on horseback. After these the general, admiral and lords, with officers of the army, on foot. Then followed the House of Commons and the assembly of divines. It was arranged that the Scottish commissioners should come between the commons and the assembly; "but," says one of them, "my Lord Maitland being drawn away to the lords, and we not loving to take our place before all the divines of England, stole away to our coatch; and when there was no way for coatches, for throng of people, we went on foot, with great difficultie, through hudge crowdings of people. While all past throu Cheapside, there was a great bonfyre kindled, where the rich Cross wont to stand, of manie fyne pictures of Christ and the saints, of relicks, beads, and such trinkets. The feast was great, valued at four thousands pounds sterling; yet had no desert, nor musick, but drums and trumpets. In the great laigh hall were four tables for the lords and commons. The mayor at the head of the chiefe in ane upper roome. Two long tables for the divines; at the head of the which we were sett, with their proloquutor. All was concluded with a psalme, whereof Dr. Burgess read the line. There was no excess in any we heard of. The speaker of the commons house drank to the lords, in name of all the commons of England. The lords stood all up, everie one with his glass, for they represent none but themselves, and drank to the commons. The mayor drank to both in name of the citie. The sword-bearer, with his strong cap of maintainance still fixed on his head, came to us with the mayor's drink." *

We have seen that ten weeks were spent by this assembly in discussing the thirty-nine articles. Before, however, this debate was ended, an order came from both houses of parliament requesting their immediate attention to the subjects of discipline and a directory of worship. This was in reality the great purpose of their meeting. After a day of solemn fasting and prayer, they agreed to take up the subject of church government; and, to avoid any unnecessary differences of opinion at the outset, they began with church officers. Various debates followed, in the midst of which the parliament, embarrassed by these delays, sent a message requesting a speedy decision respecting two points, — the ordination of ministers and induction into vacant benefices. (It was now October.) Ministers, regular and irregular, deprived by the

* Baillie, Feb. 18, 1644.

tyranny of Laud, were starving, and asked to be replaced or maintained; and the great difficulty pressed upon the assembly how to deal with those whom they might account regular, so as not to do flagrant injustice to those whose tenets they accounted heretical. An impossible equation truly! though some attempt was made to solve it. Then came the questions of ordination and discipline, debates on which lasted till the end of the year. Parliament became more impatient; the assembly was required to make more haste! But this was not so easy. A body of independents, consisting of Philip Nye, Thomas Goodwin, D.D. (not to be confounded with John Goodwin), Sydrach Simpson, Jeremiah Burroughes, and William Bridge (called "the five dissenting brethren"), with a few others, proved themselves, according to the views of the Scottish commissioners, extremely troublesome and pertinacious. It was April before the assembly, having long dwelt upon the doctrinal part of ordination, came to consider the manner in which it should be conducted. When this was settled by a majority of votes, and the report presented to parliament, that superior assembly altered certain parts of it likely to prove offensive to the leading sectaries, and sent it back amended to the assembly, who refused to receive it. The remonstrances of the convocation caused it to be restored to the condition in which they had presented it; and it thus became the law of the land, a committee being appointed for the ordination of ministers, consisting of ten of the assembly with thirteen city ministers.

But rocks and quicksands of every variety yet beset the course of these theological navigators, sailing in search of a land of happy uniformity. Defeated in voting, the independent party made use of the press. "Foreseeing," says Baillie, "they behoved ere long to come to the point, they put out, in print, on a sudden, an Apologetical Narration of their way, which long had lain ready beside them, wherein they petition the parliament, in a most sly and cunning way, for a toleration; and withal lend too bold wipes to all the reformed churches, as imperfect yet in their reformation, till their new model be embraced." In this publication, undeserving of Baillie's censure, the writers state their own sufferings for the sake of the truth; avow their wish to stand only by the Word of God; acknowledge "multitudes of the assemblies and parochial congregations" (of the Church of England) to be "the true churches and body of Christ, and the ministry thereof to be a true ministry," "and that they had held, and would hold, communion with them as the churches of Christ," &c. Calm and dignified as this publication was, it irritated the opposite party almost into frenzy, and upon this rock the whole vessel afterwards became irrecoverably stranded. A sharp and somewhat acrimonious conflict began, in the midst of which, the battle of Marston-moor having been now gained, an order of the commons reached the assembly, "to refer to the committee of both kingdoms the accommodation or toleration of the independents." "This," says Baillie, "is the fruit of their disservice, to obtain really an act of parliament for their toleration, before we have got anything for presbytery, either in assembly or parliament."

It is evident that, however defective the views of the independents might be, they were considerably in advance of the assembly in general. Yet they distinctly acknowledged the power of the magistrate in backing the sentences of the various churches, and say that to hold an exemption from the power of the civil magistrate is dishonorable to Christianity; whilst they disclaimed the notion of a national church in any other sense than as a collection of individual congregational bodies,* and claimed the right of "gathering churches," though out of the members of other communions, — a demand necessarily fatal to the scheme of a general uniformity. Such were the views propounded in the "Apologetical Narration."

To follow the debates of this famous convocation through all the points which came under its notice is, within our limits, impossible. Cynically enough, yet truly, Carlyle thus describes it: "Uniformity of free-growing, healthy forest-trees is good; uniformity of

* Hetherington's Westminster Assembly, p. 201.

clipt Dutch-dragons is not so good! The question, Which of the two? is by no means settled, — though the assembly of divines and majorities of both houses would fain think it so. The general English mind, which, loving good order in all things, loves regularity even at a high price, could be content with this presbyterian scheme, which we call the Dutch-dragon one; but a deeper portion of the English mind inclines decisively to growing in the forest-tree way, — and, indeed, will shoot out into very singular excrescences, quakerisms, and what not, in the coming years. Nay, already we have anabaptists, Brownists, sectaries and schismatics, springing up very rife; already there is a Paul Best, brought before the House of Commons for Socinianism; nay, we hear of another distracted individual, who seemed to maintain, in confidential argument, that 'God was mere reason.' There is like to be need of garden-shears, at this rate! The devout House of Commons, viewing these things with a horror inconceivable in our loose days, knows not well what to do. London city cries — 'Apply the shears!' — the army answers, 'Apply them *gently;* cut off nothing that is sound.' The question of garden-shears, and how far you are to apply them, is really difficult; — the settling of *it* will lead to very unexpected results. London city knows with pain that there are 'many persons in the army who have never yet taken the covenant,' the army begins to consider it unlikely that certain of them ever *will* take it." *

It is very clear that in this assembly the independent party argued for a more complete toleration than had been yet seen, or than their opponents were at all willing to grant. "People in the country," — as distinguished from those in London, — says Baillie, "complained that the assembly did cry down the truth with votes, and was but an anti-christian meeting, which would soon erect a presbytery worse than bishops." Nye contended strongly against presbyterial church government. Baillie says, "The day following, when he saw the assembly full of the prime nobles and chief members of both houses, he did fall upon the argument again, and

* Carlyle's Cromwell, vol. I., pp. 341, 342.

boldly offered to demonstrate that our way of drawing a whole kingdom under one national assembly was formidable, yea, pernicious, and thrice over pernicious to civil states and kingdoms. All cried him down, and some would have had him expelled the assembly as seditious." Again, "Our next work is to give our advice what to do for the suppression of anabaptists, antinomians, and other sectaries." "The independents, in their last meeting of our grand committee of accommodation, have expressed their desires for toleration, not only to themselves, but to other sects."

It is equally clear, however, that the toleration which these five "dissenting brethren" advocated so strongly was not a perfect equality in matters of religious opinion.

In a treatise entitled "Irenicum; to the Lovers of Truth and Peace," written evidently after these agitations of this Westminster Assembly, Jeremiah Burroughes (one of the five) says:

"But for all that hath been said, are there not yet a sort of men who though they would colour over things, and put faire glosses upon their opinion and wayes, saying they would not have such an absolute liberty as to have all religions suffered, yet doe they not come near this in their tenets and practice? Doe not men in a congregational way take away all ecclesiastical means that should hinder such an absolute liberty as this? for they hold, every congregation hath sole power within itself, and they are not tyed to give any account to others, but merely in an arbitrary way. *Will not this bring in a toleration of all religions*, and a very anarchy?

"First: I *know none holds this;* and how farre men in a congregationall way are from it shall appear presently." He then shows "wherein consists the power of the magistrate in matters of religion," and that "they which are for a congregationall way doe not hold absolute liberty for all religions." He adduces the examples of Jewish worship, in support of the doctrine that it is the province of the magistrate to interpose, though not in all cases; and says, "I doe not in these deliver only mine owne judgement, but by what I know of the judgements of all those brethren with whom I have occasion to converse by conference, both before and since: I stand charged to make it good to be their judgments also; yea, it hath been both their's and mine for divers years,"* &c. This, from one of the "five brethren," is surely decisive.

Some of the mistakes on this point have evidently arisen from confounding the name of Dr. Thomas Goodwin with that of John Goodwin, of Coleman Street. The latter published a work arising out of the "Apologetical Narration," which proves him, says Baillie, "to be a bitter enemie to presbytery, and to be openly for a full liberty of conscience to all sects, even Turks, Jews, papists." Again: "The independents here, finding they have not the magistrate so obsequious as in New England, turn their penns, as you will see in MS." (John Goodwin), "to take from the magistrate all power of taking any coercive order with the vilest heretics. Not only they praise your magistrate, who for secret policie gives some secret tollerance to diverse religions, wherein, as I conceive, your divines preache against them as great sinners; but avows by God's command, the magistrate is discharged to put the least discourtesie on any man, Turk, Jew, papist, Socinian, or whatever, for his religion. I wish Apollonius† considered this well. *The five he writes to will not say this;* but MS. (John Goodwin) is of as great authoritie here as any of them."‡

In a work published by Baillie, a year or two later, he refers to the same John Goodwin's "Theomachia," and quotes the following passage:

"Concerning other civil means for the suppression and restraint of these spiritual evils, errours, heresies, &c., as imprisonment, banishment, interdictions, fineings, &c., both reason and experience concur in this demonstration, that such fetters as these, put on the

* Burroughes' Irenicum, pp. 18, 44.

† Apollonius wrote a book entitled "A Consideration of Certain Controversies agitated in the Kingdom of England;" he sent from the Wallachian churches to declare the sense and consent of their churches to the Synod at London, 1645.

‡ Baillie's Letters.

feet of errors and heresies, to secure and keep them under, still have proved wings whereby they raise themselves the higher in the thoughts and minds of men, and gain an opportunity of further propagation."

So far was the generality, even of men of the most expanded minds, from apprehending the true principles of religious freedom at this period, that Milton himself, though a noble defender of religious toleration in general, places exceptions to its universal extension, and regards Romanism and idolatry as not to be comprised in its benefits.* The exceptions taken in those days excite our regret, rather than our wonder. Sir Harry Vane, taught by Roger Williams, appears to have been the only one in the assembly who assserted anything like consistent sentiments. He pleaded for "a full libertie of conscience to all religions," and opposed the clause which required subscription to the covenant before ordination.† To the anabaptists, as they were then termed, the high praise is due, that at this period and before it they had been clear in the principle, "that it is not only unmerciful, but unnatural and abominable, yea, monstrous, for one Christian to vex and destroy another for difference on questions of religion." ‡ They asked again, "Whether it be not better for us that a patent were granted to monopolize all the cloth and corn, and to have it measured out unto us, at their price and pleasure, which were yet intolerable, as for some men to appoint and measure out to us what and how much we shall believe and practise in matters of religion?" "If the magistrate must punish errors in religion, whether it does not impose a necessity that the magistrate have a certainty of knowledge in all intricate cases? And whether God calls such to that place whom he hath not furnished with abilities for that place? And if a magistrate in darkness, and spiritually blind and dead, be

* See John Milton: a Biography. By Cyrus R. Edmonds.

† Baillie, Oct. 25, 1644.

‡ Religion's Peace; or, a Plea for Liberty of Conscience. Published 1646, with a preface to the presbyterian reader.

fit to judge of light, of truth, and error? And whether such be fit for the place of the magistracy?"*

Such are specimens of the kind of questions addressed by baptists to the consideration of the Assembly of Divines, at the period of which we write.

It is scarcely surprising that, among the most grievous heresies of the day, anabaptism was hence regarded as of singular malignity. The following extract from a title-page of the period will speak for itself:

ANABAPTISME THE TRUE FOUNTAINE
OF
INDEPENDENCY } { ANTINOMY
BROWNISME } { FAMILISM
AND THE MOST OF THE OTHER ERROURS
WHICH FOR THE TIME DOE TROUBLE
THE CHURCH OF ENGLAND, UNSEALED,
&c., &c., &c.,
BY ROBERT BAILLIE, MINISTER AT GLASGOW.
1647.

This work, dedicated to "the Right Hon. the Earl of Lauderdail" and others, is an attempt to confound the anabaptists of that day with the abettors of the outrages and abominations of Münster. One of their enormities is thus held up to horror,—"They are a people very zealous of liberty, and most unwilling to be under the bondage of any other."

It is easy to charge upon the independent members of this Westminster Assembly factiousness and crotchetiness. It is intimated by the free-church historian, Dr. Hetherington, that Nye and his brethren were introduced by the intrigues of Cromwell purposely to thwart the progress of the deliberations. But this is entirely gratuitous. The fact evidently was, that the men who had originally met to promote a protestant uniformity found themselves

* Necessity of Toleration in matters of Religion: Certain Questions proposed to the Synod, &c. By Samuel Richardson, 1647.

further and further, as the discussion advanced, from the object they sought. The justice of differing claims opposed the course they had at first meditated. Experience taught them truth; they found that they themselves were on the brink of exclusion, as afterwards happened, from the new establishment; and they plainly saw what disastrous effects would follow, if the "sectarian" parties, now increased and increasing, were excluded by the parliament they were even now in arms to support. They had aimed to form an establishment, based, to some extent, on the voluntary consent of differing parties. It was like extracting "sunbeams from cucumbers." The effort dislocated the puritan party; the presbyterians, resolved to have their doctrine and discipline, seized the earliest period possible, and brought in their covenanted king!

The history of what the Westminster Assembly, or rather the parliament under their guidance, did accomplish, must be briefly told. They suppressed the liturgy, — forbade the use of the common-prayer in public or in private, under the penalty of five pounds for the first offence, ten pounds for the second, and a year's imprisonment for the third. They set up a directory for public worship, according to the presbyterial model, including sitting at the communion, and burying without the necessity of a religious ceremony; and imposed a fine on those who did not observe this directory, of forty shillings, whilst such as should "preach, write, or print anything in derogation of it," forfeited a sum of not less than five pounds, nor more than twenty pounds. They ordered all prayer-books found in churches to be disposed of according to the pleasure of parliament. They enforced the observance of the Sabbath, ordaining "That no person, without cause, shall travel, or carry a burden, or do any worldly labor, upon penalty of ten shillings for the traveller, and five shillings for every burden;" and "if children are found offending in the premises, their parents and guardians to forfeit twelve pence for every offence."* They put down the observance of Christmas, by a special decree, which commanded a fast in its stead; they determined "what degrees

* Neal, chap. IV.

of knowledge in the Christian religion were necessary to qualify persons for the communion, and what sorts of scandal deserved suspension or excommunication." They passed a presbyterian form of church government, "as narrow," says Neal, "as the prelatical; and as it did not allow a liberty of conscience, claiming a civil as well as ecclesiastical authority over men's persons and properties, it was equally, if not more insufferable."* The Assembly of Divines claimed presbyterian government as a divine right, and, therefore, independent of parliamentary control; but this the parliament would not acknowledge. The same assembly denied the right of the independents to form separate congregations, till they forced the moderate Burroughes to declare, on behalf of the independents, that, "if their congregations might not be exempted from the coercive power of the classes, if they might not have liberty to govern themselves in their own way as long as they behaved peaceably towards the civil magistrate, they were resolved to suffer, or go to some other place of the world, where they might enjoy their liberty." Prynne himself, the victim of Laud, declared, "that if the parliament and synod establish presbytery, the independents and all others are bound to submit, under pain of obstinacy." But the debate on this subject was never ended. They imprisoned one of their own members, Dr. Featley, as a spy, mainly for his attachment to the Church of England, sequestrated his livings, and he died in their hands. They demanded of the king that he would sign the covenant; confirm the proceedings of the Assembly of Divines; establish an oath whereby papists should be required to renounce the pope's supremacy, provide for the education of the children of papists by protestants, prevent the hearing of mass, enforce the observance of the Lord's day, and declare those who had taken arms against the parliament incapable of preferment or employment, without consent of the houses of legislature, — the king intriguing, in the mean time, with the independents on the one hand, and the presbyterians on the other. They abolished "archbishops and bishops, and for-

* Neal, chap. VI.

bade their ecclesiastical jurisdiction, or the use of their titles." They denounced lay-preachers, and published an ordinance to prevent "the growth of errors, heresies and blasphemies;" they authorized the larger and shorter catechisms, and confession of faith, and Rouse's metrical Psalms; they declared stage-players punishable as rogues, and decreed that they should be publicly whipped, whilst all spectators should be fined five shillings for every offence; they proclaimed that any person holding certain heresies, — atheism, Socinianism, universalism, free-will, quakerism, &c., — should be, for some offences, committed to prison, and, unless he abjured, should suffer the pains of death; whilst for others, he should be imprisoned till he found sureties that he would maintain such doctrines no more! Such was presbyterian uniformity!

Many baptists were exposed — among them Hanserd Knollys — to severe persecutions, were stoned, fined, imprisoned and outraged. The sufferings of the episcopal clergy were great. Provision was, indeed, made for them out of the sales of lands heretofore in the possession of bishops and chapters of cathedrals, and from a fifth of tithes and livings; but the allowance became difficult, and, from their suspected monarchical tendencies, dangerous to be procured. The course taken against Roman Catholics was even more severe.

Such were the fruits of a national establishment which, in the first instance, presbyterians and independents had united to form! The lamentable result shows that the evils of persecution are not justly chargeable upon any mere opinions, whether episcopalian or any other, but upon the principle of state-alliance itself. That involves so monstrous an injustice, as to metamorphose the best of men into the most unrelenting. Laud himself, when his actions are fairly put by the side of his principles, was not so bad as he seemed; and it was not wonderful that these really good men should, when judged by the same standard as that which was applied to him, appear, though none ever less deserved the charge, self-seekers and hypocrites. It is the infallible effect of power used for spiritual purposes, that it contaminates and degrades the men who use it. We can no more apologize for the conduct of the

Long Parliament, than we can for the burning of Servetus, the sufferings of Bartholomew-day, or the horrors of the inquisition. The degrees of penalty might differ ; the substantial principle was the same.

The assembly of divines dwindled away, after the business of the committee of accommodation, till the death of the king. A fragment of it remained after that period, for the examination of ministers. The dissolution of the Long Parliament was at hand, and the convocation perished with it. It was high time!

The Earl of Manchester was deputed by the House of Lords, at some time hereafter, to congratulate Charles II. on his return.

Philip Nye was very prominent in political movements during the period of the commonwealth. When commissioners were appointed to treat with the king in the Isle of Wight, Nye was one of their chaplains; and when the citizens of London were actively endeavoring to procure a treaty with the king, he endeavored by a counter-petition to prevent it. Nye was one of the Triers for appointing ministers, and is represented as having a living at Acton, and lectures in Westminster and London. He opposed the return of Charles, and it was for some time questioned whether he should be excepted from the king's indulgence. Nye drew up a complete history of the old puritan dissenters, but the manuscript was burnt in the fire of London. After the Restoration, he preached to a church who met chiefly in private houses, till the indulgence granted by Charles II. He died in September, 1672, aged seventy-six, and was buried in St. Michael's, Cornhill.

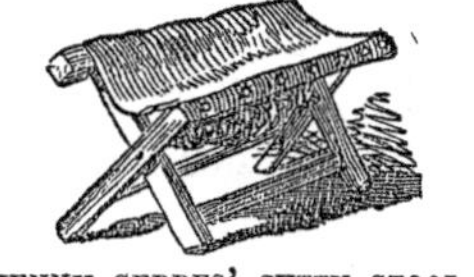

JENNY GEDDES' CUTTY STOOL.

CHAPTER VI.

THE CROWNLESS MONARCH.

"Strongest of mortal men!
* * * His fiery virtue roused
From under ashes into sudden flame!"
Samson Agonistes.

HUNTINGDON.—THE BIRTH-PLACE OF CROMWELL.

THE "whirligig of time," which "brings about its revenges," has within the last two years restored the town of Huntingdon to its ancient place on the great north road. When stage-coaches began to mend their pace, and to cease to stop on their journey, it was of some consequence to avoid the angle which the road made at that point, and Huntingdon was dispossessed of its pride of place, till the Great Northern Railway was recently brought through it. Yet Huntingdon boasts of some antiquity. It was one of the head-quarters of the Iceni, — possibly of the ancient British queen, Boadicea, herself; its "castle hills" were probably the site of the fortress which gave to the Duriliponte of Antoninus, afterwards called, in Saxon, Godmanchester (Good-man's-castle), its importance; and its name occurs in Saxon chronicles as Huntandene, and sometimes as Huntantum. Henry of Huntingdon lived here, and Edward the Elder rebuilt, near the town, a castle given by Stephen to David, Earl of Huntingdon and King of Scotland, of which the intrenchments remain, though the building was destroyed by Henry II., as affording too safe a retreat to his disaffected barons. In subsequent times, when the steam-engine was a mere toy in the hands of the Marquis of Worcester, when delays in travelling were as much sought as they are now avoided, that passengers might repose their bodies, bruised by the jolting and ill-managed roads, and refresh their exhausted frames; when night journeys were full of dangers, and the passage from York to London was measured but by days; Huntingdon formed a convenient resting-place, and abounded in inns, after the model then most approved, replete with all conveniences which the luxury of the times could furnish.

Huntingdon has now lost much of its ancient *prestige*. Its monasteries are dismantled, and their localities almost unknown: instead of the fifteen churches once standing in it, it now boasts only two; and the hospitals which formerly distinguished it have altogether disappeared. Nor will the traveller be attracted to the town by any very picturesque environs. On one side of the river Ouse, there are, indeed, gentle and agreeable undulations, though they are deserving of no higher name, and the foliage of several respectable trees is full and luxuriant. But the traveller who stands on the ancient bridge with his back to the town, and looks out on the expanse before him, may begin to understand what is meant by the phrase, so mysterious to the uninitiated, *the fens.* He will see a kind of Sahara, in which the fault, however, is not too little water, but too much, and out of which a few distant churches stand up as land-marks. Through this level the river "creeping like snail," slowly saunters along; and if its waters do contrive to reach the sea near Lynn, it is by dint of more means and appliances than we can now stay to record. It was some similar region to that now within sight that a celebrated preacher called "the focus of suicides;" and the few willows scattered in groups over the wide flat correspond sufficiently to his similitude of "nature hanging out signals of distress." Certainly, if there be any poetry on this side of the town, it is such as only Cowper, who for some time resided here, could have found; and but that "the blue sky," always beautiful, "bends over all," one may well wonder at the interest awakened in some whom we have known by the view. If great thoughts have ever come into minds in this region, they must have arisen from interior inspiration, not by any natural and obvious association with the scenes themselves. But one great name is prominent in the history of this heretofore celebrated town, a name long cast out as worthless, but now believed to be not wholly a lie; and the whole region is memorable for having produced a phenomenon, regarded once as a mere flashing meteor which had passed away into darkness, but now, in spite of Heylins and Clarendons, and Heaths and Humes, and house-of-parliament decorators, proved to have had an orbit of its own, and to have been, nay, yet to be, one of the superior planets of our system. Need we pronounce the name of Cromwell?

But it is not at Huntingdon that the visitant will discover any enthusiastic memory of that remarkable man, or even many traces of his whereabouts. Except the bridge, a few ancient gateways, the two surviving churches, and one or two scattered and mouldering fragments besides, there is little to feed an antiquarian's curiosity. Something about the whole town, indeed, reminds one of the past. But this is owing rather to the narrowness of the streets, and the projecting upper stories of the houses, than to any actual antiquity in the buildings. The majesty of Huntingdon, if it ever had any, is faded away.

Passing through the single street of which this now quiet country town is composed, and leaving behind us the area called the market-place, we reach, after a short walk, a house on the right, now shut in by high walls and overtopped by pleached lime-trees; a pleasant spot, suggestive of privacy and wealth; a true banker's residence; and here, we are told, the Protector was born. Whether this was really a brewery, is doubtful; but it is very probable that, in his day, malting and brewing to some extent may have been carried on upon the premises to supply the wants of tenants and dependants. At all events, the narrow lane which runs by the side of the mansion, contiguous to its adjacent out-buildings, and the vicinity of a little brook hard by, would have been very suitable for such purposes. But the family of Cromwell was not baseborn.

Let us now take the reader by the hand, and invite him to a pleasant walk up the gentle slope which overhangs the town, and across a bridge now traversing the Great Northern Railway. Thick groves of young and flourishing trees, enclosed within extensive oaken fences, mark the beautiful residence of one of our English aristocracy, the Earl of Sandwich. If the reader can propitiate the dragons who guard the entrance, he will find himself, after traversing a considerable park, before a residence of the olden time, views of which catch the eye of the railway traveller as he approaches Huntingdon from the south. This is the ancient residence of the family of Cromwell, — Hinchinbrook House.

"I was by birth," said Cromwell, in one of his speeches to parliament, "neither living in any considerable height, nor yet in obscurity." His family was well born, had some relationship with

Thomas Cromwell, Earl of Essex, and "mauler of monasteries" in the times of Henry VIII., and was represented by many branches round about the country. The church of All-Saints, Huntingdon, yet preserves traces of some of them; namely,

"Johan Cromwell, daughter of Mr. Oliver Cromwell, buried 13 April, 1600."

"James Tinsty, servant to Sir George Cromwell."

"Mistress Oliver Cromwell, of Godmanchester, buried the 27 July, and her funeral was the 12th of August." (Sic!)

"Richard, the son of Mr. George Cromwell, buried the 18 Nov. 1601."

"Mr. George Cromwell, Captain, buried the 24 of December, 1601."

Hinchinbrook was somewhat memorable in the history of royal progresses. Henry Cromwell entertained Elizabeth at this family mansion in 1563, and was knighted by the queen in testimony of her remembrance of his hospitalities. He had a large family, six sons and five daughters; the eldest son succeeded to the estate; the second daughter was the mother of Hampden; the youngest son, Robert, was father of the protector.

This Robert Cromwell, whose elder brother, Oliver, it is to be remembered, was Lord of Hinchinbrook, married a Miss Steward, of the Isle of Ely, a descendant of the royal family of the Stuarts, though the name had become, in process of time, a little changed. She was a woman of equal energy and virtue; simple in her habits, firm in character, a faithful wife, and a true mother, who, in the later years of her life, occupied apartments in the palace of Whitehall, and at the age of ninety-five breathed forth her "good-night" to her son, who stood by her bed-side.

Of these parents was born Oliver Cromwell, named after his uncle at Hinchinbrook. Four days afterwards, the infant was baptized in the parish church of St. John's, which then stood opposite to his father's house, but the site of which is now a mere cemetery. The baptismal registry is still extant:

"*Anno Dom.*, 1599.

"*Oliverus, filius Robti Cromwell gentis et Elizabeth ux: eius, natus vicesimo quinto die Aprilis, et Baptisatus vicesimo nono eiusdem mensis.*"

Of the house in which this great man saw the light, scarcely any, if any, trace is now extant. Rumor speaks of a remnant of the old Gothic edifice; but it is mere rumor. The existing building is of comparatively modern date; and as one walks round, and looks into the precincts, all which one can connect with Cromwell is an ancient wall, probably belonging to the monastery on the locality of which Mr. Robert Cromwell's house was built, but which it gratifies the fancy to connect with the boyish antics of the future statesman. Many traditions, two of which we give as we find them, have become attached to Oliver's memory. One is, that when the little infant was carried up to Hinchinbrook, that his relatives might see him, a monkey took him from the cradle, and carried him up to the leads of the house. Another is, that the child was saved from drowning by Mr. Johnson, curate of Cunnington, who, in after life, told Oliver that he wished he had let him be drowned, rather than see him take arms against his king.

In the year 1603, Hinchinbrook was the scene of great preparations and festivity at the reception of James I., who was then travelling southward to take possession of the crown of England. The king stayed here two nights. In honor of this visit, Oliver, the protector's uncle, built the portion of the mansion which yet forms the most conspicuous part of the edifice, and displays the royal arms carved in stone.

HINCHINBROOK HOUSE,* — THE SEAT OF CROMWELL'S ANCESTORS.

The entertainments with which majesty was greeted were profuse and magnificent. The king was in excellent humor at having at length gained possession of "the promised land;" and the tables of his nobility not only supplied him with good cheer, — no insignificant matter in his eyes, — but afforded him an opportunity for displaying his boasted conversational powers. He had created knights all the way that he came, and in the great hall of Hinchinbrook he dubbed little Oliver's uncle Sir Oliver. His majesty departed laden with the presents of his munificent host.

The following anecdote is from Noble: "They have a tradition at Huntingdon, that when King Charles I., then Duke of York, in

* From an engraving in Noble's Life of Cromwell.

his journey from Scotland to London, in 1604, called, in his way, at Hinchinbrook, the seat of Sir Oliver Cromwell, that knight, to divert the young prince, sent for his nephew, Oliver, that he, with his own sons, might play with his royal highness; but they had not been long together, when Charles and Oliver disagreed; and, as the former was then as weakly as the latter was strong, it was no wonder that the royal visitant was worsted. And Oliver, even at this age, so little regarded dignity, that he made the royal blood flow in copious streams from the prince's nose. I give this only as the report of the place." Certain it is that this story is currently believed at Huntingdon.

The grammar-school of the town at which young Oliver was educated still preserves some traces of the original edifice, though considerably altered, and almost re-built. His master was Thomas Beard, D.D., "preacher of the word in the town of Huntingdon," — certainly an anti-papist, and probably somewhat of a puritan. Men's minds were at that time full of the gunpowder plot, — a then recent occurrence. It was an event which could not but make a profound impression on the imagination of young Oliver; nor would he fail to connect it, in after years, with the promotion of Dr. Laud to the archdeaconry of Huntingdon. We find Cromwell's first recorded public speech dwelling on the tolerance given to "flat popery at Paul's Cross;" and this self-same Dr. Beard cited as his authority for his statements. Dr. Beard, like his contemporary, Dr. Busby, was a firm believer in the medicinal virtues of the birch. A plate of him is said to exist, representing the pedagogue, rod in hand, with two scholars in the back-ground, and "*As in presenti*" coming from his mouth. This kind of regimen seems to have been frequently employed towards the young pupil. "His master, honestly and severely observing his faults, did, by correction, hope to better his manners; and, with a diligent hand and careful eye, to hinder the thick growth of those vices which were so predominant and visible in him." Such is the testimony of an enemy, and it must, therefore, be received with some abatement. The subsequent acknowledgment of Oliver himself, — "You know what manner of life I led," — seems to imply that his early youth was not remarkable for its regularity or propriety. That bridge across the brook at the back of his father's house, — those castle hills whereon the youth of Huntingdon love to congregate, — that full and deep river bestrode by the antique bridge, over which the royal forces afterwards made their way into the town, — could, perhaps, tell many a tale of follies which in another's case would have been dismissed and forgotten, but which it suited the purpose of "Carrion Heath" to retail in all their varied or disgusting features.

These are meagre materials out of which to form a conception of the first seventeen years of Oliver's life; but they are all now extant of any credit and respectability. The 23d of April, 1616, witnessed, passing along the raised causeway which extends from Huntingdon to Godmanchester, a father and a son travelling to Cambridge, that that son might be admitted fellow commoner of Sydney Sussex College; and here for a time we lose sight of our young hero. Yet, if tradition may be credited, there were not wanting reports that this son turned out somewhat wild; in fact, "a roysterer." A year after, his devout and worthy father is taken sick, and Oliver is summoned in all haste to his death-bed. This event breaks up his college career. To fit him for the duties of after life, he spends some time in London, gaining a knowledge of law in Lincoln's-inn. Stories of his wildness still prevail at Huntingdon. But it is now impossible to verify them. In 1620, just after he had reached his twenty-first year, he returns home, married to a lady suitable for a life-companion, and not entirely destitute of fortune. He now takes up his position in his native town; becomes the father of a family; opens his house to persecuted puritan ministers; is oppressed by convictions of conscience approaching almost to insanity; sets himself to retrieve and repair some of his former errors; pays back money which he had formerly won at play; declares himself ready to make restitution to any whom he had wronged; erects, behind his house, a building which might be used as a chapel; grows in the opinion of his townsmen; is an unsuccessful candidate, in 1625, for his native borough; but is returned in the third parliament of Charles I., ready to take his part in the mighty movement of those tumultuous times.

Could we discover some newspaper of 1628, containing, in the modern fashion of detail, the whole history of such an election, — the movers and seconders of the candidates, the speeches of the day, the feeling existing in that ancient borough respecting the court, its advisers and its measures, the list of votes as they were polled, the account of the chairing of the members according to the fashion of those times, — how invaluable would such a document be!

The following mysterious entry occurs, in reference to this year, in the Register of All-Saints', Huntingdon:

> "1628.
> Hoc anno Oliverus Cromwell pœnitentia escā totā amissā.*
> J. T."

The initials are those of J. Tomlinson, then the rector. The Latin is none of the best, and it defies the present author's power of interpretation. It may refer to the uncle, Sir Oliver, whose extravagance had compelled him, in the preceding year, to sell Hinchinbrook into the family of the Montagues. Or does it refer to the nephew, and is it confirmatory of those traditions which relate how he sold his wife's jointure, with her consent, in payment of his debts? and does it tell us that he had arrived at the end of his substance, being then a penitent? South's abusive representation of Cromwell may be here remembered: "Who that had seen such a bankrupt, beggarly fellow as Cromwell first entering the Parliament-house, with a thread-bare cloak and a greasy hat, and perhaps neither of them paid for," &c. We must regard this interpretation of Mr. Tomlinson's bad Latin as not altogether improbable. But conjecture is useless. This much alone is clear, that from this time the whole course of Cromwell's life

* Qu? escâ totâ amissâ.

became completely changed. That change he avows in a letter written subsequently to his cousin, and already partially quoted: "You know what manner of life mine hath been. O! I lived in and loved darkness, and hated light; I was a chief, yea, the chief of sinners. This is true; I hated godliness, yet God had mercy on me. O the riches of his mercy!" The Christian man who honors the transforming power of religion will not shrink from this side of the alternative.

What tempestuous matters were agitated in this parliament needs not here be told. The relationship between Cromwell and Hampden, with St. John's marriage to Oliver's cousin, would necessarily place the young Cromwell in the thickest of the fight; and the only speech in a committee of this parliament which is extant shows with what eagerness he took up the cause of protestantism. Parliament was vehemently and angrily dissolved. "I know," said the king, "there are dutiful subjects in this house as any in the world; it being but some few vipers among them that did cast this mist of misunderstanding before their eyes." "To conclude, these vipers must look for their reward of punishment." Was Cromwell then in the king's eye, as a young spawn of this brood?

Eleven years now elapse before the electors of Huntingdon are again called to exercise their franchise. After three years were ended, Cromwell ceased to be a resident in his native town, and we must move with him five or six miles lower down the river. His mother remained at Huntingdon, making the best of the property belonging to the family. She was well known as a good parent, a frugal housewife, and a clever manager of her brewery — if brewery it were.

St. Ives, though not itself actually fen-country, is the cattle-market of the fens. It has many points of resemblance to Huntingdon, being situated like it upon a rising bank of land immediately above the river Ouse, and overlooking a large extent of flat country. On one side of the river the fields are all pastures, rich, green, and succulent. An antique bridge, with only breadth enough to admit of a single carriage, spans the river by six arches, and bears upon it the remains of a chapel, now transformed into a beer-house. The town preserves an air of grave and sober antiquity, here and there yielding to the innovations of modern time. A venerable house, which stands by the side of the bridge, gives the town, as one enters, a somewhat foreign air. Carlyle supposes that in the seventeenth century it consisted, not, as now, mainly of one long street, having houses on each side, but principally of a row of houses overlooking the river, with an intervening green. That author's visit to the town must have certainly been made under unfavorable circumstances. The river is not "black as Acheron;" its waters are limpid and transparent, though somewhat deep, and the metallic *streaks* to which he refers must have arisen from some accidental and unusual defilement. The church is pleasantly situated on a gentle elevation at the end of the town, immediately above a branch of the stream; and, though it has no architecture of high pretensions, is a good and substantial edifice. Like many such structures, its interior has been sadly disfigured by modern alteration; but it preserves some traces of the ancient carved pews which once filled it, probably about the date of James I., and the pulpit is perhaps referable to the same period. The whole structure has a mildewy air, which corresponds with the times of which we write.

Such was the town in which Cromwell, then a grazing farmer, spent five years of his varied life. The lands occupied by him were on the end of the town opposite to the church. It is believed at St. Ives that he lived in an old house called Slepe-hall. Cromwell certainly rented the estate; and though the house, lately standing but now removed, was more modern than the time at which he lived, the traces of an older building have been very apparent in its removal, and a chain of testimony points to this prëexisting hall as his residence. The barn belonging to it is unquestionably an ancient piece of masonry; the timber-work of the roof is very curiously constructed; and a strong and confident statement attaches his tenantship to the building, whilst some inhabitants of St. Ives remember the rings to which, it was asserted, Cromwell's horses were customarily attached.

CROMWELL'S BARN AT ST. IVES.

Cromwell was overseer of the St. Ives' green, — perhaps then used as a cattle-market, — and his name appears in the parish records of the town in this capacity. Carlyle says, graphically, as he points to the lands "past which the river Ouse slumberously rolls:" "Here of a certainty Oliver did walk and look about him habitually during those five years, from 1631 to 1636, — a man studious of many temporal and many eternal things! His cattle grazed here, his ploughs tilled here, the heavenly skies and infernal abysses over-arched and under-arched him here!" *

He had certainly materials enough for reflection. Not to speak of the inward conflicts of his own mind, — conflicts arising from

* To this period of Cromwell's life we may imagine Milton's stately eulogium to refer:

"He had grown up in peace and privacy at home, silently cherishing in his heart a confidence in God, and a magnanimity well adapted for the solemn times that were approaching. Although of ripe years, he had not yet stepped forward into public life; and nothing so much distinguished him from all around, as the cultivation of a pure religion, and the integrity of his life."

the views of truth he had been recently led to take — deep, earnest, heaven-born impulses, — society around him was raging like a volcano. Laud's horizon, though as yet he knew it not, was growing darker and darker. Prynne's case, with that of Burton and of Bastwick, was deeply touching the sympathies of men's minds. Episcopacy was beginning to be introduced in Scotland. The efforts made by well-wishers of religion to purchase advowsons, that godly ministers might preach the truth, had exposed many to the terrors of the Star Chamber. The Book of Sports was revived. The writs of ship-money had been issued, and Hampden had stood resolute in its refusal. The thunder-storm was rising!

Cromwell had now a numerous family, the eldest son a youth of great hope. What destiny he might imagine for his son — what for himself — who can tell! As he walked to that old church, his neck enveloped, if tradition may be believed, in red flannel (for the air of the place did not agree with his constitution), what devout thoughts regarding his own spiritual state, and what distaste, probably, for the preacher who gave him husks instead of grain! How would he muse upon the religious destitution around him! How converse upon the subject with "Dr. Wells, a man of goodness, and industry, and ability to do good every way"! How listen to his words, perhaps on the very spot now occupied by nonconformists in a similar manner! His fervor was contagious; fervor cannot be hid. It communicated itself to his tenants and friends. Cromwell prayed with them, expounded to them, sounded the very depths of their hearts. And then we think how, amidst the dreadful chaos of his emotions, there came across his mind the thought which loyalty forbade him to utter, and Christianity to think of (it was a Jewish age!)* — the sword! Till the grave

* We have before us a pamphlet entitled "The Truth of the Times Vindicated; whereby the lawfulness of Parliamentary proceedings in taking up of arms is justified, &c., by William Bridge, Preacher of God's Word, at Yarmouth," the arguments of which are almost entirely drawn from Judaism. Owen, too, was strongly belligerent. An appeal to arms on behalf of Christianity is, perhaps, one of the greatest anomalies on record.

reveal its secrets, we can never know precisely what these workings were! They have passed away like the waters of the river on whose banks they were conceived. But fit is it that St. Ives should have Cromwell's monument. Mistaken as in some points he was, there has been a prophet among them! Not many towns have given a resting-place to a king in his own right!

He who falls in with the lying, canting strain, which proclaims Cromwell to be nothing but a designing hypocrite, has small knowledge of the anatomy of human nature. It is true that he might deem considerable retention of his thoughts to be legitimate — even virtuous; and that he might carry that opinion more strongly than we should care to justify. But his private utterances are not at war with his public ones. The complexion of his inward musings, so far as they can be gleaned from his most confidential letters, does not differ from that of his public actions. Religion was not with him a garb put on as a holiday suit; it was an earnest and deep conviction. *He* must be strangely constituted, who, while reading Cromwell's letters, and then viewing his private life, can discern nothing in him but unmingled dissimulation. He declares himself not to have been ambitious of power. What is there to prove the contrary? Amidst the earlier part of Charles' reign, his talents might have won for him distinctions of a high order; yet until the age of forty we see him little more than a dignified farmer. So far from eagerly grasping after place and power, it was the force of circumstances alone which brought him out from his obscurity, and set him on high as the object of universal attention. That men's noses were slit, and men's ears cut off, because of their love to a spiritual religion, was no fault of Cromwell's. It was no fault of his that a nation, long downtrodden, rose up, with an almost unanimous energy, to assert their rights and liberties. In the first instance, Cromwell was but following in the wake of others, and he certainly indicated no eager desire to be prominent in the reclamations of the times. But that, when the quarrel had reached its crisis, and the demands of the period called out loudly *for a man*, Cromwell, feeling himself inspired for great actions, put himself into the position to which an outraged nation was calling him, is his highest honor. "I have been called," he said, in a subsequent address to the House of Commons, "to several employments in the nation, and I did endeavor to discharge the duty of an honest man in those services, to God and his people's interest, and to the commonwealth; having, when time was, a competent acceptation in the hearts of men, and some evidence thereof." If any man were ever summoned by Providence to the post he afterwards occupied, Cromwell was that man. When once aroused, there were with such a man no prolonged pauses of hesitancy:

> ——— "On each glance of thought
> Decision followed, as the thunder-bolt
> Pursues the flash."

To determine and to do were with him almost simultaneous; and when Charles had consummated his oppression, by the attempt to seize the five members, and war had become inevitable, he was at once, and the first, in action. His influence, his purse,* his sword, were at the nation's call; and on August 15, 1642, we find him under arms, taking vigorous measures for the defence of the kingdom, seizing the magazine in the castle of Cambridge, and hindering "the carrying off of plate from that university."† The king was soon to learn what an enemy his unrighteous acts had made.

Cromwell is now appointed captain, and soon after colonel, of the sixty-seventh troop of the parliament's forces; the commander-in-chief being the Earl of Essex. He is present at the indecisive

* He states himself to have contributed to this service between eleven and twelve hundred pounds. Carlyle, vol. I., p. 226.

† This service was of great importance to the commonwealth. It was not only twenty thousand pounds cut off from the royalists, but the addition of twenty thousand pounds to the funds for raising the parliamentary army; and this was at the time most valuable. Cromwell was assisted in this movement by Wauton, father of Valentine Wauton, who afterwards became his brother-in-law, and one of the captains of the Ironsides.

battle of Edge-hill, and he is already coming to conclusions far in advance of his position. His rapid tactics have on more than one occasion "prevented the designs of the royal army." But he groans inwardly at the want of adequate support from those who ought to aid him, and says to Hampden, yet living, "Your troops are most of them old, decayed serving-men, and tapsters, and such kind of fellows; and their troops are gentlemen's sons, younger sons, and persons of quality; do you think that the spirits of such base and mean fellows will be ever able to encounter gentlemen that have honor and courage and resolution in them?" Forthwith, therefore, he began to organize his Ironsides, and to try what religious conviction would do, when set in array against punctilious loyalty. "My troops," he writes, "increase. I have a lovely company; you would respect them, did you know them. No anabaptists? They are honest, sober Christians; they expect to be used as men!" "I had rather have a plain russet-coated captain, that knows what he fights for and loves what he knows, than that which you call a gentleman, and is nothing else." Of these Ironsides there appears to have been nearly fifty troops organized from the surrounding districts, as the "St. Neot's troop," &c. The captains of these troops probably included Evanson, Whalley, Norton, Sidney (Algernon?) O. Cromwell, jr.,* H. Cromwell, Montague (afterwards Earl of Sandwich), and others. These troops seem to have been formed at different periods. It was the desire of Cromwell that his Ironsides should be, in the phrase of that day, "a gathered church."† Now and then an old Bible turns up from the relics of a past age, which formed an absolute necessary of their baggage and equipment. The report is that a fine of twelve-pence was levied for every oath, and that plunder, drinking and disorder, were severely discountenanced. An air of stern morality‡ pervaded the whole superintendence of these troops,

* This was Cromwell's eldest son. He appears to have been killed near Knaresborough, in 1644.

† Calamy's Baxter.

‡ Even Clarendon bears witness concerning these soldiers—"An army whose

and indeed the conduct of Oliver himself. He had got into his possession a horse seized by force. "I understand," he writes, "there was some exception taken at a horse that was sent to me. If the owner be not by you judged a malignant, and you do not approve of my having of the horse, I shall as willingly return him again, as you shall desire. Not that I would for ten thousand horses have the horse to my own private benefit, saving to make use of him for the public," &c.

For an account of the rapidity of Cromwell's marches and counter-marches, at this crisis everywhere full of decision, we must be content to refer our reader to the pages of his biography themselves, which record how he dashed into St. Alban's in the midst of a certain royal commission of array, broke down the intrenchment of Lowestoffe, delivered Lincolnshire from the power of the royalists, and, by concentrating thus a strong force in the eastern counties, kept the war most effectually from that quarter of the kingdom. Many similar adventures at this period demonstrated equally his skill and prowess.

We have seen what was the substance of the solemn league and covenant taken at this time by the English parliament, in conjunction with the Scottish nation. Cromwell himself does not appear to have been in London to affix his signature among the rest to that celebrated document. But that he was prepared to act in the full spirit of it, the following incident will show: Lord Manchester is, at this time, sergeant-major of the associated counties, Cromwell being his lieutenant, and also governor of Ely. Parliament has determined on the removal of all "monuments of superstition and idolatry," and Cromwell resolves to enforce the command in his own vicinity. The scene is Ely Cathedral, a very ancient edifice, bearing traces of having been repaired and restored at various periods, and of having narrowly escaped total destruction in the wars with the barons, during the reign of King John.

sobriety of manners, whose courage and success, made it famous and terrible over the world; which lived like good husbandmen in the country, and good citizens in the city." Rebellion, vol. IV., p. 729.

Cromwell, who has caused fortifications to be raised near the Horse-Shoe, to secure the passes out of Lincolnshire, which were held on behalf of the king, resolves to proceed in enforcing the orders of the parliament with promptitude. A letter has accordingly been despatched to "The Reverend Mr. Hitch, at Ely," requiring him, "lest the soldiers should in any tumultuary or disorderly way attempt the reformation of the Cathedral Church," "to forbear altogether" the "choir service, as unedifying and offensive;" and conveying, moreover, this advice: "I advise you to catechise, and read and expound the Scripture to the people; not doubting but the parliament, with the advice of the assembly of divines, will direct you further. I desire your sermons where usually they have been, but more frequent. Your loving friend, Oliver Cromwell."*

The warning was disregarded; the choir service went on. The little city, to whose knowledge we may suppose this military threatening had come, was in a hubbub of anxious expectation as to what the event might be. Cromwell issued no idle orders. One day, therefore, he makes his appearance in the church, his hat upon his

* The second volume (third edition) of Carlyle's "Letters, &c.," which presents to the public the remarkable collection entitled the Squire-papers, contains the following letter, bearing date a little while preceding:

"*Christmas Eve*, 1643.

"To Mr. Squire.

"Sir: It is no use any man's saying he will not do this or that. What is to be done is no choice of mine. Let it be sufficient, it is the parliament's orders, and we to obey them. I am surprised at Montague to say so. Show him this; if the men are not of a mind to obey this order, I will cashier them, the whole troop. I heed God's House as much as any man, but vanities and trumpery give no honor to God, nor idols serve him; neither do painted windows make men more pious. Let them do as parliament bid them, or else go home: and then others will be less careful to do what we had done with judgment. I learn there is four men down with the sickness in the St. Neot's troop now at march. Let me hear; so ride over, and learn all of it.

"Sir, I am your friend,

"Oliver Cromwell."

Squire has endorsed, — "They obeyed the order."

head. He gazes sternly at the resolute looks of the little congregation, and says aloud, "I am a man under authority: I am commanded to dismiss this assembly." He is disregarded; the service goes on. He becomes more peremptory. "Leave off your fooling, and come down, sir!" was the distinct and sufficient command. It was no longer to be disputed, and the company gloomily retired.

This was a sad scene, but not unlike a hundred previous ones, which had removed catholic worshippers to make way for their protestant successors. It was a lesson to those who stood by parliamentary enactment, that the power which had made could also unmake. Such are the alternations to which a state-church is necessarily liable in times of public excitement. For the sake of peace, of the decencies of a spiritual religion, and of truth itself, let it not be exposed to such questionable hazards! What has Christ's gospel to do with steel caps or glittering partisans, or why needs it be subjected to their influence? Cromwell learned afterwards to suspect the system under which he was then acting; but if there be a parliamentary church at all, and if the parliament, which gives life to that church, deem certain opinions sacrilegious and unchristian,—and if, moreover, those who believe in the authority of such a church refuse to adhere to the principle which their own doctrine recognizes,—what then? It is not for us, who deny the right of the state's interference, to be responsible for all its possible consequences.

Already the "solemn league and covenant" is beginning to work ill. Cromwell himself becomes one of the first to distrust its efficacy. For, not two months after this transaction at Ely, we have a letter of remonstrance to Major-general Crawford, on behalf of some poor anabaptist in the army, who it seems has been laid under arrest because of his unpopular opinions; giving us clear evidence how a man like Cromwell, taught by experience and reflection, may begin to outgrow a garment which seemed to fit him only a few short weeks before:

"Surely, you are not well advised thus to turn off one so faithful to the cause, and so able to serve you as this man is. Give me leave to tell you, I cannot be of your judgment (if a man notorious for wickedness, for oaths, for drinking, hath as great a share in your affection as one who fears an oath, who fears to sin), that this doth commend your election of men to serve as fit instruments in this work!"

"Ay, but the man 'is an anabaptist.'" "Are you sure of that? Admit he be, shall that render him incapable to serve the public?" * * "Sir, the state, in choosing men to serve it, takes no notice of their opinions; if they be willing faithfully to serve it, that satisfies. I advised you formerly to bear with men of different minds from yourself: if you had done it when I advised you to it, I think you would not have had so many stumbling-blocks in your way."

What will the Westminster assembly of divines, now earnestly sitting, say to such doctrine? Baillie shall answer for himself: "The independents have so managed their affaires, that of the officers and sojours in Manchester's armie, certainlie also in the generall's, and, as I hear, in Waller's likewise, more than the two parts are for them, and these of the farr most resolute and confident men for the parliament party. Judge ye if we had not need of our friends' help."* "In this long anarchie, the sectaries and heretics increase marvellouslie; yet we are hopefull, if God might help us, to have our presbyteries erected as we expect shortly to have them, and gett the chiefe of the independents to joyn with us in our practicall conclusions, as we are much labouring for it; and are not yet out of hope, we trust, to winn about all the rest of these wild and enormous people."† "The humor of this people is very various and inclinable to singularities, to differ from all the world, and one from another, and shortly from themselves. No people had so much need of a presbytrie."‡

But instead of matters inclining, as the war went on, to this mode of adjustment, they gradually moved further and further from the desired point. After the battle of Marston Moor, fol-

* Baillie, April 26, 1644. † Ibid., April 29, 1644.
‡ Ibid., May 9, 1644.

lowed by the second battle of Newbury, Cromwell and Manchester differed, divided, became antagonists. Whilst Essex and Manchester commanded, the war was indeed little likely to be brought to a close. Cromwell exhibited in the House of Commons charges against his superior officer, and was charged in return with having said, "There will never be a good time in England till we have done with lords." The self-denying ordinance was accordingly passed; was at first rejected by the lords, but afterwards obtained their concurrence. One of the features of this bill was, that religious men might be permitted to serve in the army without taking the covenant; another was, that no member of either house should take any office of command, civil or military. The adherents of the covenant were deeply shocked by Cromwell having declared that, if he met the king in battle, he would as soon fire his pistol at him as at any other man. Essex, Manchester, and others, immediately resigned their commissions. Cromwell, by some means not very apparent, retained, or was recalled to, his post of service. The season of uniformity and dilatoriness had passed. The battle of Naseby followed. Charles was completely routed on the field, and the publication of his correspondence, seized on the spot, proclaimed to the nation his utter insincerity,* and his determination to have called in a catholic army to reïnstate him on the throne. "I give thee power," he says to one of his generals, "to promise in my name that I will take away all the penal laws against the Roman Catholics in England, as soon as God shall enable me to do it; so that by their means and favors I may have such powerful resistance as may deserve so great a favor, and enable me to do it." It was equally evident that the king was intending to bring in a foreign force for the subjugation of his

* The want of "reliableness," to use a Scottish phrase, was remarkable in the Stuarts. It was a vice of James I. Part of Rochester's epigram was equally applicable to the father, the son, and the grandson:

"Here lies our sovereign Lord the king,
Whose word no man relies on."

people.* This battle, after some further adventures, in which Cromwell's energy was conspicuous, ended the first civil war, June 14, 1645, with the defeat of the king.

Charles now put himself into the hands of the Scottish army, encamped before Newark. The solitary man who, with clipped beard, and in a mean disguise, came to seek a refuge in the camp of his enemies, was yet a king; and the Scotch army was not insensible of the advantages his possession gave them. But the king proved in their hands intractable.† He would not abandon episcopacy; the Scotch would not abandon their covenant; and between the presbyterian and the independent party Charles endeavored to intrigue, so as to get "his ain again." "The king's madness," writes Baillie, "has confounded us all. We are in a woeful evil taking; we know not what to doe, nor what to say." ‡ "The king's answer has broken our heart; we see nothing but a sea of new and more horrible confusions. We are afraid of the hardness of God's decree against that madd man, and against all his kingdomes." § The result was, that the Scottish army delivered him over into the hands of the English, receiving two hundred thousand pounds in payment of the arrears due to the army, and marched home. They would not serve a monarch who rejected the covenant of Christ. His majesty left Newcastle, and was escorted to a kind of honorable imprisonment in Holmby House.

The 10th March, 1647, was appointed by the commons — who as yet adhered to the notion of the possibility of a general uniformity, and had just passed the presbyterian platform of church government — as a day of fasting and humiliation against "blasphemies and heresies." It was the first overt manifestation of a discord which soon became notorious. Cromwell felt the blow; and a letter of his, addressed to Fairfax, who had now superseded Manchester, shows the state of his feelings: "Never were the

* "The King's Cabinet, &c., Opened." Published by special order of parliament, 1645.

† Baillie, Aug. 4, 1646. ‡ Ibid.

§ No fewer than twenty garrisons were taken this summer by the army.

spirits of men more embittered than now. Surely the devil hath but a short time. Sir, it's good the heart be fixed against all this. The naked simplicity of Christ, with that wisdom he is pleased to give, and patience, will overcome all this * * *. Upon the fast-day divers soldiers were raised (as I heard), both horse and foot, near two hundred in Covent Garden, to prevent us soldiers from cutting the presbyterians' throats. These are fine tricks to mock God with." Uniformity was crumbling already in the hands of its manufacturers! The city and the army had become antagonists. A new contest was rising—presbyterianism *versus* independency; by which word independency let the reader understand is meant the party contending, not so much for a particular form of church polity, as for religious liberty in general. Among the latter party, Cromwell was daily becoming mightier. He had even ventured, when watching the developments of the strugglers for uniformity in the House of Commons, to say to Ludlow, "These men will never leave till the army pull them out by the ears!"

We must hastily pass over the complicated history of this crisis. Presbyterianism is established, at least in London and in Lancashire; but the discontents between the city and army are every day increasing. Those who cannot understand the questions at issue will be forward in connecting these dislocations with Cromwell's intrigues. But there was a vital question involved; and that question was, whether Cromwell and his army would allow the religious liberty, for which they had struggled so manfully, to be crushed by the heel of a dominant establishment, by what religious name soever that establishment might be called. Ludlow relates that, in a conversation with Harrison, he asked that general what had led him to unite with Cromwell in his movements against the parliament; and the reply was, "that he had done it because he was fully persuaded they had not a heart to do any more good for the Lord and his people." The king had been taken by the army from Holmby House, not unwillingly; and it was the question of a moment whether he could not be set upon his throne on terms which might give to Cromwell's party a guarantee for the religious liberty they sought. But Charles proved now, as always, impracticable. His coronation oath would not allow episcopacy to be abolished, though it had suffered the daily infraction of Magna Charta.

At length, the king fled from Hampton Court to the Isle of Wight; and, by a resolution of the two houses that they would treat with him no more, was virtually dethroned, and made a prisoner in Carisbrook Castle. The Scotch raised an army to deliver the king from sectaries, and the second civil war began. This war will be understood to have been a contest for liberty against parliamentary uniformity.

We cannot better describe the position of affairs than by an extract from Neal: "The army* had been six months in the field, this summer, engaged against the cavaliers and Scots, who being now reduced and subdued, they began to express a high dissatisfaction with the present treaty, because no provision had been made for their darling point, *liberty of conscience.* Here they had just reason for complaint, but ought not to have relieved themselves by the methods and at the expense they did. They were thoroughly incensed against the king and his cavaliers on one hand, and the high presbyterians on the other. It appeared to them that the king's sentiments in religion and politics were not changed; that he would always be raising new commotions till things returned to their former channel, and in the present treaty he had yielded nothing but through constraint; and that when he was restored to his throne, after all the blood that had been shed, they should neither be safe in their lives or fortunes. On the other hand, if *protestant uniformity* should take place by virtue of the present treaty, their condition would be little mended; for (said they), if the king himself cannot obtain liberty to have the common prayer read privately in his own family, what must the independents and

* It is important to remember that the body termed "the army" was not at this period a band of mercenaries, but a collection of sober citizens, whom religious persecution had driven to take up arms against the king.

sectaries expect? What have we been contending for, if, after all the hazards we have run, presbytery is to be exalted, and we are to be banished our country or driven into corners?"*

In the present crisis, days of fasting and prayer were instituted by the army at their head-quarters in St. Albans. The result was the presentation of a remonstrance, demanding that the king be brought to justice; that the Prince of Wales and the Duke of York be required to surrender, or be declared incapable of governing; and that henceforth no king be admitted but by the people's free election.

Other prompt measures followed up this remonstrance. A party of horse was marched to the Isle of Wight to secure the king. The army, with Fairfax at its head, posted itself in London, and the troops were quartered about Whitehall and St. James', with the assurance that the property of the people should not be disturbed.

It is impossible for us to follow Cromwell through the vigorous Scottish campaigns by which (contemporaneously with the above movements) this second civil war was distinguished. An extract from a letter, addressed by Cromwell to the House of Commons, is, however, worth the quotation: "I do think the affairs of Scotland are in a thriving posture as to the interests of honest men; and Scotland is like to be a better neighbor to you now than when the great pretenders to the covenant, and religion, and treaties,— I mean Duke Hamilton, the Earls of Lauderdale, Traquhar, Carnegy, and their confederates,—had the power in their hands. I dare to say that that party, with their pretences, had not only thought the treachery of some in England (who have cause to blush) endangered the whole state and kingdom of England, but also brought Scotland into such a condition as that no honest man, who had the fear of God, or a conscience of religion and the just ends of the covenant and treaties, could have a being in that kingdom." This extract will show on what principles Oliver Cromwell's campaign was undertaken.

* Neal, vol. III., p. 485.

During the subsequent proceedings, Cromwell was a constant attendant in his place in the House of Commons. He had narrowly escaped being committed to the Tower in June, 1647, by leaving London early. At this time, he is described by Mrs. Hutchinson as being "uncorruptibly faithful to his trust and to the people's interest." Ireton, Cromwell's son-in-law, had, up to a late period, been of opinion that Charles might even yet be brought to a safe adjustment. But an expression of the king's, added to many others, undeceived him. On one occasion the king said, "I shall play my game as well as I can." To which Ireton replied, significantly, "If your majesty has a game to play, you must give us also the liberty to play ours." It would appear that Cromwell had for some time hesitated respecting the proceedings to be taken in reference to the king. He said, "If any man moved this of choice or design, he should think him the greatest traitor in the world; but, since Providence and necessity had cast them upon it, he should pray God to bless their counsels, though he was not provided on the sudden to give them advice." Burnet says, "Ireton was the person that drove it on. Cromwell was all the while in some suspense about it." *

Were we compiling a general history, it would be necessary to enter at large upon the constitutional and moral questions which were involved in the execution of the king. As it is, we must leave them to the reader's own consideration, simply observing that, to regard the matter aright, it must be looked at in connection with the recent deaths of Strafford and Laud, and that the religious party who advocated the former stand upon disadvantageous ground in condemning the latter. Nor will we stay to record the deliberate and public manner in which that deed was executed, as an act which its perpetrators by no means shrank from avowing; nor tell how the death of the king pierced the nation to the centre of its sympathies, and tended materially to shake the foundations of the new commonwealth. No edifices are more insecure than

* Burnet's History of His Own Times, vol. I., p. 46.

those which are cemented with blood. A terrible spirit of Judaical severity pervaded the whole transaction, — a spirit only legitimate when inspired by direct divine sanction, and, lacking that, formidable and most dangerous. Cromwell was not the proposer of the measure; but, by the part he performed in it, he voluntarily undertook its large responsibility.*

The remnant of the assembly of divines at Westminster protested unanimously against the execution of the king, and on behalf of the solemn league and covenant which was intended to secure his person. A remonstrance to this effect was signed by the most eminent London ministers. Neal says, "None of their ministers, that I know of, declare their approbation of the proceedings of the council of officers in the trial of the king, except Hugh Peters and John Godwin." Many of the independent ministers, though dissatisfied with the treaty of Newport, because it denied toleration to them, joined with their brethren in protesting against the king's execution; whilst the commissioners of the Scottish Kirk denounced the proceeding, and wrote a letter to the ministers of London, exhorting them to persevere in their opposition to the House of Commons, and to a general toleration. It is evident that at this time the parliament had not determined what form of government was most desirable, and that the execution of the king was not the act of any one party alone, seeing that there were then in the house "men of all parties, — episcopalians, presbyterians, independents, anabaptists, and others."

Cromwell's defence of his course will be found in the memoir prefixed to the state letters of Lord Broghill. The writer says, "One time particularly, in the year 1649, when Lord Broghill was riding with Cromwell on one side of him and Ireton on the other, they fell into discourse about the late king's death. Cromwell declared that if the king had followed his own mind, and had had trusty servants about him, he had fooled them all;

* Dr. Owen preached before parliament on the day following the decapitation of the king. But he evidently avoided expressing any distinct opinion on the procedure.

and further said that once they had a mind to have closed with him; but upon something that happened, they fell off from their design again. My lord, finding Cromwell and Ireton in good humor, and no other person within hearing, asked them if he might be so bold as to desire an account: 1. Why they once would have closed with the king? and 2. Why they did not? Cromwell very freely told him that he would satisfy him in both his queries. The reason, says he, why we would once have closed with the king was this: we found that the Scots and the presbyterians began to be more powerful than we; and if they had made up matters with the king, we should have been left in the lurch, — therefore we thought it best to prevent them, by offering first to come in upon any reasonable conditions. But while we were busied with these thoughts, there came a letter from one of our spies who was of the king's bedchamber, which acquainted us that on that day our doom was decreed; that he could not possibly tell what it was, but we might find it out if we could intercept a letter from the king to the queen, wherein he declared what he would do. The letter, he said, was sewed in the skirt of a saddle, and the bearer of it would come with the saddle upon his head, about ten o'clock that night, to the Blue Boar Inn, in Holborn; for there he was to take horse and go to Dover with it. This messenger knew nothing of the document in the saddle, but some persons in Dover did." The letter is intercepted. "As soon as we had it we opened it, in which we found the king had acquainted the queen that he was now courted by both factions, the Scotch presbyterians and the army, and which bid fairest for him should have him; but he thought he should close with the Scots sooner than the other, &c. Upon this, added Cromwell, we took horse and went to Windsor; and, finding we were not likely to have any tolerable terms from the king, we immediately, from that time forward, resolved his ruin."

The constitution of England was now completely changed. The House of Commons was proclaimed the supreme authority; the Prince of Wales was disinherited; the House of Lords abolished;

the office of king declared unnecessary and dangerous; the executive power lodged in a council of state; the oaths of allegiance and supremacy abandoned, and supplanted by the "engagement," — a declaration that the person taking it would be "true and faithful to the government established without king or house of peers." Cromwell, with his army, departed for Ireland, to quell the catholic insurrection.

Before he embarked, he addressed a letter for the parliament, recommending the abandonment of penal laws relating to religion. The house accordingly brought in an act "for the approbation of able and well-qualified persons to be made ministers, who cannot comply with the present ordinance for ordination of ministers." At the same time an act was passed, at the instance of General Fairfax and his council of officers, to abandon all penal statutes which offended weak consciences, excepting, however, from the indulgence, all papists, or favorers of the late hierarchy, and providing for the punishment of immorality and profaneness. No minister was capable of presentation to any living, unless within six months he took the engagement publicly before his congregation.

This was very partial justice, if indeed it was justice at all. Many ministers, accordingly, refused to abide by the test, and would not keep the fast-days appointed by the government. In these protests the presbyterians were especially prominent. In the mean time, the Scotch commissioners, supported by the English presbyterians, were treating with young Charles in Holland, with a view to obtaining his subscription to the covenant.

Cromwell's campaign in Ireland was, like its author, stern, prompt, terrible; undertaken and executed upon principles sufficiently intelligible, but open, like the rest of his actions, to large questioning. The cruelties which had been practised upon protestants had inflamed his spirit. He felt that so dangerous a party as excited "papists" must be dealt with as the highest class of enemies; and, anticipating a general movement in Scotland consequent upon the death of the king, it was requisite that no time should be lost. Cromwell was not by nature cruel; on the contrary, the letters which are preserved at this date, in reference to the marriage treaty he had just concluded on behalf of his son, afford evidence of the softest tenderness. But, whilst some of his protestantism was principle, some of it was passion; and Cromwell's military mind saw but one way to an object, and that the shortest. His red right hand avenged the persecutions of his brethren. We hasten over a page which the religion of Christ, in its gentleness, forgiveness, and loving persuasion, trembles to peruse. Ireland was subdued: the flame of its disaffection quenched in blood. The spirit of the campaign is sufficiently indicated by Cromwell's own manifesto: "You, unprovoked, put the English to the most unheard-of and most barbarous massacre,—without respect of sex or age,—that ever the sun beheld. And at a time when Ireland was in perfect peace, and when, through the example of English industry, through commerce and traffic, that which was in the natives' hands was better to them than if all Ireland had been in their possession, and not an Englishman in it. And yet then, I say, was this unheard-of villany perpetrated by your instigation, who boast of 'peace-making' and 'union against the common enemy.' What think you, by this time, is not my assertion true? Is God, will God be, with you?

* * * * * *

"He that bids us 'contend for the faith once delivered to the saints' tells us that we should do it by 'avoiding the spirit of Cain, Corah, and Balaam:' and by 'building up *ourselves* in the most holy faith,' not pinning it upon other men's sleeves. Praying 'in the Holy Ghost:' not mumbling over matins. Keeping 'ourselves in the love of God:' not destroying men because they will not be of our faith. 'Waiting for the mercy of Jesus Christ:' not cruel, but merciful. But, alas! why is this said? why are these pearls cast before you? You are resolved not to be charmed from 'using the instrument of a foolish shepherd.' You are a part of Antichrist, whose kingdom the Scripture so expressly speaks should be 'laid in blood;' yea, 'in the blood of the saints.' You have shed great store of that already; and ere it be long, you must all of you have 'blood to drink;' 'even the dregs of the cup of the fury and the wrath of God, which will be poured out unto you.'

* * * * * *

"First, therefore: I shall not, where I have power, and the Lord is pleased to bless me, suffer the exercise of the mass where I can take notice of it. 'No,' nor 'in any way' suffer you that are papists, where I can find you seducing the people, or by any overt act violating the laws established; but if you come into my hands, I shall cause to be inflicted the punishments appointed by the laws, to use your own terms, *secundum gravitatem delicti,* upon you; and shall try to reduce things to their former state on this behalf. As for the people, what thoughts they have in their own breasts I cannot reach; but shall think it my duty, if they walk honestly and peaceably, not to cause them in the least to suffer for the same. And shall endeavor to walk patiently and in love towards them, to see if at any time it shall please God to give them another or a better mind. And all men under the power of England within this dominion are hereby required and enjoined strictly and religiously to do the same."

Leaving Ireton, his son-in-law, as the lord-deputy of Ireland, Cromwell next marched, Fairfax having resigned his command, against the Scotch. A new position had been taken by that nation. They had proclaimed Prince Charles their king; had "compelled him voluntarily," as Carlyle says, to take the covenant; and Charles is now on his way to be crowned among them. Anticipating a little, we may remark that we have now before us "a sermon preach'd at Scoon, Jan. 1, 1651, at the coronation of Charles the Second. By Robert Dowglass, minister at Edinburgh, moderator of the commission of the General Assembly." The text is 2 Kings 11: 12, 17,—"And he brought forth the king's son and put the crown upon him, and gave him the testimony, and they made him king, and anointed him, and they clapt their hands and said, God save the king. And Jehoiada made a covenant between the Lord and the king, and the people that they should be the Lord's people, between the king also and the people."

In the course of this sermon the preacher declaims against anabaptists, photinians, levellers and republicans, and tells the king that he has covenanted to maintain the true reformed religion, "to extirpate popery, prelacy, superstition, heresy, schism, and profaneness;" to punish "malignants and evil instruments." "Sir, you are in covenant with God and his people, and are obliged to maintain presbyterian government as well against Erastians as sectaries." "Another example I give you, yet in recent memory, of your grandfather, King James. He happened to be very young in a time full of difficulties; yet there was a godly party in the land who put the crown upon his head. And when he came to some years, he and his people entered into the covenant with God: he was much commended by godly and faithful men; comparing him of young Josiah standing at the altar renewing a covenant with God. And he himself did thank God that he was born in a reformed faith, better reformed than *England*, for they retained many popish ceremonies: yea, better reformed than Geneva, for they keep some holy days: charging his people to be constant, and promising himself to continue in that reformation, and to maintain the same. Notwithstanding of all this he made a foul defection: he remembered not the kindness of them who had held the crown upon his head: yea, he persecuted faithful ministers for opposing that course of defection. He never rested till he had undone oath, and was girded with the sword, the lord great constable saying:

"Receive this kingly sword for the defence of the faith of Christ, and protection of his kirk and of the true religion, as it is presently professed within this kingdom, and according to the national covenant and league and covenant, and for executing justice and equity," &c. &c. Then the king, after other ceremonies, was crowned, and when he was seated on the throne the minister "spoke to him a word of exhortation." The lords after this, holding their hands between the king's hands, swore the following oath:

"By the eternal and almighty God, who liveth and reigneth forever, I become your liege man, and truth and faith shall bear unto you, and live and die with you, against all manner of folks whatsoever, in your service, according to the national covenant and solemn league and covenant." The ceremony was concluded by another exhortation, and by prayer, singing, and the benediction.*

Such, though the period has been a little antedated, was the king, and such the system which Scotland was now in arms to promote! It was, as before, a war for a national presbyterial establishment. Against this system, and against this future king, Cromwell is now marching to Scotland, not without visions of what may happen should he be successful in keeping him from his hereditary crown!

Cromwell's Scottish campaigns are most interesting and instructive. They exhibit the same man that we saw in Ireland, impulsive, energetic, absolute; but they exhibit him in his better aspects.

He is afterwards seen lying at Berwick; Leslie, the Scottish general, in front of Edinburgh. From this point the English general addresses a manifesto to the people of Scotland: "Your own guilt is too much for you to bear; bring not, therefore, upon yourselves the blood of innocent men, deceived with pretences

* The Phœnix.

of king and covenant; from whose eyes you hide a better knowledge. I am persuaded that divers of you, who lead the people, have labored to build yourselves in these things; wherein you have censured others, and established yourselves 'upon the Word of God.' Is it, therefore, infallibly agreeable to the Word of God, all that *you* say? I beseech you, in the bowels of Christ, think it possible you may be mistaken."

How Cromwell becomes cooped up in the peninsula on which Dunbar is situated; how his forces are discouraged at their position, whilst Cromwell, undaunted in trouble, comforts himself with hope; how Leslie looks upon Oliver as altogether undone; how the weather is wet and stormy, most unfavorable for such military movements as it is necessary for Cromwell to take; how Leslie is, in an unguarded moment, tempted from his position on the overlooking heights; how the quick eye of the future protector detects the error of his antagonist; how he attacks the Scottish general with an overwhelming force, routs and almost destroys his army, and compels Leslie to enter Edinburgh as a fugitive, we cannot stay to record.* It is the turning-point of the whole campaign. The covenant is tottering again! It is finally lost at the great battle of Worcester, where Charles narrowly escapes being taken by his foes. His hopes are for the present baffled. The crown has faded before the vision of the covenanted king!

Who wielded the power of that throne is known. By what means he ascended to its high eminence it is not our province to record. It will be sufficient to mark the aspect which the protectorate of Cromwell bore towards the great questions of religious liberty.

* It must be observed, however, as characteristic of the spirit of Cromwell's legislation, that when he arrived in Edinburgh, while he put down the General Assembly, he gave the Scotch ministers full liberty to occupy their own pulpits, though they declined to avail themselves of it. "I verily believe," says Kirkton, in his History of the Church of Scotland, "there were more souls converted to Christ in that short period of time, — that is, during the administration of Cromwell, — than in any season since the Reformation, though of triple its duration."

In the thirty-seventh article of "the instrument of government" which appointed Cromwell protector, it was provided that "all who professed faith in God by Jesus Christ should be protected in their religion." This, though by no means complete, was a great advance upon the toleration of any preceding period. Popery and prelacy were indeed excluded; but rather on the supposition that they were political than because they were religious systems. Parliament, however, either with a view to restrict Cromwell's desired toleration, or because they designed to bring forward a measure for the propagation of the gospel,* appointed a committee of fourteen persons, among whom were Owen, J. Goodwin, Marshall, Nye, Manson and Baxter, to determine what were the fundamentals of Christianity. It was a disputatious meeting; Baxter, who, in the case of the assembly of divines, complained of the logomachies of the sectaries, being the most pertinacious in it. But their labors were stopped by the dissolution of the parliament. Cromwell himself, according to the testimony of Baxter, declared that "he could not understand what the magistrate had to do in matters of religion; he thought that all men should be left to the liberty of their own consciences, and that the magistrate could not interpose without ensnaring himself in the guilt of persecution." And these were the protector's own words: †

"Have we not lately labored under the weight of persecution, and is it fit then to sit heavy on others? Is it ingenuous to ask liberty, and not to give it? What greater hypocrisy than for those who were oppressed by the bishops to become the greatest

* Orme's Life of Owen, p. 150.

† During his protectorship, Cromwell called a conference in his drawing-room respecting the toleration of the Jews, a measure advised by some of his highness' judges. The conference was composed of judges, citizens, and divines. Among the latter were Owen, Goodwin, Cudworth, and Bridge. The laymen affirmed; the divines denied. Cromwell's patience was, at length, wearied; he told them he had hoped they would throw some light on the subject, but that they had rendered the matter more obscure than before; he, therefore, wished no more of their counsels, but desired an interest in their prayers. The project came to no result.

oppressors themselves so soon as their yoke is removed? * * As for profane persons, blasphemers, such as preach sedition, contentious railers, evil-speakers, who seek by evil words to corrupt good manners, and persons of evil conversation, punishment from the civil magistrate ought to meet with them," &c.

The notion of a "Christian nation" — that lamentable confounding of an external with a spiritual religion — was clearly uppermost in Cromwell's mind, and it was a gigantic error. But within these limits he intrenched himself most firmly:

"Men who believe in Jesus Christ — that is the form that gives being to true religion. * * Whoever hath this faith, let his form be what it will, he walking peaceably, without prejudice to others under other forms, it is a debt due to God and Christ; and he will require it if that Christian may not enjoy his liberty. If a man of one form will be trampling upon the heels of another form, — if an independent, for example, will despise him under baptism, and will revile him, and reproach, and provoke him, — I WILL NOT SUFFER IT IN HIM. If, on the other side, those of the anabaptist" (sentiment) "shall be censuring the godly ministers of the nation who profess under that of independency; or if those that profess under presbytery shall be reproaching or speaking evil of them, traducing and censuring them, — as I would not be willing to see the day when England shall be in the power of the presbytery to impose upon the consciences of others that profess faith in Christ, — so I will not endure any reproach to them. But God give us hearts and spirits to keep all things equal!"*

These were noble sentiments! And, though they were dashed with matters not altogether palatable to modern tastes, such as the maintenance of ministers by a state provision, — at present by the tithes of the old episcopal clergy, † — they give us a striking view

* Speech to Protector's Second Parliament. Carlyle, vol. IV., pp. 123, 124.

† The appointment of Tryers, which were thirty-eight in number, and consisted of independents, presbyterians and baptists, was, perhaps, as good as any such measure could be. Baxter himself praises the body and their usefulness to the community. But such a measure must be attended, it is evident,

of what was the true nature of Cromwell's ambition, — that of being not a monarch of precedents and conventionalities, of gilded crowns and red cushions, but, in the largest sense of the term, a king of men!

None is prepared rightly to estimate Cromwell's character and conduct, without the fairest examination of the elements with which he was required to deal, and of the unpropitious demands by which he was surrounded. Even the greatest admirers of the superiority of right over policy will not find the question compressible into a very narrow compass. But it was the day when "there was no king in Israel, but every man did that which was right in his own eyes." Cromwell did what was right in *his* eyes, and he saved the nation from anarchy and confusion. Yet, successful as, in its immediate results, his strong-handed policy might have been, the admirer of right *versus* might may still believe that a different course would have been attended with less ultimate reäction. But Cromwell was no yielding Apollo, who would let every upstart Phaeton step into his chariot, and possess himself of the reins of a most difficult government. He believed himself, like one of the judges of ancient Israel, called, by an authority which superseded ordinary precedent, to a certain work, and he did that work. We do not defend the integrity of the whole premiss; but, admitting it, it is impossible to deny the completeness of the conclusion. "We are ready," said he, "to excuse most of our actions, — and justify them too, as well as to excuse them, — upon the ground of necessity. The ground of necessity, for justifying men's actions, is above all considerations of instituted law; and if this or any other state should go about — as I know they never will — to make laws against events, against what *may* happen, I think it obvious to any man they will be making laws against Providence; events and issues of things being from God alone, to whom all issues belong."*

by great occasional injustice. It was only at Owen's strong intercessions that Pococke, the Orientalist, and Fuller, the church historian, retained their positions in the church.

* Speech to Second Protectorate Parliament, 1656. Carlyle, vol. IV., p. 95.

Of Cromwell's conviction of this divine call, how questionable or dangerous soever the precedent thus established may be, there is not the slightest valid reason for doubt. That he was accessible to fanaticism may be granted; that he was a deep designing hypocrite is a calumny, such as could only arise out of the doctrine of Charles' divine right to tread down his subjects on the one hand, or out of an ignorance of the spiritual liberty which Cromwell sought to promote, and which he mainly *did* promote, on the other.

These points in Cromwell's character may be extensively illustrated by reference to his extant memorials. The following extract from a letter, which appears among the "Squire Papers" of Carlyle's edition, is remarkable, and we leave the reader to estimate it for himself.

"To ————

"*London*, *July*, 1642.

"DEAR FRIENDS: Your letters gave me great joy at reading your great progress in behalf of our great cause.

"Verily, I do think the Lord is with me! I do undertake strange things, yet do I go through with them, to great profit and gladness, and furtherance of the Lord's great work. I do feel myself lifted on by a strange force, I cannot tell why. By night and by day I am urged forward on the great work. As sure as God appeared to Joseph in a dream, also to Jacob, he also has directed — (*some words eaten out by moths.*) Therefore I shall not fear what man can do unto me. I feel He giveth me the light to see the great darkness that surrounds us at noon day. * *

"I hoped, in a private capacity, to have reaped the fruit and benefit, together with my brethren, of our hard labor and hazards; the enjoyment, to wit, of peace and liberty, and the privileges of a Christian and a man, in some equality with others, according as it should please the Lord to dispense unto me. And when, I say, God had put an end to our wars, or at least brought them to a very hopeful issue, very near an end, — after Worcester fight, — I came up to London to pay my service and duty to the parliament which then sat; hoping that all minds would have been disposed to answer what seemed to be the mind of God, namely, To give peace and rest to his people, and especially to those who had bled more than others in the carrying on of the military affairs. I was much disappointed of my expectation; for the issue did not prove so. Whatever may be boasted or misrepresented, it was not so, not so!"

Again:—

"I appeal to the Lord, that the desires and endeavors we have had — nay, the things will speak for themselves: the liberty of England, the liberty of the people; the avoiding of tyrannous impositions, either upon men as men, or Christians as Christians; is made so safe by this act of settlement — the Protectorate — that it will speak for itself. And when it shall appear to the world what really hath been said and done by all of us, and what our real transactions were — for God can discover; no privilege will hinder the Lord from discovering!"

It is difficult to understand on what supposition, except that of divine right, Cromwell's conduct in desiring to be king, even supposing that he did desire it, is to be represented as of such inconceivable enormity. As protector, he enjoyed more real power, though less state, than he could have possessed had he brought himself, by the acceptance of the royal title, within the definitions and provisions of British law. To be king, was not, therefore, his interest. But he evidently desired it, in order to settle his government, to put an end to the distracting influences which raged around him, and to render the recovered liberties of the English people permanent. But such a thing might not be. The officers of the army, conspicuous among whom were Fleetwood and Desborough, his own son-in-law and brother-in-law, resisted it, and presented a petition drawn up by Dr. Owen,* and signed by a majority of the officers near town, which determined the question. England by this course lost a race of monarchs called to the throne by the popular voice; went back to its old oppressors; smarted

* Owen appears to have lost, by this act, Cromwell's favor. Orme's Life of Owen, p. 165.

beneath the rod of their vengeance or their folly; and, after a few years, called for another revolution, to throw off its oppressive burden.

It was a frequent declaration of Cromwell's, that the course of his life was one great aim to promote religious freedom. Was he insincere in this affirmation? Let his conduct in the matter of the Piedmontese bear witness!

The persecutions instituted by the Duke of Savoy against the poor protestants who occupied the mountains and valleys of Piedmont were of the most atrocious description. The duke published an order, dated January 25, 1655, commanding all protestants to depart from their homes to such places as he should appoint, within three days, on pain of death and confiscation. This was in the depth of a most severe winter, and many perished in the mountains from hunger and cold. The most cruel barbarities were perpetrated on those who remained. Many men and women were hewn in pieces, others were ravished and murdered. Some, hung on hooks, were left so to expire. Some had their mouths filled with gunpowder, which was made to explode. Some were flayed alive; some burned alive; and a variety of other tortures, too numerous or too barbarous to relate, signalized the infuriate malice borne by Italian Romanists to gospel truth. It was, in fact, all but an extermination; churches were set on fire, full of miserable fugitives, and families hunted like wild beasts. The news reached England just as Britain was on the eve of concluding a treaty with France. Louis XIV. was then nominally king, but he had not yet asserted his own authority, and Cardinal Mazarin, in conjunction with Ann of Austria, wielded the sole power. Cromwell refused to sign the treaty till he had despatched an ambassador on the part of the Piedmontese to the court of Turin. With all the protector's hardness and sternness, when the occasion called for them, pity was an essential ingredient in his nature.* The news

* The following extract from a letter of Cromwell's illustrates both these aspects of his character: — "To Cornet Squire, 15th March, 1642. Dear Friend, — I have no great mind to take Montague's word about that farm. I

of the sufferings of these Piedmontese had melted him to tears; he sent them two thousand pounds from his privy purse, appointed a day of national humiliation, and a collection, in order to relieve their wants, and resolved that, in the absence of all other power to compel justice for these sufferers, England should and would see them righted. Forty thousand pounds were contributed, with generous readiness, for the relief of these poor victims of oppression.

But Cromwell did more — he insisted that, before he would sign the treaty with France, Mazarin should interpose with the Duke of Savoy to procure a cessation of these outrages. In vain did the cardinal represent that the matter stood in no relation to the treaty, and that the Vaudois had committed a hundred times worse cruelties on the catholics than they had suffered from them. Cromwell was not the man to give way. He told Mazarin that he had already allowed his own troops to be engaged on the side of the persecution. The French ambassador threatened to take his leave. Cromwell, entirely unmoved, allowed him to go. He at the same time announced to the court of Turin that if remonstrances failed he was prepared to take up arms. Encouraged by the example of England — Denmark, Sweden, Holland, and some of the German States, said the same. The result was, that the Duke of Savoy sent the English ambassador to Cromwell, with a message most respectfully worded, declaring that "the persecutions had been much misrepresented and exaggerated, and that they had been occasioned by his rebellious subjects themselves; nevertheless, to show his great respect for his highness, he would pardon them, and restore them to their former privileges." Such was the issue of a negotiation, by which the descendants of the ancient Waldenses were protected by the strong hand of Crom-

learn behind the oven is the place they hide them (the arms); so watch well and take what the man leaves; and hang the fellow out of hand [out a hand], and I am your warrant. For he shot a boy at Pilton-bee by the Spinney, the widow's son, her only support: so God and man must rejoice at his punishment."

well's freedom-loving administration! The interval of quiet lasted so long as Cromwell lived, and no longer.

An instance not dissimilar occurred in reference to the city of Nismes, in the province of Languedoc. The protestants had set up a reformer as magistrate, which the catholics strongly opposed. On the day of election the protestants took possession of the town-house, which they occupied with armed men; and when the magnates of the city came to give their votes, the protestants poured out a volley of musket-shot upon them. The provocation was certainly very great, and the catholic party immediately proceeded to great severities against them. The inhabitants of Nismes, seeing an army marching against their city, and fearful of the consequences which their rash conduct had entailed on themselves, sent a messenger to Cromwell, to desire his interposition on their behalf. That very night, Cromwell despatched a courier to the English ambassador at Paris, who prevailed on the cardinal to pardon the offending reformers, and to stop the troops, which were already on their march to chastise them, so that when the messenger returned, he found the negotiation complete, and the city absolved.

Such were some of the leading features in the ecclesiastical history of Oliver Cromwell. In no line of regal descent, his kingship stands distinct, peculiar, alone, — for his successor was the merest cipher, — denied by the republican, and more strongly denied by the royalist, a gap in sculptured lineage, and a blot in history; yet acknowledged by such men as Louis XIV. and Mazarin, who made the rest of the world fall down and worship them. That Cromwell's character — independent, decisive and self-reliant, as he was — prompted him to actions which, had they been performed by royalists, he would have been the first to condemn; that the doctrine of the divine law of necessity, as he held it, made him dangerously a law to himself; that he showed "the terror of his beak, the lightning of his eye," not always to punish the daring Prometheus who was wielding the fire of heaven, but sometimes to fright men away from the dead carrion of his own interests* and power, we fear truth and candor must admit. But he was a vessel moulded out of no common clay. He had the quick, intuitive perceptions which seem akin to inspiration. As we search the dunghill on which his memory has been ignominiously thrown, the jewels which adorned him flash out upon our eyes. His enemies dwell upon his despotism, his friends applaud his love of religious liberty; both verdicts may be conjoined in the paradox which is his true description. He was a despot for religious liberty. He held that religion was above all law, excepting always that false religion which rendered law impossible. Whilst he crushed the uniformity which would have paralyzed moral action, he taught that spiritual liberty was the vital element of a nation's glory, and that greatness belonged to character, and was not identical with the punctilios of a denominational creed. He did not, it is true, realize a complete notion of the thing he aimed at, and he sometimes perplexed and confounded himself. But he showed the way to a possibility of which the nation never lost sight; the conviction of which made men impatient of the harsh rule of the second Stuart, and prompted the subsequent movements of the great revolution. It must never be forgotten that much of the obloquy heaped upon this great man arises not only from the malignity of the royalists,† but from the narrow views of the disappointed seekers of presbyterian uniformity. The day of Cromwell's degradation is, however, over. In vain do men any longer trample on his memory; his name will not die.

We cannot close this chapter without adverting to two scenes in

* The testimony of so eminent a man as Howe must not be forgotten, in this connection.

† The reader of the history of the commonwealth needs not to be told that many of the tales which obtained credence relative to the personages of that period are absolutely naked inventions. Owen was charged with having gone about Oxford girt with a sword; he declares that he never, to his remembrance, wore a sword in his life. The same divine is spoken of by Tillotson as having been present at Cromwell's death-scene. Every probability attests that this was entirely without foundation. These may be taken as specimens of the rest.

the protector's private life, which form a counterpart more than corresponding to the descriptions of his royal antagonist's domestic virtues. One is the death of Cromwell's earnest, loving, true-hearted mother:

"On Friday, Secretary Thurloe writes incidentally: 'My Lord Protector's mother, of ninety-four years old, died last night. A little before her death she gave my lord her blessing, in these words: The Lord cause his face to shine upon you, and comfort you in all your adversities, and enable you to do great things for the glory of your most High God, and to be a relief unto his people. My dear son, I leave my heart with thee. A good-night! — and therewith sank into her long sleep.' Even so. Words of ours are but idle. Thou brave one, mother of a hero, farewell! Ninety-four years old! The royalties of Whitehall, says Ludlow, very credibly, were of small moment to her; at the sound of a musket, she would often be afraid her son was shot, and could not be satisfied unless she saw him once a day, at least. She, — old, weak, wearied one, — she cannot help him with his refractory pedant parliaments, with his anabaptist plotters, royalist assassins, and world-wide confusions; but she bids him be strong, be comforted in God. And so good-night! And in the still eternities and divine Silences, — Well, are they not divine?"*

The companion scene is not less affecting; it describes the death-bed of Oliver's favorite daughter, the Lady Claypole. "For fourteen days he watched by her bed-side, he and her noble mother, and the loving circle of sisters, including their young Frances, with her widow's tears still undried. For fourteen days the fond father, unable to attend to any public business, refused to quit her bedside. On the 6th day of August she lay at rest, in her last sleep, and the weeping circle sought consolation where they had oft before found it in less trying hours of bereavement."

Oliver bore the trial with the fortitude of a Christian parent, and yet it broke his heart. About a fortnight afterwards, Thur-

* Cromwell's Letters and Speeches, vol. III., p. 406.

loe wrote to Henry Cromwell, and, after describing the funeral of his sister Elizabeth, he adds: — "Your lordship is a very sensible judge how great an affliction this was to both their highnesses, and how sad a family she left behind her; which sadness was truly very much increased by the sickness of his highness, who at the same time lay ill of the gout and other distempers, contracted by the long sickness of my Lady Elizabeth, which made great impression on him."

But Cromwell's life, shattered by this new sorrow, approached its close. The sunset was impressive, really sublime.* Did ever hypocrite — conscious of his manifold hypocrisies — so die? "Children, live like Christians; I leave you the covenant" (of grace) "to feed upon." — "Lord, thou knowest that if I desire to live, it is to show forth thy praise and declare thy works." — "It is a fearful thing to fall into the hands of the living God." His calmness, therefore, was not without a doubt; but the doubt was transient! "All the promises of God are in *Him*, yea, and in him Amen, to the glory of God by us in Jesus Christ." — "The Lord hath filled me with as much assurance of his pardon as my soul can hold." — "I am a conqueror, and more than a conqueror, through Christ that strengtheneth me." And then he breathes forth the following prayer: — "Lord, though I am a miserable and wretched creature, I am in covenant with thee, through grace. And I may, I will, come unto thee for this people. Thou hast made me, though very unworthy, a mean instrument to do them some good, and thee service; and many of them have set too high a value upon me, though others wish and would be glad of my death; Lord, however thou do dispose of me, continue and go on to do good for them. Give them consistency of judgment, one head, and mutual love; and go on to deliver them, and with the work of reformation; and make the name of Christ glorious in the world. Teach those who look too much on thy instruments to

* Mr. Carlyle has done much service by his disinterments; by none more than by his publication of Harvey's "Collection of several passages concerning his late Highness, Oliver Cromwell, in the time of his sickness."

depend more on thyself. Pardon such as desire to trample on the dust of a poor worm, for they are thy people, too; and pardon the folly of this short prayer. Even for Jesus Christ's sake. And give us a good-night, if it be thy pleasure. Amen!"*

But the days of Cromwell — such is the tenure upon which human life is held — were numbered! Whilst Europe was resounding with the fame of those splendid achievements which had raised Great Britain to an unprecedented eminence, — whilst powerful empires were crouching at his feet, and his incomparable energy was beating down the hydra-like attempts of modern and ancient factions, but before he had time fully to concentrate and establish the power out of which future liberty was to spring, — he died. He left behind him a name inseparably bound up with England's pride and power, and a fame which will outlive reproach, and may well dispense with statuary. Whatever his faults, — and his very strength was his weakness, — he taught a secondary nation to become the first in Europe, by developing its latent powers and resources. What can be more honorable to Cromwell than the fact that he, in the seventeenth century, had approximated as nearly to religious liberty as most senators have done in the nineteenth; and that he only stopped then where they are stopping now? With clearer views than his predecessors, his contemporaries, or his immediate successors, he saw, to a large extent, that freedom was an essential element of virtue and of power, and that a nation was great, not when it prescribed opinions, but when it acted on the divine rule of bearing with the mistaken, and diffusing free air and sunshine around it.

Happy shall we be if whilst we profit by the errors, we shall exceed the lessons, of so great an instructor!

* Carlyle's Cromwell, vol. IX., p. 400.

CHAPTER VII.

THE RETURNING TIDE.

"The flagrant inconsistency of all protestant intolerance is a poison in its veins which must destroy it." — MACKINTOSH.

AMONG the eminent men who flourished during the period of the great civil wars, none was more worthily conspicuous than Richard Baxter. His name, his piety, his usefulness, have been bequeathed by him as a precious legacy to Christ's church, to show how much more religion is than an empty name; how near a Christian on earth may be to a saint in Paradise; and how the deepest concern in public movements does not necessarily fret away a heaven-born piety. His portrait is almost as well known as his name. The pinched skull-cap, from under which the jet-black locks flow down with puritanical severity; the sharply-chiselled features, indicating an equal familiarity with thought and emotion; the somewhat severe expression of the dark lineaments, over which a divine radiance is yet diffused, like some stern fastness glowing in the brilliance of a summer's sun, — are in the memory of the least intelligent. To dwell upon the history of such a man, even to its most detailed incidents, and to observe how his errors and littlenesses become faint, when regarded by the side of a devoutness which has scarcely a parallel, would be, to any well-constituted man, a delightful task; but it is one we cannot in this chapter undertake to perform, — nor is it necessary.

The ancient town of Kidderminster is at present, owing to its being off the great lines of railway, no very accessible spot. It stands in a basin of the red sandstone formation, and its vicinity is delightfully diversified with hill and valley. Nothing can be more delicious than the green foliage, alternating with the ruby-colored soil which abundantly produces it, — a contrast of color always harmonious, and in this neighborhood peculiarly beautiful. Kidderminster is less injured than most towns by the progress of modern improvement. The natural features of the place are, indeed, beyond the possibility of change; but, besides these, old structures meet the eye continually. The eminence from which our sketch

KIDDERMINSTER, WITH THE CHURCH OF BAXTER.

is taken — Bewdley-road — must exhibit in 1851 nearly the same aspect it presented in the days of the devout nonconformist. The steep declivity down which the road passes into the town, displaying ancient houses, hollowed out of the living rock, as if they had been parts — though very ungraceful ones — of some modern Petra; the antique tower, conspicuous in the central distance, built of the red rock, to which the corrosions of weather impart a peculiar mellowness; the ill-constructed houses, sometimes almost buried under the cliffs, and then as picturesquely lifting themselves high in air, — impart a physiognomy to the ancient place extremely uncommon.

Here, then, the holy man lived and labored. On each side of this old street the voice of thanksgiving might be heard, on a Sabbath-evening, from the various families assembled at their evening devotions. The grave form of the thin, sickness-worn divine, or of his congenial assistant, may be imagined, proceeding from house to house, as he pursued his work of conversation or catechising among the numerous parishioners. The crowds gathering weekly to the church bore witness to the value the hearers set upon the living truth, enforced as it was by Baxter's earnest oratory, and still more by his exemplary life. His time — for at this period he had neither wife nor family — was altogether devoted to his flock. Though his means were small, his liberality was great. Vice was frowned down. The Sabbath was so observed, that the traces of that observance yet remain, or did until very recently, in the habits of the people. All Baxter's hearers were not, indeed, converted, and enemies and maligners still remained; but they were mostly silenced; and Kidderminster presented, in his days, the nearest approach, perhaps, which any town has ever exhibited, to a Christianized community. And what rendered this the more remarkable was, that this reformation took place at a time when internal discord was eating into the heart of the land.

No change can be greater than that which has befallen the interior of Baxter's church itself. It stands on one side of the town, and on the edge of a precipice, which renders it a commanding object. But all within is transformed. A taste, in some respects of the best kind, but of the most tractarian pattern, has remodelled the whole edifice; and the advance to Romanism is conspicuous upon every panel and adornment. But in the "New Meeting" Baxter's ancient pulpit yet survives, having been purchased, among a mass of old rubbish, when, some years ago, the church was undergoing alteration. What visitor can look upon it unmoved? It is an ornamented structure, as rich as carving and gilt could make it, of the date of James I., when Inigo Jones gave the taste for Grecian architecture in Gothic churches. Carved in alto-relievo, on its sounding-board are the appropriate words:

SING UNTO THE
LORD PRAISE
HIS NAME DECLARE
HIS WORKS A
MONG THE PEOPLE
PSALMS THE CV.

Below, in a similar style, is the conspicuous name of its donor:

ALICE DAWX WIDOW GAVE THIS.

Kidderminster has no other monument of Richard Baxter. It is impossible that it could possess a better.

Baxter had not been long settled in Kidderminster, when the great civil war began. He was at this time twenty-six years of age. The king kept as far as possible from the counties which formed the eastern association; and drew most of his retainers from Shropshire, Herefordshire, Worcestershire, and Wales. As, to be a puritan, or to be suspected of being one, exposed a man to all kinds of abuse and exaction from the royal partisans, many who would have lived in quiet, had such a course been possible, were compelled to ally themselves with the parliamentary troops, and seek refuge under their protection. Among those who were in this predicament was Baxter himself. When the king's declarations were read in the market-place of Kidderminster, the rabble grew so riotous and outrageous, that he was compelled to leave the town. He retired for a while to Gloucester, where he became involved in sectarian disputes, tending to sharpen his acrimony against ecclesiastical schismatics. He subsequently found a refuge in Coventry, where he resided for a time with a friend, preaching once a week to the soldiers of the garrison, and to various ministers and others, who had taken refuge in the town from the flames of popular fury. Many of his old hearers, also, had here sought a quiet retreat.

After the battle of Naseby, Baxter went to visit the army, and to see some of his friends. "He staid," says Calamy, "a night with them, and got such intelligence as to the state of the army as amazed him. He found plotting heads were hot upon what intimated their intention to subvert both church and state. Independency and anabaptistry extremely prevailed among them; antinomianism and arminianism were equally distributed. * * Many common soldiers, and some of the officers, were honest, sober, and orthodox men; but a few proud, self-conceited, hot-headed sectaries had got into the highest places, and were Cromwell's chief favorites; and by their very heat and activity bore down the rest, or carried them along with them, and were the soul of the army, though much fewer in numbers than the rest. * * Separatists and sectaries were the persons most honored; but Cromwell and his council joyn'd with no party, being for the liberty of all."

This, it will be remembered, is the testimony of a presbyterian, relating the impressions made upon Baxter, himself a presbyterian, by the agitation of the times. The evil was, indeed, manifest, and was a grief to every well-wisher to the church of God, as well as a serious impediment to all united and concentrated action. But the remedy was one entirely beyond the power of Baxter, or of those who thought with him, to apply; and the course they took only exasperated the malady they would fain have cured. The state had, certainly, no appliances which could heal so wide a wound.

This visit, however, made a deep impression upon Baxter's mind. When Cromwell had first formed his band of Ironsides, "which was to be a gathered church," he had invited Baxter to become their chaplain. He, perhaps, afterwards, as he reasoned out his own position more clearly, had ceased to desire it; but when now Baxter witnessed the influence of this band, and saw the increase of sectarianism among them, he regretted that the invitation had not been accepted, and readily fell in with the entreaty of Colonel Whalley to undertake a similar charge in his regiment. He went, therefore, into the army, hoping to stem the torrent of sectarianism, from which he boded the most disastrous consequences. "His life among them," says Calamy, "was a daily contending against seducers." "He was almost always disputing with one or other of them, — sometimes for civil government, and sometimes for church order and government; sometimes for infant baptism, and often against antinomianism, and the contrary extreme. *But their most frequent and vehement disputes were for liberty of conscience, as they called it;* that is, that the civil magistrate had nothing to do in matters of religion, by constraint or restraint; but every man might not only hold and believe, but preach and do, in matters of religion, what he pleased."* Their spirit was no doubt sufficiently factious and disorderly, especially if we remember that conspicuous among them were the levellers, who afterwards rose up against Cromwell himself. But it is evident that to Baxter "liberty of conscience" was rank heresy. No man better loved the order and power implied in the phrase "church and state" than Baxter. He therefore complained that he was kept in ignorance of the meetings and councils of Cromwell and his officers, and "found reason to apprehend that, if there had been a competent number of ministers, each doing his part, the whole plot of the furious party might have been broken, and king, parliament and religion, preserved." Let us hear Baxter's own words relative to the assembly of "dry vines," as the sectaries in the army then called it, and to the period in general which his autobiography so energetically describes:

"A few dissenting ministers of the Westminster assembly began all this, and carried it far on. * * Afterwards they increased, and others joined themselves to them, who, partly by stiffness, and partly by policy, encreas'd our flames, and kept open our wounds, as if there had been none but they considerable in the world. And

* Calamy's Life of Baxter.

having an army and city agents, fit to second them, effectually hindered all remedy, till they had dash'd all to pieces as a broken glass. O, what may not pride do, and what miscarriages will not false principles and faction hide! One would have thought that if their opinions had been certainly true, and their church order good, yet the interest of Christ, and the souls of men, and of greater truths, should have been so regarded by the dividers in England, as that the safety of all these should have been preferred, and not all ruined, rather than their way should want its carnal aim and liberty; and that they should not tear the garment of Christ all to pieces, rather than it should want their lace."

These words describe a not uncommon error, especially among some good men, who regard the unity of the church as implying the sacrifice of its less important truths. How Baxter himself acted when the current ran in the contrary direction we have seen already. None was more liable to the charge of an undue pertinacity than himself. But in this case the plea which the presbyterian party urged against the sectaries was but that which the episcopal had urged against the puritans. How easy it is for the inflicter of an injury to cry out, Peace! *

It would be a gross mistake to imagine that Baxter meant to impute to these sectaries in general a spirit of lawless disorder, so far as the great object for which they were in arms was concerned. "They all agreed to preserve the kingdom; they prospered more in amity than uniformity. Whatever their opinions were, they plundered none with them, they betrayed none with them, nor disobeyed the state with them; and they were more visibly pious

* It is right that Baxter's praises should be set over against his censures. In another passage he says, speaking of the independents, "Most of them were zealous, and very many learned, discreet, and godly men, fit to be serviceable in the church. * * I saw also a commendable care of serious holiness and discipline in most of the independent churches." Life, part I., p. 140.

and peaceable in their opinions than those we call more orthodox." *

An accusation was got up against Baxter, that at this period he had killed a papist with his own hand. But the report was utterly unfounded.

Whilst with the army, Baxter was visited with a dangerous sickness. His constitution was naturally most delicate, his blood being so attenuated that it frequently oozed out from his fingers' ends; but on this occasion he was seized with so violent a bleeding at the nose, as to put his life in great peril, and entirely to destroy his schemes for drawing off the sectarian party from their proposed plans. He was pitied in this distress by Lady Rous, who cared for him and tended him with great assiduity, till he was able to return to Kidderminster. This sickness is memorable as having led to the publication of that devout and incomparable work, "The Saint's Rest;" one chapter of which more than compensates for all the venial errors into which Baxter was ever betrayed.

He now resumed his labors at Kidderminster. At this time he sided with neither party; opposing on the one hand the covenant, and on the other the engagement. Conscientious always, he was, probably, in a state of indecision as to his duty. One great object of his life was now, however, secured; he was free to resume his beloved work at Kidderminster. For fourteen years he had, as he tells us, "after wars and sickness, liberty in such sweet employment." Nothing can better describe his pastoral life than the account he gives of it himself. His self-denying earnestness; the pungency of address which he carefully cultivated; the intense ardor with which he spoke, to use his own well-known words, "as a dying man to dying men;" the faithfulness of his rebukes; the loftiness of his seraphic piety; the unyielding firmness with which he maintained all which he believed to be true; and the energy with which he seconded in private all which he delivered

* Sprigge's "Anglia Rediviva," quoted in Orme's Baxter, p. 53. Sprigge was chaplain to Fairfax, himself a presbyterian.

in public, might almost form an appendix to "the Acts of the Apostles."

During his residence at Kidderminster, he once preached at court before Cromwell. His subject was 1 Cor. 1 : 10, "against the divisions and distractions of the church." He says, "My plainness was displeasing to him and his courtiers, but they put it up." Cromwell sent to converse with him, endeavoring, in "a long and tedious speech," to reconcile him to the new government; but Baxter, who was a firm royalist, could not be won. Cromwell afterwards summoned him to a conversation on liberty of conscience: a subject which the protector understood much better than the divine. But this interview was equally fruitless. Baxter was remarkable for tenacity of opinion, and the matter ended as it had begun.

The following passage exhibits Baxter's views of Cromwell's administration of religious liberty. It will be read with mingled pleasure and pain:

"When Cromwell was made Lord Protector, he had the policy not to detect and exasperate the ministers and others who consented not to his government. Having seen what a stir the engagement had before made, he let men live quietly, without putting any oaths of fidelity upon them, except members of his parliaments; these he would not allow to enter the house till they had sworn fidelity to him. The sectarian party in his army and elsewhere he chiefly trusted to, and pleased; till, by the people's submission and quietness, he thought himself well settled; and then he began to undermine them, and by degrees to work them out. Though he had so often spoken for the anabaptists, he now found them so heady, and so much against any settled government, and so set upon the promotion of their way and party, that he not only began to blame their uneasiness, but also to design to settle himself in the people's favor by suppressing them."*

When Richard Cromwell succeeded his father, Baxter gave his

* Life, part I., p. 74.

allegiance to the new government. In his simplicity, he sufficiently indicates the ground of his adherence. "He began to favor," says Baxter, "the sober people of the land, to honor parliaments, and to respect the ministers called presbyterians." The last assertion probably contains the gist of the whole matter. The independent party saw no small fear for religious liberty. They dreaded a return to uniformity, and to the conditions of the solemn league and covenant. In the movements of the period which followed, Joseph Caryl, Dr. Owen and Philip Nye, were conspicuous. They sent a deputation to Monk at Holyrood House, in the name of the independent churches, to which Monk was regarded as belonging, and they offered to raise one hundred thousand pounds for the use of the army, that their religious liberty might be protected.* But the presbyterian party prevailed. Monk veiled his intentions until, at last, backed by the Earl of Manchester, Lord Hollis, the presbyterian ministers of London, and others, he declared for the king. Baxter appears to have taken little part in the movement, beyond that of interceding with the general that debauchery and profaneness might be put down. The king sent over a proclamation against these evils, (!) to the great joy of the future nonconformists, who lost no time in reading it in their churches.

The day much desired, but long delayed, of the restoration of Charles II. to the throne, had arrived. Under what pretexts he now ascended it needs not to be detailed. With a base hypocrisy, far transcending the worst transactions attributed to Cromwell by his bitterest enemies, he had caused certain presbyterian ministers to overhear him in his devotions, like Richard III. of old time, praying for the presbyterian church, and for the success of the covenant. Notwithstanding unfavorable rumors of his levity, the reality of this scene was believed. Thus far, at least, his scheming proved successful; if that could be called success which involved conditions he had neither the inclination nor the power to fulfil. "We do grant," he had said from Breda, "a free and general

* Orme's Life of Owen, pp. 282, 283.

pardon, which we are ready, upon demand, to pass under our great seal of England, to all our subjects of what degree soever, who, within forty days after the publishing hereof, shall lay hold on this our grace and favor, and shall by any public act declare their doing so, and that they return to the loyalty and obedience of good subjects, except only such persons as shall hereafter be excepted by parliament: * * we desiring and ordaining that thenceforward all notes of discord, separation and difference of parties, be utterly abolished among all our subjects, whom we invite and conjure to a perfect union among themselves, under our protection, for the re-settlement of our just rights and theirs in a free parliament; by which, on the word of a king, we will be advised. * * We do declare a liberty to tender consciences; and that no man shall be disquieted, or called in question, for differences in matters of religion which do not disturb the peace of the kingdom."* Under these assurances, the king returned on the 29th May, 1660. It was a period of mad intoxication. Could men have lifted the veil which concealed the secret history of the period, they would have ascertained what would have abated their ardor. For, on the king's journey towards London, Monk had placed in his hand a list of about seventy persons recommended as privy-councillors, at the same time assuring his majesty that in doing so he only complied with the necessities of his position, and did not suppose the persons so recommended would be accepted by his majesty.

On that day,—a day memorable in the annals of national infatuation and royal perjury,—Charles advanced from Canterbury to London, amidst the loud shouts of a rejoicing nation. All the most splendid concomitants usual upon royal progresses attended him. But there were also peculiar features in this welcome. When he reached Blackheath, his eye rested upon the army,—the people's national guard, the same army which had beaten down his royal father, and changed the kingdom into a commonwealth,—drawn up

* This phrase is memorable, and will account for the subsequent eagerness shown to implicate the religious parties in the various plots of the period.

in their most imposing array, to hail him as their undisputed sovereign. At St. George's-fields he was met by the lord mayor and aldermen of the city of London, who, after inviting him to a collation in a tent provided for that purpose, took part in the gorgeous procession which escorted his majesty over London-bridge to Whitehall. The streets were hung with tapestry; the train-bands of the city, and the several companies in their liveries, lined the way as far as Temple-bar; and beyond that a similar array was formed, consisting of the train-bands of Westminster, and portions of the army. The procession itself was prolonged and superb. It was led by troops, some in doublets of cloth of silver, some in buff coats, with sleeves of silver lace, and rich green scarves, and some in blue. Trumpeters with the king's arms, sheriffs' men in rich cloaks laced with silver, six hundred of the different companies of London, in black velvet coats, with gold chains, on horseback, attended by footmen in liveries, followed. Then, kettle-drums, trumpeters, and rich red liveries; twelve ministers, succeeded by the king's life-guards; the sheriffs; the aldermen, in scarlet robes; the lord mayor, with the sword and badges of his office; the Duke of Buckingham, and the general of the forces; whilst, after these, came the king himself, riding between the Dukes of York and Gloucester. All men pressed forward to see the son of the royal martyr, and the hero of the Boscobel oak, and to look upon that swarthy countenance* radiant with joy. He was followed by a troop of horse, bearing white colors, and a great multitude of noblemen and gentlemen. Hearts were beating; bonfires blazing; everywhere was heard the *refrain*, "The king shall enjoy his own again."

Thus, on his birth-day, was Charles II. conducted to the palace of his fathers. Here the lord mayor took leave of him. The king then went to the lords, where he was addressed, on behalf of that house, by the Earl of Manchester, in the following terms:

* Charles was so far from being handsome, that his mother, Henrietta Maria, said at his birth, "He is so ugly, that I am ashamed of him."

"Dread Sovereign," said the once parliamentary general, "I offer no flattering titles, but speak the words of truth; you are the desire of three kingdoms, the strength and stay of the tribes of the people, for the moderating of extremities, the reconciling of differences, the satisfying of all interests, and for the restoring of the collapsed honor of these nations."

He then proceeded to the banqueting-house, where the commons awaited him, and Sir Harbottle Grimstone said, on their behalf, "With an humble confidence, I shall presume to acquaint your majesty that I have further in command to present to you at this time a petition of right, and humbly, on my bended knees, to beg your assent thereto. Sir, it hath already passed two great houses, — heaven and earth, — and I have *vox populi* and *vox Dei* to warrant this bold demand. It is that your majesty would be pleased to remove your throne of state, and set it up in the hearts of your people; and, as you are deservedly the king of hearts, there to receive from your people a crown of hearts."

To these addresses the king replied, "that next to the honor of God, from whom he chiefly owed the restoration to his crown, he would study the welfare of his people, and not only be a true defender of the faith, but a just assertor of the laws and liberties of his subjects." A pledge akin to lovers' promises, which are kept, according to Ariosto, in jars in the moon.

A further scene ensued. The dignitaries of the church, in their long-disused habits, awaited him in Westminster Abbey, to give thanks for his restoration. The king, however, pleaded fatigue, and made his oblations in his own apartment. After which, he who, on his arrival, had received from certain presbyterian ministers the present of a large Bible, with clasps of gold, which he declared should be the guide of his life, went to the lodgings of Mrs. Palmer, afterwards Lady Castlemaine, his avowed mistress, to spend his evening.

The first acts of Charles were full of promise to the presbyterian party. Several of their ministers, among whom were Calamy, Reynolds, Spurstow and Baxter, were appointed royal chaplains, and some of them preached before the king. The time had now come, as they imagined, for the realization of their fondest hopes. Baxter's warm heart had longed for a scheme of comprehension. He had hoped for it, even in the days of Cromwell, and his correspondence with Howe, who was preacher at Oliver's court, had signified the sincerity and ardency of his desires for such an issue. Under Cromwell the motto had been "state and church;" there was now hope that it would be "church and state" once more. A deputation, accordingly, waited on the king, in which Baxter was the chief speaker. Charles gave so gracious a reception to these representatives, that old Mr. Ash burst into tears of joy!

As, on the king's arrival, it had been decreed that all the acts of the Long Parliament, not having received the royal assent, were null and void, the nation, by a huge transition, fell back upon those laws which, existing before the proceedings of the commonwealth, brought the people once more under compulsory episcopacy. A year had not passed before these former laws began to be rigorously enforced. The old clergy now took possession of their former livings, — the court paying no regard to the petitions that those who had been sequestrated for malignancy or for scandal might not be replaced. But, where the old incumbent was dead, the king confirmed the living to the present possessor. It was evident that, at this time, a modification of the liturgy might have comprehended a large portion of both parties, — perhaps have quieted for a moment the exhausted and gasping nation.

We have, in a former part of this volume, made mention of a palace, situated on the banks of the river Thames, and once the residence of John of Gaunt, Duke of Lancaster. It had now fallen into the possession of the Bishop of London, and was, at the early part of the reign of Charles II., the scene of a remarkable conference, called for the purpose of effecting what, in those days, was termed a comprehension: in other words, of so adjusting the liturgy of the church establishment as to accommodate it to the consciences of religious men of different persuasions. In this scheme Baxter was specially prominent. He, and the presbyterian party which he led, entertained no objection to episcopacy as such, though they would have desired to modify its prelatical form; nor would they have rigorously objected to the Book of Common-prayer, provided that certain alterations could have been made in it, to relieve their consciences from its more offensive portions. To discuss the possibility of such an adjustment, the Savoy conference had been summoned by the king.

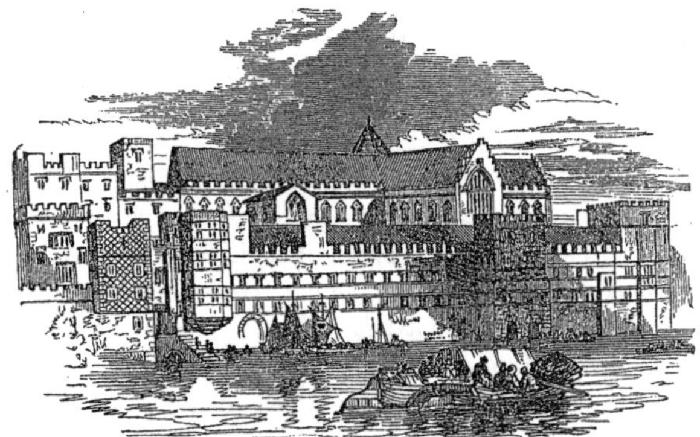

THE SAVOY PALACE — SCENE OF THE CONFERENCE.

It was attended by the Archbishop of York, with twelve bishops on the one side, and eleven nonconformist ministers, chosen either by Reynolds (Bishop of Norwich) or by Calamy, on the other. The scene was singular, but characteristic of the temper of the times. The Archbishop of York, opening the conference, avowed that he did not know its precise object, and referred to Sheldon, the Bishop of London; he, a merciless enemy of nonconformity, with ill-disguised contempt, said that it was not the episcopal, but the nonconformist party, who had desired the alterations in the liturgy; and that, therefore, nothing could be done till they exhibited their objections and amendments.* In vain was it urged

* This prelate, upon being told that the presbyterian ministers were not likely to accept the terms of conformity offered to them, is reported to have said, "I am afraid they will." The presbyterian party was the only body

by the nonconformists that this would be a tedious business, and at variance with the purposes of the king's commission, which required them to meet together and to consult. The bishop was inexorable, and Baxter reluctantly agreed to adopt his proposal. Sheldon's motives are obvious. He wished to throw the odium of attacking the Common-prayer upon the nonconformist party. If, in stating their objections, they should agree among themselves, — which was doubtful, — it would not be difficult to represent them as captious and destructive. The temper of the times was with prelacy, and against presbyterianism. The nonconformists, however, addressed themselves to the task of stating their objections, whilst to Baxter was given that part which referred to the substitution of new forms for the old. In the course of a fortnight, he prepared a revised liturgy — a formula, expressive, in all its parts, of a spiritual religion, but immeasurably inferior, as a piece of composition, to the compendium it was designed to supplant. Indeed, none but an untaught and untrained man, like Baxter, would have presumed to offer the labor of a few short days, as a rival to a liturgy which, whatever its faults, was much of it the production of men of various ages, eminent for profundity, piety, and religious taste.

A tedious logomachy followed. The conclusion was, indeed, from the first, foreseen; but, for the sake of appearances, a little show of debate seemed necessary. We need not follow the history into its particulars. Like all similar convocations, it was a heartless juggle, a farce scarcely possible to be thought serious.

The whole affair was, on the part of the presbyterians, a signal failure. The episcopalians would not abate the smallest ceremony of the church; the puritans retired disappointed and disgusted.

The open and then unoccupied area of Charing Cross was the scene, about this time, of a cruel and inhuman punishment. This

whose rising power was then dreaded. The policy of the day was to keep them down, not merely because of their religious views, but in order to diminish their influence in elections.

was the carrying out of "An Act for the attainder of several persons guilty of the horrid murder of his late sacred majesty King Charles I." Harrison, Carew, Scroope, Jones, Clement, Scot, Hugh Peters, Cooke, Axtel and Hacker, were the names of the ten who, out of twenty-nine convicted for having been concerned in the late king's death, underwent the severest penalty. At the same time, the writings of Milton and John Goodwin, defending the death of the king, were suppressed by proclamation. The most inhuman and cowardly outrages were committed on the bodies of those who had been concerned in the late revolution. The mouldering remains of Cromwell, Ireton and Bradshaw, were dragged to Tyburn, and there hanged and decapitated, whilst the heads were exposed on the top of Westminster Hall. Nor did even the bodies of Cromwell's mother and daughter escape indignity. By the authority of the king's warrants, the corpses of all who had been buried in Westminster Abbey since 1641, including those of Pym, Blake, Twisse, Marshall, and others of scarcely less fame, were exhumed, and cast into a pit in St. Margaret's church-yard. The revenge was paltry and impotent. At the same time, the Solemn League and Covenant was declared illegal by parliament; and the well-known law, entitled the "Corporation Act," which prohibited all persons from bearing offices of magistracy without taking the oaths of allegiance and supremacy, was passed. The ancient flame was again kindled.

The convocation was now, by command of the king, employed on the revision of the Book of Common-prayer, in conformity, it was pretended, with the wishes of the Savoy conference. Between the court, stimulated by Clarendon, on the one hand, and the presbyterians on the other, they found this a task of no common difficulty; but they resolved to ignore the objections of the latter, and to listen only to the former. "They made," says Tenison, afterwards Archbishop of Canterbury, "about six hundred small alterations or additions; but, if there was reason for these changes, there was equal, if not greater, reason for some further improvements." They added forms of prayer for the 30th of January and the 29th of May; also, prayers to be used at sea, and a new office for the administration of adult baptism. New holidays were appointed, and more lessons from the Apocrypha, such as the history of Bel and the Dragon, were inserted. The prayer for "our most religious and gracious king" was also added. It was the opinion of Burnet and Baxter that these alterations only rendered the Prayer-book more open to objection.* But it was thus sent up to the houses of legislature.

Symptoms of the rising storm were already apparent. Nonconformists were indicted for not reading the common-prayer, and hearers were complained of for neglecting their parish churches. Worshippers in conventicles were exposed to all kinds of annoyance; insulted on their way, their windows broken with stones, and their religious rites often disturbed by the blowing of horns, and other similar outrages. The spread of immorality and profaneness was most extensive; and the court was given up to profligacy and licentiousness. Dunkirk, which had been gained by Cromwell with so much *éclat*, was sold to the French king for five hundred thousand pounds; Lambert and Sir Harry Vane, jr., were brought to trial, one for taking arms against the king, the other for compassing his death; the former was imprisoned for life, the latter executed on Tower-hill, not being allowed to speak to the people from the scaffold.

At length, after sundry debates, and by a majority of six votes, the commons passed the infamous bill for "the uniformity of public prayers and administration of sacraments, and other rites and ceremonies, &c. &c., in the Church of England." The act was ordered, either by a strange fatality, or in daring defiance, to take effect from the Feast of St. Bartholomew, Aug. 24, 1662.

One of the provisions of this act was, that before St. Bartholomew's day every parson, vicar, or other minister whatsoever, should, on pain of deprival, declare openly and publicly his approval of the Book of Common-prayer, according to the following formula:

"I, A B, do hereby declare my unfeigned assent and consent

* Neal, vol. IV., c. 6.

to all and everything contained and prescribed in and by the book entitled the Book of Common-prayer," &c.

At the same time, the act provided that all persons holding preferment or office in the church, and every schoolmaster keeping any public or private school, and every person instructing youth in any private family, "should declare it unlawful to take arms against the king; should promise to conform to the liturgy; and should disclaim, as unlawful, the Solemn League and Covenant." Those who were not clergymen, but only teachers, were, in case of non-compliance with the act, visited with heavy penalties.

One of the first persons on whom the weight of this enactment fell was Richard Baxter. He had refused to accept a bishopric; and had made an endeavor to return to the curacy, the duties of which he offered to perform without recompense, and he carried with him the express desires of the king and Lord Clarendon in his reïnstatement. Had their desires, however, been sincere, the issue probably would have been widely different. As it was, the Bishop of Worcester, Dr. Morley, refused to appoint him. Baxter now joined Dr. Bates, and preached for him once a week at St. Dunstan's; and, whilst that church was under repair, at St. Bride's, Milk-street, and Blackfriars. His preaching began to be regarded with much suspicion. He was watched, waylaid, and positively prohibited from preaching at Kidderminster any more.

Such was Baxter's position at the time of the passing of the Act of Uniformity. That act received the royal assent on the 19th May; it was to take effect from the 17th August, which was the Sunday before St. Bartholomew's day; but the revised Prayer-book was not printed till the middle of August, leaving a space of only a few hours for conveying both the announcement and the test through the country. Even in our own day, such wanton haste in the smallest legal matter would be regarded as a serious indignity; what, then, must so great a measure have been at that period, when few papers were published at all, none of them more frequently than twice a week, and when the roads were always bad, and sometimes impassable? Bishop Burnet says, "The vast number of copies, being many thousands, that were to be wrought off for all the parish churches of England, made the impression go so slowly, that there were few books set out to sale when the day came. * * The matter was urged on with so much precipitancy, that it seems implied that the clergy should subscribe implicitly to a book they had never seen; and this was done by too many, as the bishops themselves confessed." We have said that Baxter was the first on whom the weight of this act fell. The explanation he gives himself. "The last sermon that I preached in public was on May 25th; the reasons why I gave over sooner than most others were, because lawyers did interpret a doubtful clause in the act as ending the liberty of lectures at that time; because I would let authority soon know that I intended to obey in all that was lawful; because I would let all ministers in England understand in time whether I would conform or not: for had I staid to the last day, some would have conformed the sooner, from a supposition that I intended it." From this time, therefore, Baxter ceased to be a minister in the Church of England.

We may well imagine with what beating, and sometimes bursting hearts, many of those who were then holding livings in the Church of England anticipated the twenty-fourth of August in that year. How many a father would feel his eyes fill with tears, as he looked to the prospect of penury for his helpless offspring! How many a pastor would think, with an anguish which no words can describe, of the separation which was soon to sever him from his flock, the object of so many solicitudes and prayers! Before the eyes of those most sensitive to feel such a reverse would rise up the visions of hated idleness, of galling persecution, of dreary and aching want! The secession of the Free Church within our own day is justly regarded as a noble instance in modern times of men who preferred truth to interest. But St. Bartholomew's was a still severer test; for the power enlisted against the puritans of that day threatened to exterminate them altogether. Who could tell what might be the next step which should follow one so severe? But there was no alternative. They were good men, and behind them stood conscience, an impassable wall of adamant. The test before them — at least, before those of them who had time to inspect it — admitted of no subtlety or evasion which it was consistent with their high character to adopt. They were not required to approve a part of the system, nor even the system as a whole, but to declare their "unfeigned assent and consent to all and everything;" though even passages of that same Prayer-book asserted that some parts of the church's own discipline were not all that could be desired! * Failing in their adhesion, they would lose station, honor, usefulness, emolument, subsistence — for the time fixed upon for compliance was just before the yearly tithes would be due, and the non-compliant would thus sacrifice a year's income; — "their houses would be turned to aliens, their inheritance to strangers." † But the act set forth so many conditions, and prescribed them so absolutely, that no alternative remained.

Were there none who at such a conjuncture thought even more deeply? Were there none whose soliloquies were not unlike the following: There is something judicial in our position; when we proclaimed uniformity, we lifted on high the stone which is to fall on our own heads! The instrument of torture, which, like a new Perillus, we prepared, is turned, by a not unjust retribution, on ourselves! So would *we* have crushed all sectarianism except our own! When we gave ecclesiastical power to the state, did we not know that forms of religion in its hands would vary as the administration of the state itself? We came in upon the ruin of another system; that other system now returns upon us! ‡

With all their errors, however, we love, we admire, we reverence, the holy men of those days! But, whilst we pity their

* See the Commination service.

† Such was the text from which Bridge preached at Yarmouth to a party of religious emigrants at an earlier period.

‡ It must not, however, be forgotten that, in the ejectment of the prelatical clergy, a fifth part of the sequestrated revenue was assigned for their support. In the present case there was no such provision.

sufferings, let us not forget that there were others more to be pitied than they. What stings and agonies must have passed, however transiently, through the mind of Charles,* who knew that, with all this pretended zeal for protestant uniformity, he, even now, believed all protestantism to be a lie! What unenviable moments were those in which Clarendon called to mind how he had once fought the battles of religious liberty, by the side of the very men whom, for the paltry bribe of seeing his daughter acknowledged as a duchess, perhaps as a queen, he was now laboring to destroy! Who would envy Lauderdale, who had once sat as a commissioner in the Assembly of Divines, enacting the very provisions for their part in which these men and their successors were now about to suffer! And there were more pitiable objects than even these. Men who were renouncing the high franchises of eternity for a miserable pittance; forcing down the feather-weight of worldly advantage, to make it heavier than the deeply-loaded scale of conscience and of God; intentionally shutting out the light of their clearest understanding; taking refuge in quips and evasions, from which their inmost souls recoiled; and pronouncing with faltering voice the words which sunk them irrecoverably in their own self-esteem, no less than it did so in the esteem of their observant flocks. Among the many who subscribed in utter levity, and the many more who had made over their consciences already to the ruling power, there were doubtless such men as these. The honor and dignity of Christianity were, however, amply redeemed by the fact that their number was not greater. On the 24th of August, 1662, the Church of England was poorer by two thousand conscientious ministers!

No day in the annals of the church in modern times ever witnessed such an amount of pathetic and earnest Christian preaching as the Lord's day before that Feast of St. Bartholomew! The deepest solemnity pervaded these last utterances. The whole

* Perhaps we do Charles II., in such supposition, more than justice. Many parts of his history would seem to indicate him as a specimen of that morbid moral anatomy in which conscience is altogether wanting.

fervor of puritan piety blazed up in these last farewells. The preacher stood above suspicion. The hearer gave emphasis to every word of the voice he was to hear no more. Whole audiences were bathed in tears. The fire of religion fed its flames from the very elements which were employed to quench it!

But the most extensive suffering succeeded. Several became houseless, homeless, and almost destitute of food. Those who had congregations were in continual need of their contributions, to aid them in paying fines, or in maintaining them whilst in prison. Some died of dejection; some took shipping for Holland or New England; many found their ejection followed by years of hardships, imprisonments and fines; some endured persecutions from the succeeding incumbents, under the name of suits for dilapidations; some took to authorship, or sought a precarious subsistence by teaching in secret and in danger; some lost the favor of their own families by their firmness, and lived a life of bitter reproach from their connections; a few practised physic; whilst many who had seemed at the Restoration on the eve of a high church preferment began a course of trial and contumely which ended only in the grave. Happy were they who, like Woodward and Ash, died before this harsh act took effect!

Nor was the effect of such enactments less disastrous upon the Church of England herself. "The author of 'The Five Groans of the Church' complains," says Neal, "with great warmth, of above three thousand ministers admitted into the church who were unfit to teach because of their youth; of fifteen hundred debauched men ordained; of the ordination of many illiterate men; of one thousand three hundred and forty-two factious ministers, a little before ordained; and that of twelve thousand church livings, or thereabouts, three thousand or more being impropriate, and four thousand one hundred and sixty-five *sinecures;* so that there was a poor remainder left for a painful and honest ministry." The consequences are admirably depicted by Macaulay:

"During the domination of the puritans, many of the ejected ministers of the Church of England could obtain bread and shelter only by attaching themselves to the households of royalist gentlemen; and the habits which had been formed in those times continued long after the reëstablishment of monarchy and episcopacy. In the mansions of men of liberal sentiments and cultivated understandings, the chaplain was doubtless treated with urbanity and kindness. His conversation, his literary assistance, his spiritual advice, were considered as an ample return for his food, his lodging, and his stipend. But this was not the general feeling of the country gentlemen. * * A young Levite — such was the phrase then in use — might be had for his board, a small garret, and ten pounds a-year; and might not only perform his own professional functions, might not only be the most patient of butts and of listeners, might not only be always ready in fine weather for bowls and in rainy weather for shovel board, but might also save the expense of a gardener or a groom. * * With his cure he was expected to take a wife. The wife had ordinarily been in the patron's service; and it was well if she was not suspected of standing too high in the patron's favor. * * Not one living in fifty enabled the incumbent to bring up a family comfortably. As children multiplied and grew, the household of the priest became more and more beggarly. Holes appeared more and more plainly in the thatch of his parsonage and on his single cassock. * * His boys followed the plough, and his girls went out to service. Study he found impossible; for the advowson of his living would hardly have sold for a sum sufficient to purchase a good theological library; and he might be considered as unusually lucky, if he had ten or twelve dog-eared volumes among the pots and pans on his shelves. Even a keen and strong intellect might be expected to rust in so unfavorable a situation." *

Bishop Burnet says that these men were mean and despicable in all respects: the worst preachers he ever heard; ignorant to a reproach, and many of them openly vicious; that they were a disgrace to their order, and to the sacred functions, and were, indeed, the dregs and refuse of the northern parts. The few who were

* Macaulay's England, vol. i., pp. 327—329.

above contempt or scandal were men of such violent tempers that they were as much hated as the others were despised.

Those who desire to peruse the reasons for the nonconformity of these two thousand will find them amply detailed in Calamy's Abridgment of Baxter (c. x.). The objections were mainly specific; they seldom rose to the dignity of a fundamental truth. But the case was one which rendered a single objection, how small soever its weight, "though in the estimation of a hair," decisive. The assent and consent to all and everything is so narrow a sieve, that not the smallest gnat will pass it.* Yet the objections sometimes hovered on the edge of a great principle. "Many of them," says Calamy, "apprehended that the method of the national establishment broke in upon œconomical government. The master of a family is an emblem of a prince in the state. Some branches of his power and authority are evidently superior. The parental authority is the highest that nature gives. We may suppose it to reach a great way, when we consider that it is designed to supply the place of reason; whereas, in the exercise of a prince's authority, he is supposed to have subjects that use their reason; and must be dealt with accordingly. * * If neither prince nor bishop may choose for my children a tutor, a trade, a physician, or diet, or clothing, or impose husbands and wives without my consent, how should either of them come by a right to impose a minister upon them without my will and choice? Especially when his management of holy things is a matter of such vast importance, and wherein their salvation and my interest are so nearly concerned?"

The course taken by Baxter, relative to the Act of Uniformity, is an epitome of his whole character. Where it affected himself, and touched his own disinterested conscientiousness, he was ready to show himself the first sufferer; where the case of others could be met by palliatives, instead of decided and clear-headed courses,

* Yet the unworthy continuator of Mackintosh's History of England can see in this course, taken by the nonconformists, nothing but "frivolous objects" and "perfidious artifices!"

he was prone to recommend the former. But Baxter was a disciple of the schoolmen, and was so addicted to casuistical subtleties, that he might have attempted to solve the problem, "How many angels can stand on the point of a needle without jostling?" His heart, not his judgment, was the best director of his conduct. At this time he gave serious offence to some of his most attached hearers at Kidderminster, by advising them still to remain in the establishment, though they were altogether disgusted with its spirit, and were presided over by a man thoroughly incompetent for his task. When, at length, their unworthy clergyman was dead, many of his old parishioners thought that Baxter would now conform, in order to receive the next presentation. But they were in error; he was no self-pleaser.

The design of the king — if, indeed, so heartless a voluptuary could be said to have a design,— was evidently to eject the presbyterians, and to let in the catholics.* The former part of the scheme had been successful. Charles now endeavored to accomplish the latter; and he published, on the 26th of December following the Act of Uniformity, a declaration expressive of his purpose to grant some indulgence, — not excluding the papists, "many of whom," he said, "had deserved well of him." But here he met with an unexpected opposition. The parliament set themselves in array against such a dispensation of penal laws, on the sole authority of the crown; and the king, fearing for his next subsidy, was compelled to retreat. The sectarian party of the nonconformists had rejoiced in the prospect of the alleviation; but the presbyterians, firm to their principle of an ecclesiastical establishment, resolved rather to petition against their own toleration than to abandon their idol of uniformity. In this crisis, Philip Nye came to Bax-

* "I will not yield to any," said this perjured and despicable man, "no, not to the bishops themselves, in my zeal for the protestant religion, and my liking for the Act of Uniformity." Speech to parliament, Feb. 28, 1662.

With equal infamy, he declared, towards the close of his reign, in the course of a proclamation, that "he had always adhered to the true religion, established in these realms, against all temptations whatsoever."

ter to solicit his coöperation for greater liberty. Baxter, however, declined, and the nonconformist ministers in general followed his example. They preferred to be left to perish, rather than that the help given them should be the means of saving some papist from a similar predicament. It must, however, be remembered that, in thus acting, political causes had no small influence. The presbyterians suspected already the protestantism of the house of Stuart. They identified catholicism with despotism, and held the penal argument to be the most cogent, if not the most convincing. Much, therefore, of what followed must be regarded, so far as this party was concerned, in the light of a voluntary martyrdom.

The revived doctrine of church and state, having silenced the ministers, proceeded to attack the flocks.* Worshippers were laid under penalties so confused and ambiguous, that none could precisely determine the extent of his danger. The act of the 35 Elizabeth was put in force, requiring all persons to attend at church, under the severest penalties. Justices were empowered to dissolve all unlawful assemblies, and to take as many of the congregation into custody as they might deem proper. A jury was unnecessary. A single justice of the peace and the oath of an informer were sufficient. The work of persecution was taken up with great eagerness by those whose former sufferings had exasperated their tempers. But the better part of the episcopalians soon cooled. Dr. Laney, Bishop of Peterborough, "looked through his fingers," to use his own phrase, at the nonconformists in his neighborhood. Saunderson had a list of culprits marked out for prosecution; but, when he was dying, he ordered it to be burnt. Dr. Cosins, Bishop of Durham, though once bitter, became of a more pacific tone;

* "Before the Conventicle Act took place, the laity were courageous, and exhorted their ministers to preach till they went to prison; but when it came home to themselves, and they had been once in jail, they began to be more cautious, and consulted among themselves how to avoid the edge of the law in the best manner they could." Neal, vol. IV., chap. 7. So true is human nature to itself, in every age!

Gauden (author of Ikon Basilike), Wilkins, Reynolds, and some others, were never guilty of these outrages.

What, in the anguish of these trials, were the feelings of ministers and people, may be sufficiently learned from the following extracts. The first describes the sentiments of Oliver Heywood:— "I am so well satisfied in my refusing subscription and conformity to the terms enjoined by law for the exercise of my public ministry, that, notwithstanding all the taunts, rebukes and affronts, I have had from men; the weary travels for many thousand miles; the hazardous meetings, plunderings and imprisonments; the banishment from my own house, coming home with fear in the night, &c., — notwithstanding all this, I am so fully satisfied in my conscience that my nonconformity as a minister is the way of God, and I have so much peace in my spirit that what I do in the main is according to God's Word, that, if I knew of all these troubles beforehand, and were to begin again, I would persist in this course to my dying day, and, if God call me to it, would seal it with my blood."

Again. "Our adversaries envy us all our pains, and toils, and hazard, for our dear Lord and the good of sinners. They enjoy their rich livings, fair parsonages, and fruitful glebes; they step out of their houses into their churches, read their easy service, say their eloquent orations, eat the fat and drink the sweet; are companions with gentlemen and peers of the realm; have their thousands a-year; make laws for us; and yet think much at our having a poor livelihood, and a little honest work; weeping and wrestling with God and sinners to do good. They call us schismatics and seditious; they exasperate magistrates against us, punish, banish, and imprison us; confiscate our goods, excommunicate and censure us, and think and say we are not worthy to live; while we live peaceably, pray for them, and dare challenge them if ever they found fault in us, save in the matters of our God. O Lord, judge between them and us, and plead the cause of thy servants!"

"In consequence of the Conventicle Act," says Dr. Fawcett, in his life of Heywood, "the jails in the several counties were quickly filled with dissenting protestants. If the money was not immediately paid, there was a seizure of their effects. The goods and wares were taken out of the shops, and cattle were driven away, and sold for half their value. If the seizure did not answer the fine, the minister and people were hurried to prison, and put under close confinement for three or six months. Religious assemblies were frequently held at midnight, and in the most private places; and, notwithstanding all their caution, the poor people were frequently disturbed. Yet it is very remarkable that, under all their hardships, they never were known to make the least resistance, but went quietly along with the officers, when they could not fly from them."

The well-known Vavasor Powell gives, about the same period, a similar description of the measures taken in Wales:

"There have been very violent proceedings, especially in some counties, where some poor and peaceable people have been dragged out of their beds, and, without regard of sex or age, have been driven on their feet some twenty miles to prison, and forced, though in the heat of summer, till their feet were much blistered, and they ready to fall with faintness, to run by the troopers' horses, receiving many blows and beatings. Others, as if they had been brute beasts, were driven into pinfolds or pounds, where they were kept several hours, their persecutors, in the interim, drinking in an ale-house, and forcing the poor people to pay for it, though they were not suffered to taste; afterwards bringing them to the sea-side, and leaving them in the night in danger of being swallowed up by the sea, and blasphemously saying that a dog that was with them was the spirit that led them. Others were committed to prison at pleasure, and kept there many months; and yet their cattle and sheep, to the number of above six hundred, were taken from them and sold. Some were forced, when they were called to the quarter sessions, to walk in chains, which should not by law, upon any such grounds, be put upon them, unless they had attempted to make an escape, or break prison. Others, who were quietly met together, after their usual manner for many years, to worship God and edify one another, were cast into prison without any examination, showing cause, or commitment, that they could understand, contrary to the laws of this and other nations.

"Nay, such was the enmity of the seed of the serpent against the seed of the woman, that, though the king was pleased by his proclamation to grant Christian liberty for some time, yet upon the next Lord's day following after the receipt of the said proclamation, some of the officers of one corporation dragged and hailed some poor women, who were hearing the word of God, into an ale-house, and kept them there till after night, and until they made them pay for the ale which these disturbers did drink."

The following (somewhat miscellaneous) extracts from "the Records of a Church of Christ meeting in Broadmead, Bristol, 1640—1687," will amply describe the character of the times: "Upon the 26th day of September, 1664, Mr. Ewin and brother Simpson were released out of prison; which long and tedious imprisonment so decayed our pastor, and his straining his voice in prison to preach, which he would every Lord's day, that the people that gathered together under the prison walls might hear, he being about four pair of stairs high from them, that when he came out of prison, after the first sermon he preached abroad, he fainted away, and declined continually, (so) that it hastened his days." * *

"Thus we were hunted by the Nimrods; but the Lord hid us many Lord's days at brother Ellis', in Corn-street, that we had some peace, though the meeting was numerous; yet we were assaulted there many a time by men, but saved by God. One time, upon a week-day meeting, which was likewise there for a long time, a guard of musketeers was sent for to take us into custody; and then, being in the evening, we were conveyed into a cellar under ground, that went into Ballance (Baldwin) street, and so we escaped, and they (were) disappointed through the Lord." * *

"Another time, at brother Ellis' upon a Lord's day, the mayor and aldermen, with officers, beset the house, and at last broke open the back door, and so came in; but, in the mean time, our brother, having before contrived, by a great cupboard, to hide a garret door, he sent up most of the men out of the meeting into the said garret, and some were concealed. But the mayor and Sir John sent away thirty-one of the members and auditors to prison, to Bridewell, for a month, upon their first conviction."

Bristol witnessed at this time the conspiracy of an intolerant bishop, a drunken vintner, and an attorney, against the nonconformists. The bishop took his place daily on the justice-bench, and threatened the religious men of his town with all kinds of severity. To meet the storm, the various nonconforming churches, two baptist, the presbyterian, and the independent, combined into a kind of protective association:

"It pleased the Lord to suffer Hellier aforesaid" (the attorney), "the first day, as he began against us, to be caught in a snare. For when he came to Mr. Gifford's meeting, it happened, by providence disposed, that at that morning another brother, that did use to preach every other Lord's day there, namely, brother Harford, was then preaching when Hellier came in. But Hellier goes before the mayor, and swears that it was Andrew Gifford was preaching then, upon the 27th of September last. So there was a warrant, as well as for other ministers, so for Andrew Gifford. Which warrants being delivered to the chief constable of James' ward, who would not execute the warrants, but would make evasions; and some Lord's days would get out of town, when he might take up the ministers, who still kept their preaching; but we suffered the chief constable to take brother Andrew Gifford, because we knew him to be clear of that information. And he being brought before the mayor, Hellier had the confidence to swear, upon the holy record, that this was the man, swearing to his person, although it was another; and notwithstanding it was put to him several times to consider, lest he was mistaken, yet he swore positively that was the man. Thus Hellier took a false oath, and there were ten present that did witness the contrary, and four took their oaths it was another did then preach; so the magistrates said Hellier had sworn false. And so they troubled us for several months, but we kept our meetings, and our pastors preaching, still pleading our rights by law."

* * * * * *

"Now, three of our ministers being imprisoned, some of each congregation of the brethren met together to consult how to carry on our meetings, that we might keep to our duty, and edify one another now our pastors were gone. Some even were ready of thinking to give off, viz: of the presbyterians; that they could not carry it on, because of their principle, (which) was not to hear a man not bred up at the university, and not ordained. But the Lord appeared, and helped us to prevail with them to hold on and keep up their meetings. And for the first, and (for) some time. we concluded this: to come and assemble together, and for one to pray and read a chapter, and then sing a psalm, and after conclude with prayer; and so two brethren to carry on the meeting one day, and two another, for a while, to try what they would do with us. So we did, and ordered one of the doors of our meeting-place to be made fast, and all to come in at one, but open it when we go forth; and to appoint some youth or two of them, to be out at the door, every meeting, to watch when Hellier or other informers or officers were coming; and so to come in, one of them, and give us notice thereof. Also, some of the hearers, women and sisters, would sit and crowd in the stairs, when we did begin the meeting with any exercise, that so the informers might not too suddenly come in upon us; by reason of which they were prevented divers times." * * * "To prevent spies that might come into the room as hearers, and yet that no strangers or persons we knew not might not be hindered from coming into our meeting, whether good or bad, to hear the gospel, we contrived a curtain to be hung in the meeting-place; that did enclose as much room as above fifty might sit within it; and among those men, he that preached should stand; that so, if any informer was privately in the room as a hearer, he might hear him that spake, but could not see him, and thereby not know him. And there were brethren without the curtain, that would hinder any from going within the curtain, that they did not know to be friends; and let whoso would come into our meeting, to hear without the curtain. And when our company and time were come to begin the meeting, we drew the curtain, and filled up the stairs with women and maids that sat in it, that the informers could not quickly run up.

"And when we had notice that the informers or officers were coming, we caused the minister, or brother, that preached, to forbear and sit down. Then we drew back the curtain, laying the whole room open that they might see us all. And so all the people begin to sing a psalm that, at the beginning of the meeting, we did always name what psalm we would sing, if the informers, or the mayor or his officers, come in. Thus till when they came in we were singing, so that they could not find any one preaching, but all singing. And, at our meeting, we ordered it so that none read the psalm after the first line, but every one brought their Bibles, and so read for themselves; that they might not lay hold of any one for preaching, or as much as reading the psalm, and so to imprison any more for that, as they had our ministers. Which means the Lord blessed, that many times when the mayor came they were all singing, that he knew not who to take away more than another. And so when the mayor, Hellier, or the other informers, had taken our names, and done what they would, and carried away whom they pleased, and when they were gone down out of our rooms, then we ceased singing, and drew the curtain again, and the minister, or brother, would go on with the rest of his sermon, until they came again, which sometimes they would thrice in one meeting disturb us, — or until our time was expired. This was our constant manner during this persecution, in Olive's mayoralty, and we were by the Lord helped, that we were in a good measure edified, and our enemies often disappointed. *Laus Deo.*" *

As the public mind became aroused, the lay nonconformists looked with increasing disapprobation on the conduct of Baxter and others, who, instead of manfully protesting against the perse-

* Broadmead Records.

cuting system, conformed as far as was possible. None suspected Baxter's motives; but he was a paradox: a combatant for peace, and disputatious for charity.

The summer of 1665 was memorable for its close and oppressive heat. The connection between cometary influences and a sultry atmosphere has been often observed, and it was this year very remarkable. No less than three comets had appeared during twelve months, and astrologers derived from the phenomena appalling auguries, whilst even religious men looked on in fear and dismay. It added to Baxter's horror at the wickedness of the times, that such portents could be disregarded. The great plague of London followed. The metropolis singularly invited such a desolation. Its ill-built wooden houses, huddled promiscuously on each other, and forbidding, from the nature of their construction, the access of free air,—its imperfect sewerage, and the absence of all adequate sanitary laws,—had often before this period provoked this fatal epidemic; but it now burst forth with fury to which all previous experience offered no parallel. The crowded horrors of that period have been amply and graphically drawn by Defoe in his memorials of the plague year. During a single night ten thousand persons died. At the time of this infliction Baxter was a resident, with his new wife, in the house which had belonged to Hampden, now occupied by his son. But he did not behold the fearful desolation unmoved; and the British Museum still preserves a broad-sheet, entitled, "Short Instructions for the Sick, especially those who, by Contagion, or otherwise, are deprived of the presence of a Faithful Pastor. By Richard Baxter." When the sound in health fled from the pestilential city in crowds, and the parochial ministers deserted their posts through fear of contagion, a little respite was hoped for by the nonconformists, and many of them gladly availed themselves of the opportunity to prosecute, in the midst of disease and death, their heavenly calling. Yet the malice of Clarendon, and Sheldon, now Archbishop of Canterbury, was proof even against such a visitation; and they employed themselves in the interval in forging "the Five Mile

Act." This act set forth a certain oath, declaring the conviction of the person taking it that it is unlawful to take up arms against the sovereign, and promising not to attempt an alteration of the government either in church or state; and it provided that those who refused to take such an oath should not come within five miles of any corporate city, or within five miles of any town or place in which they had been heretofore settled, or in which they had preached, under enormous penalties. By this act the non-conformists were a second time driven from their homes.

In the following year another tremendous visitation occurred. "September 2, 1666, began," says Baxter, as quoted by Calamy, "that dreadful fire, whereby the best and one of the fairest cities in the world was turned into ashes and ruins in three days' space. The season had been exceeding dry before, and the wind in the east when the fire began. The people, having none to conduct them aright, could do nothing to resist it, but stood and saw their houses burnt without remedy, the engines being presently out of order and useless. The streets were crowded with people and carts, to carry away what goods they could get; and they that were most active and befriended got carts and saved much, while the rest lost almost all they had. The loss in houses and goods could scarce be valued. Among the rest, the loss of books was a very great detriment to the interest of piety and learning. * * To see the fields filled with heaps of goods, and sumptuous buildings, curious rooms, costly furniture, and household stuff, — yea, warehouses and furnished shops and libraries, &c., all on a flame, whilst none durst come near to receive anything; to see the king and nobles ride about the streets, beholding all these desolations, while none could afford the least relief; to see the air, as far as it could be beheld, so filled with smoke that the sun shined through it with a color like blood, &c. But the dolefullest sight of all was, afterwards, to see what a ruinous confused place the city was, by chimneys and steeples only standing in the midst of cellars and heaps of rubbish; so that it was hard to know where the streets

22*

had been, and dangerous of a long time to pass through the ruins, because of vaults and fires in them." *

True to their function, the nonconformist ministers availed themselves of the occasion to open houses for divine service, which were crowded with worshippers.

Some of these churches were built of boards, and were called *tabernacles*. Most of the leading dissenting churches of London originated about this period.

In the following year, Clarendon, then lord chancellor, was impeached and discarded. His retirement was the consequence of intrigues disgraceful to the court and revolting to the nation. The Duke of Buckingham, the most abandoned of debauchees, succeeded him in the favor of the monarch, and the nonconformists gained some respite by the change. The king, influenced by Buckingham, and intent on gaining a popish ascendency, endeavored to moderate the stringency of preceding enactments. But the parliament refused to be won. The attempt made about this time to effect another scheme of comprehension irritated Sheldon, who addressed a circular letter to the bishops, demanding from them an account of the nonconformist ministers in their several dioceses. Under this proceeding Baxter was seized and imprisoned. He demanded a writ of habeas corpus, which, because he was favored by the court, was granted. Many friends at this conjuncture offered to assist him with their purses, but he refused all aid except for his law and prison charges.

Baffled in his attempts to affect a compromise with the episcopalians, Baxter next endeavored to make one with the independents. A correspondence on the subject took place between him and Dr. Owen, but it reached no issue, partly from a want of agreement between the two correspondents regarding the power of the civil magistrate.

* Calamy's Baxter. Calamy had reason to be interested in this event. His grandfather, Mr. E. Calamy, who refused a bishopric under Charles II., was so affected by the sight of the ruins, that it brought on his death. He had been imprisoned for nonconformity.

In the year 1766 Baxter's friends built him a new meeting-house, in Oxenden-street. He had not preached more than once in this building when new persecutions awaited him. Baxter was surprised in his own house, and served with a warrant under the corporation act, and five more warrants claiming one hundred and ninety-five pounds for four sermons. His extreme illness rescued him from prison, but the warrant was executed upon his books and goods. Fearing new seizures, he was compelled to go into private lodgings. Again he tells us, "While I lay in pain and languishing, the justices of the session sent warrants to apprehend me, about a thousand more being in catalogue to be bound to their good behavior. I refused to open my chamber-door to them, their warrant not being to break it open; but they set six officers at my study door, who watched all night, and kept me from my bed and food; so that the next day I yielded to them, who carried me, scarce able to stand, to the sessions, and bound me in four hundred pounds."

Other parts of the reign of Charles II. are full of incidents illustrative of the principles set forth in this volume; but these must be briefly told. England became, under the pressure of the king's unprincipled necessities, a mere appanage of France. Charles endeavored to prepare the way for Roman Catholic ascendency. The parliament, jealous of his intentions, labored for the passing of penal enactments. Nonconformists, who would have rejoiced at even indulgence, hesitated to accept it when offered by the king "in virtue of his supreme power in matters ecclesiastical." The contest between the king and his parliament gave birth to the Test Act, which provided that all persons holding office, civil or military, should take the oath of supremacy, declare against transubstantiation, and receive the sacrament according to the forms of the Church of England. Then came the rumors of a popish plot, which all feared, some believed, but none understood. The nation was hastening to ruin. The exchequer was bankrupt. Public morality was destroyed. The court was dissolute to a degree which, in the present day, seems incredible. The church, deprived of its most faithful ministers, was left a prey to clergymen who, though not without bright exceptions, were mostly careless, whilst many were dissolute, and some abandoned. The nonconformists were indulged or persecuted, according to the policy or the humor of the moment. The metropolis was a scene of constant agitation. The office of jailer alone was profitable. The Roman Catholics were dispossessed of their seats in parliament. The Duke of York, avowing himself a Romanist, was excluded from the privy council. Rumors of plots possessed men's minds. Noblemen suffered death under the suspicion of indefinable treasons. Judges and juries were alike servile and venal. The monarchy was hastening to its extinction. At length, jaded, sated, disgraced, contemned, Charles II. died in the arms of his mistress, comforted in his last moments by the thought that he should reach "heaven's gates" by means of the rites of the Roman Catholic church, — leaving a name characterized by no good quality, but easy address and careless facility; a saunterer, a reveller, a lampooner, a liar, a profligate; reckless of the nation's honor, and indifferent to his own; a bad husband, an untrusted friend, a merciless judge, a despotic king; pilloried, till the latest day of England's history, as one by whom its liberties were betrayed, its honor humiliated, its greatness prostituted and destroyed. Such was the penalty paid by a nation for its undiscerning enthusiasm; by a religious party for its tenacity after uniformity, and its struggles for the covenant; by an establishment for "its most religious and gracious king."

CHAPTER VIII.

THE PRICE OF RELIGIOUS CONVICTIONS.

"If we come to prohibiting, there is nothing so likely to be prohibited as truth itself." — MILTON.

JOHN OF GAUNT'S GATEWAY, LANCASTER.

OF all the scenes which the sun shines upon in the north of England, there is surely none more lovely than that which encircles the famous castle of Lancaster. The Roman poet tells us that in his day it was not the good fortune of every one to go to Corinth. Neither is a visit to the lakes within the compass of every tourist. Should the reader lack the reality, he must be contented with the pictorial, which, however, we may assure him, is a very inferior affair. The name Lancashire" indicates its origin, — the Chester (or Castle) of the Lune, which river flashes its rapid waters in a full mountain-stream above the town, where it abates its haste, and flows on more gently till it yields to the tides of the ocean beneath its walls. The castle itself stands on a considerable eminence, not, like Windsor Castle, the highest point of the landscape, but reposing on an altitude surmounted by the greater eminences of an amphitheatre of hills. The present building is not the first strong-hold by which the town has been distinguished; it is the successor of one much older, but now entirely demolished, dating back from Saxon, if not from Roman, times. From the now existing castle, however, so placed as to give protection to the shipping of its day, and a fastness of considerable celebrity in ancient story, did the county of Lancashire derive its name.

I do not know how Lancaster may look at all seasons; but I know how it looked on nearly the first spring morning of the present year. I had been directed to the Scotforth road (the name is suggestive), as presenting one of the finest views of the town; and I was not disappointed. Lord Bacon, it is said, delighted to expose himself bareheaded to the rain, avowing that he loved the spirit of nature to come over him. Since the invention of umbrellas, his taste in that respect seems to have grown obsolete. Wishing for the same thing, one would seek it now in another form, and would court the subtle essence rather in sunshine than in shower; and it is the early warmth of the year that seems best to realize it. The reader shall suppose this early spring. The hedges in their vernal beauty; the rivulet stealing down the gentle eminence "by its own sweet will," glittering and babbling in playful activity as it goes; the furze, gaudy with its rich golden blossom, yet furnishing a welcome ornament when there is not another flower within view; — let these be the foreground of my picture. The mid-ground is the valley of the Lune, stretching itself out in wide and varied luxuriance, while houses, gardens, mills, churches, trees, bridges and ships, define its course, till it pours its waters into the Irish sea, which is from this spot distinctly visible. Behind this, again, is the usually placid and unrippled bay of Morecamb, famous for those treacherous sands which have deluded and destroyed many a traveller; and further in the distance still, the eye rests on the Westmoreland mountains:

> "Rocks, hills and crags, confusedly hurled,
> The fragments of an earlier world,"

looking as if some pre-Adamite giants had been at play; or, as if there had been a thought of erecting some Titanic temple, which never proceeded further than the first excavations.

In the midst of this wide-spread panorama stands, elevated on a considerable hill, a mass of building, in such a position as that it seems the picture to which the landscape itself is but the frame, — the Castle of Lancaster. Viewed from a distance, its aspect is extremely imposing. But a nearer view dispels much of the illusion, and presents an uncomfortable piece of modern restoration. The grave mingles with the gay. Gothic windows, brilliant with plate glass, force themselves on the eye in such situations as, in the original building, would have altogether destroyed its strength as a fortress. An old Roman tower, or that which is called such, has been cased over, to preserve it, upon no conceivable principle except that which dictated the conduct of the wife of the Vicar of Wakefield, when she gave a golden guinea to each of her daughters, with a strict charge that they were on no account to use it. The inhabitants of Lancaster have the satisfaction of knowing that the tower is there. The further advantage they derive from its possession is inconceivable. But, as we stand upon this Scotforth-road, these renovations are happily unseen, nor can we here perceive what "a thing of shreds and patches" the building has become. We gladly forget the mangled present, and throw ourselves on the past. Here, in the reign of Titus the Roman emperor, Julius Agricola formed a fortress, and sent hence the military stores requisite for the northern Roman stations. Here the Picts and Scots established themselves. Here Arthur, the king of the round table, conducted a successful siege against the Saxons, who, however, subsequently regained their fortress. The Danes afterwards invested the town, and committed great devastations on the surrounding country. Roger of Poitou, one of the retainers of the fierce "conqueror," built the keep, and at last rebelled against his liege lord. King John was himself, at one period, lord of Lancaster, and its next possessor became one of the barons who wrested Magna Charta from the unwilling sovereign. One of *his* successors joined the ranks of Simon de Montfort, and was deprived of his possessions by Henry III.; another headed the barons, who opposed Piers Gavestone and the Despensers. One of the Earls of Lancaster was foremost in the battle of Poictiers, and entertained John, King of France, when brought over to England a prisoner. By marriage with the daughter of this noble, created by Edward III. Duke of

LANCASTER CASTLE. — THE PRISON OF GEORGE FOX.

Lancaster, John of Gaunt became possessed of the castle and the title. He built the entrance towers, which rise up in such majestic grandeur before the eye. His son, Henry of Bolingbroke, was one of the most remarkable of England's constitutional kings. From that day Lancaster became an appanage of the crown. Edward IV. escaped hither from York. During the civil wars Lancaster was a strong refuge of the royalists. Cromwell, in person, besieged it. Bradshaw, at the time when he sat as judge upon Charles I., was sheriff of Lancashire. The pretender was proclaimed in the market-place of the town, when the Earl of Derwentwater headed his rebel army. Charles Edward passed hither on his way to England, and visited it again on his disastrous retreat. What spot has such an associated series of historical incidents? Familiar in its day with a state only second to that of royalty itself; mixed up with the successive crises of history, whether for evil or for good; the fortress of liberty, the home of chivalry, the highway of armies, the scene of the most gorgeous hospitalities, who could have augured that its destiny would end in being what it now is, — a debtor's prison?

Amidst the many purposes to which this fastness of "time-honored Lancaster" — if we may transfer the epithet from John of Gaunt to the place whence he derived his title — has been applied, during the vicissitudes of its singular history, none, at the present moment, interests us more than its having been the prison of some of the martyrs of religious liberty. The founder of the castle in its present form, John of Gaunt, has been already mentioned as a temporary patron of England's first reformer, though he obeyed in this connection the promptings of ambition, rather than those of conscience. Our present reference to Lancaster is associated with a later period.

Among the sects which sprang up in England during the time of the great civil wars, scarcely any was more frequently mentioned than that of the "quakers." The term was one of reproach, said to have been first given to the body by some of the independents; but it covered with its contemptuous designation many men of large hearts, earnest zeal, and unquestionable integrity. Our object, in these pages, is not to advocate any definite form of religious opinion, but to endeavor to do some justice to all; and none but a prejudiced observer, looking on the personal and social virtues which the system called "quakerism" carries in its train, can fail to distinguish many points worthy of an emphatic commendation.

He would be a bold man who should assert that, in the early days of their history, the leaders of that body now called quakers never overran the bounds of prudence, or even of constitutional liberty. That they were men of the deepest religious sincerity must be apparent to the most superficial observer. It is also most evident that many of the convictions they strongly entertained were forced upon them by the irreligion, inconsistency and heartless formalism, of their times. The early Friends were as magnanimous in avowing these convictions as they were earnest in adopting them. They were under the influence of an energy for truth so powerful as to out-run ordinary calculations. But, unless we were prepared to assert, not only that conscience is above all law, but that law has nothing to do with any form in which that conscience may assert itself, even when it interferes with the liberties of others, we must demur to some of their manifestations; nor, probably, will any modern follower of the tenets of the earlier Friends greatly differ from us in doing so. When, invading the quietude of churches, they debated before the assembled congregations the doctrines which the preacher had just delivered; or when they attacked, before his flock, the personal qualifications of their minister himself, they exceeded the bounds which the largest definition of religious liberty will allow. It was not, however, against such offences as these, considered in the light of misdemeanors, and justly noticeable as such, that the civil powers of that day exclusively or even mainly proceeded, but against the right they claimed to hold opinions not recognized by any existing system. Their refusal of oaths and tithes, their preaching in markets and other public places, their declining to take off their hats before magistrates, were their main offences, and for these they suffered severely. When they had increased so much as to hold assemblies of their own, — one of them being in a house known in after years by the name of the Bull and Mouth, Aldersgate-street, — they were often violently molested, under pretence of their being engaged in treasonable conspiracies, and an order against unlawful assemblies was especially directed against them. They justly accused the government of Cromwell of great inconsistency, in thus dealing with them, especially after his professions of liberty of conscience; and many were the appeals they addressed to him on the subject. There was justice in the complaint that, "although Archbishop Laud was beheaded, yet it could not be proved that the episcopalians had persecuted so severely as these pretended assertors of liberty of conscience had done, who, being got into possession of power, did oppress more than those they had driven out."* George Fox, especially, seems to have become acquainted with most of the prisons in the kingdom. The truth was, that, during Cromwell's protectorate, most of the inferior magistrates were continued in office; and Cromwell was fearful of offending the dominant religious sects, by preventing, as he ought to have done, the injurious proceedings of those who acted in his name. So dangerous is it to commit the maintenance of religion to those who have other interests to serve.

These proceedings constitute a blot upon the administration of the protectorate.† Many laws, and, among others, one for the suppression of vagrants, were put in force against them. Men and women were imprisoned merely because they were found on the road, some of them to visit their friends, or to transact their necessary business. Others were whipped and sent with a pass from tything to tything; one, a female, was stopped about ten miles from her home, and robbed of her horse, which was sold to pay the expenses of her incarceration. As this body held different views of the Sabbath from other Christians, they were often tormented under the pretext that they abused it; and when found travelling to their own houses of worship, were frequently punished by distresses, impoundings, fines, imprisonment, whippings and confinement in the stocks. Sometimes, when preaching, they were violently assaulted; sometimes wounded with stones and sharp instruments. The popular feeling against them was certainly extremely strong; but no decisive measures were adopted to reform it, or to check its excesses. Scarcely a quaker was known to escape the violence of this general persecution.

Severe as these sufferings were, they were greatly increased by the inhumanity of those who kept custody of these poor victims of an established religion. Three quakers, imprisoned in Norwich, were compelled to lie on the floor for eight weeks in a most severe

* Sewall's History of the Quakers, vol. I., p. 151.

† The case of John Lilburn must be regarded in a light rather political than religious.

winter. Others were kept among felons, and exposed to abuse from their fellow-prisoners, who said that "if such were killed there would be no hanging for it." Others were treated in prison in a manner not only injurious, but execrable; — we spare the reader the offensive details. Women were kept in the stocks in a way most indelicate and severe, and then turned abroad in the freezing night. James Parnel, a young man of tender constitution, but a powerful preacher and vigorous disputant, was imprisoned for several months, till he died under the severity of his treatment.

Besides this, great injuries were done by depredations committed on their property in the processes of distraint for tithes. In one case, where fifty-four pounds only were demanded, the sum actually seized was one hundred and thirty-eight pounds.

The patience of these sufferers was such as to cause wonder that it did not disarm their enemies. They conducted themselves under persecution with a meekness truly exemplary. When they lifted up their public testimony, they were not always sparing of severe denunciation. Indeed, this was sometimes carried not only to an injudicious, but even to an unwarrantable extent. But, when they suffered, there was usually a total absence of passion, or of revenge. Whitelock relates two anecdotes, which may be regarded as striking illustrations of this most Christian temper. When some of the body were assaulted and ill-treated by the populace, "the quakers fell on their knees, and prayed to God to forgive the people, as those who knew not what they did; and remonstrated with them, so as to convince them of the evil of their conduct, on which they ceased from their violence, and began to reproach each other with being the occasions of it; and beat one another more than they had before done the quakers."*

The spirit of intolerance which oppressed the quakers was stronger among the presbyterian party of that day than any other. The independents were by no means altogether free. But they

* Memorials, pp. 564, 599.

were not the distinguished persecutors. The protectorate parliament, dissolved in 1654, was extremely vehement against sectarian opinions. One of their resolutions was:

That the true reformed protestant Christian religion, as it is contained in the Holy Scriptures of the Old and New Testaments, and no other, shall be asserted and maintained as the public profession of these nations."*

In a subsequent parliament we meet the following resolutions:

"Ordered, that it be referred to the sub-committee to bring in the bill for supply of the defects in the act for the observation of the Lord's day, to peruse the several ordinances and acts for abolishing of the Book of Common-prayer, and to consider wherein those laws are defective, and to bring in a bill to supply the same; and further, to prevent the using of Common Prayer, and to provide against the using of other superstitious ceremonies and practices in divine worship.

"It was further ordered, that it be referred to another subcommittee to consider how to suppress the meetings of quakers, papists, anti-sabbatarians, anti-trinitarians, and of the setters up of Jewish worship; and two worthy members were desired to take care hereof, and to bring in one or more bills to remedy the same."†

To one case, among the rest, more than an ordinary notoriety is attached. It is that of James Naylor. This man, born near Wakefield, had been once a soldier under General Lambert, and had been held in considerable repute among the body of Friends. His popularity proved too much for his understanding; and when some of his followers addressed blasphemous expressions to him, he received them with a gratification extremely inconsistent with his religious professions. "He was already," says Sewall,‡ "too much transported, and grew still more exorbitant; for, * * riding into Bristol in the beginning of November, 1656, he was

* Burton's Diary, Introduction, p. 112.

† Mercurius Politicus. Quoted in Burton's Diary, vol. III., p. 403.

‡ Hist. Quakers, vol. I., pp. 236, *et seq.*

accompanied by several persons; and passing through the suburbs of Bristol, one Thomas Woodcock went bareheaded before him; one of the women led his horse; Dorcas, Martha and Hannah, spread their scarfs and handkerchiefs before him, and the company sung, 'Holy, holy, holy is the Lord God of Hosts,' &c. * * Thus these mad people sung, whilst they were walking through the mire and dirt, till they came to Bristol, where they were examined by the magistrates and committed to prison; and not long after he was carried to London, to be examined by the parliament."

The case was sufficiently lamentable and disgraceful, and his party believed him, not improbably, to be "clouded in his understanding," and hastened to avow, as they have ever since done, their entire repudiation of his extravagances. "His sorrowful fall," says their historian, "ought to stand as a warning, even to those that are endued with great gifts, that they do not presume to be exalted, lest they also fall; but endeavor to continue in true humility, in which alone a Christian can be kept safe."

Naylor's conduct came before parliament, Dec. 3, 1656. He was accused of having "assumed the gesture, words, names and attributes, of our Saviour Jesus Christ." The case excited a deep sensation in the house. "Naylor is, in fact," says Carlyle, "almost all that survives with one, from Burton, as the sum of what this parliament did." The first speaker, Major-general Skippon, said, breaking the silence which had followed the report, "I do not marvel at this silence. Every man is astonished to hear this report. I am glad it is come hither; I hope it will mind you to look about you now. It is now come to your doors, to know how you that bear witness of Christ do relish such things. God's displeasure will be upon you, if you do not lay out your special endeavors in the things of God; not to postpone them. You are cumbered about many things; but I may truly say this, *unum necessarium.*" "I am as tender as any man to lay impositions upon men's consciences, but in these horrid things. I have always been against laws for matters *ex post facto:* but in this I am free to look back, for it is a special emergency." There were not wanting those in the house who, though they abominated the blasphemy, desired fairness to be shown to the criminal. Captain Baynes said, "However others look upon Naylor, I look upon him as a man, an Englishman." Naylor was, at length, brought to the bar of the house. He was examined, and, being removed, the debate proceeded. Skippon pressed for punishment with extreme urgency: "These quakers, ranters, levellers, Socinians and all sorts, bolster themselves under thirty-seven and thirty-eight of government,* which, at one breath, repeals all the acts and ordinances against them. I heard the supreme magistrate say, 'It was never his intention to indulge such things.' Yet we see the issue of this liberty of conscience. It sits hard upon my conscience; and I choose rather to venture my discretion than betray conscience by my silence. If this be liberty, God deliver me from such liberty!" Some difficulties occurred respecting the propriety of the phrase, horrid blasphemy. The lord-president said that it was a matter very hard for a parliament to define, and that no definition of it could be given which would not include many others besides Naylor. What would become of the familists, what of Arians, what of Arminians? "By this rule," replied Skippon, "none shall meddle at all in matters of religion." Colonel Sydenham said, "If some of those parliaments were sitting in our places, I believe they would condemn most of us for heretics." In the end it was resolved, "that James Naylor is guilty of horrid blasphemy." Many were for condemning him to death; some,—amongst others Thurloe, the secretary of state,—for punishing him as a rogue. The debate grew excited. One said, "The quakers are not only numerous, but dangerous; and the sooner we shall put a stop, the more glory we shall do to God, and safety to this commonwealth."

* These parts of the "Instrument of government" provided "that such as profess faith in God by Jesus Christ (though differing in judgment from the doctrine, worship or discipline, publicly held forth), shall not be restrained from, but protected in, the profession of the faith and exercise of their religion," &c., "provided this liberty be not extended to popery nor prelacy."

Some contended that the law for punishing blasphemers was binding only on the Jewish nation. The nature of the punishment to be inflicted, death being set aside, was much discussed. The debate turned on the questions of slitting the tongue, or boring it; of cutting off his hair; of whipping; of sending him to Bristol, the Isle of Scilly, Jamaica, the Isle of Dogs, the Marshalsea. At length the prisoner was called up to receive his sentence. It was one of terrible severity:

"That James Naylor be set in the pillory, with his head in the pillory, in the New Palace, Westminster, during the space of two hours, on Thursday next; and be whipped by the hangman through the streets of Westminster to the Old Exchange, London; and there likewise to be set upon the pillory, with his head in the pillory, for the space of two hours, between the hours of eleven and one on Saturday next, in each of the said places, wearing a paper containing an inscription of his crimes; and that, at the Old Exchange, his tongue should be bored through with a hot iron, and that he be there also stigmatized in the forehead with the letter B; and that he afterwards be sent to Bristol, and conveyed into and through the said city, on a horse, bare-ridged, with his face back, and there also publicly whipped, the next market-day after he comes thither; and that from thence he be committed to prison in Bridewell, London, and there restrained from the society of all people, and kept to hard labor, till he be released by the parliament; and during that time be debarred of the use of pen, ink and paper, and have no relief but what he earns by his daily labor."

The sentence was executed accordingly. "The 18th of December, J. Naylor suffered part of it; and, after having stood two full hours with his head in the pillory, was stripped, and whipped at a cart's tail, from Palace-yard to the Old Exchange, and received three hundred and ten stripes; and the executioner would have given him one more (as he confessed to the sheriff), there being three hundred and eleven kennels; but his foot slipping, the stroke fell upon his own hand, which hurt him much.

All this Naylor bore with so much patience and quietness, that it astonished many of the beholders, though his body was in a most pitiful condition. He was also much hurt with horses treading on his feet, whereon the print of the nails was seen. Rebecca Travers, a grave person, who washed his wounds, in a certificate which was presented to the parliament, and afterwards printed, says, 'There was not the space of a man's nail free from stripes and blood, from his shoulders near to his waist; his right arm sorely striped, his hands much cut with cords, that they bled and were swelled; the blood and wounds of his back did very little appear at first sight, by reason of the abundance of dirt that covered them, till it was washed off.' "* When the time arrived for the second part of Naylor's punishment, he was in a state so exhausted that it was necessarily deferred; and a petition was presented to the protector in this interval, signed by many who were not quakers, for clemency to be showed to the sufferer, — "leaving him to the Lord, and to such gospel remedies as he hath sanctified." It was a general impression on many minds that Naylor had been rather guilty of inconsiderateness and folly, than actual guilt. But the interposition was in vain. The commons sent several ministers, among whom were Caryl, Manton, Nye and Reynolds, to speak with the prisoner; and they, according to Naylor's account, were unable to prove that he had been guilty of blasphemy at all, and after some rebuffs, left him as they came. The rest of Naylor's sentence was afterwards executed.† This

* "A merchant's wife told me there was no skin left between his shoulders and his hips." Col. Holland, in parliament, 1656.

† "This day B. and I went to see Naylor's tongue bored through, and him marked in the forehead. He put out his tongue very willingly (?), but shrinked a little when the iron came on his forehead. He was pale when he came out of the pillory, but high-colored after tongue-boring. He was bound with a cord by both arms to the pillory. Rich, the mad merchant, sat bare at Naylor's feet all the time. Sometimes he sang and cried, and stroked his hair and face, and kissed his hand, and stroke the fire out of his forehead. Naylor embraced his executioner, and behaved himself very handsomely and patiently." — *Burton's Diary*, vol. I., p. 226.

poor wretch, who was probably under the influence of a temporary insanity, made, subsequently, a public recantation of his errors. These proceedings seem not to have been very acceptable to Cromwell. Whilst they were yet pending, he sent a message to the House, desiring to know "the grounds and reasons how you proceeded therein without our consent." The interposition was useless; the parliament would have its way. Naylor, after some time, recovered his liberty, and spent the rest of his days blamelessly and usefully. He died in Huntingdonshire, in the year 1660.

The interviews which are related to have taken place between George Fox and Cromwell himself would lead us to the conclusion that he was favorable to the religious liberty which the quakers claimed. On one occasion, Oliver said, "Come again to my house! If thou and I were but an hour of the day together, we should be nearer one to the other. I wish no more harm to thee than I do to my own soul!"* On a second occasion, after some grave conversation, the protector said "to his wife and other company, that he had never parted so with the quakers before." On the third and last interview, he went to the protector at Hampton Court "to speak with him about the sufferings of his friends." He here met him riding into the park, and says that he felt "a waft of death going forth against him, and when he came near him he looked like a dead man." Oliver invited him to his house; but when he came, Oliver was already on his bed of death.

The reader by this time will have almost forgotten that he is yet standing within view of Lancaster Castle. In one of his peregrinations, in the year 1660, Fox had come to Swarthmore, near Lancaster, immediately after the restoration of Charles II. He was here apprehended at the house of a widow named Fell, and led away to Ulverston. Here he tells us he was kept a night at the house of the constable, with fifteen or sixteen men set to watch him, in some fear lest he might make his escape up the chimney.

* Fox's Journal, vol. I., p. 265.

Next morning he was carried to Lancaster, seated on a horse, behind the saddle, with nothing by which to support himself; whilst the attendants urged on the horse by sudden strokes, so that the animal kicked and galloped, and threw his rider. Here he was put in prison. In vain did he ask for a copy of the mittimus under the authority of which he was imprisoned. He learned, however, that his accusation was that he was suspected of being "a common disturber of the peace of the nation." The justice before whom he was brought, and who had granted the warrant against him, was named Porter; he had been heretofore a zealous defender of the cause of the parliament against the king.

The widow in whose house Fox had been apprehended, with another female friend, resolved to go to London personally, to petition the king in favor of the imprisoned man. Porter declared that he would go also, till he was reminded that the part he had taken in the recent civil war would be likely to gain him small favor at court. The women, therefore, went alone, and were received by Charles with the grace and courtesy which are not seldom associated with the absence of valuable principle. They asked the king to hear the cause himself. They were fed by promises, pending the slow execution of which Fox was kept in prison. At length the sheriff said he would release him, if he would enter into recognizances to pay the charges incurred by his incarceration and his removal to London. This, however, Fox refused to do. The authorities then considered how to convey him to town. At first, they proposed to send a few horsemen as guard over him. Fox told them that, if all were true which had been laid to his charge, a troop or two would not be more than was sufficient for his security. At length they determined that he should go up, guarded only by the jailer and some bailiffs. But even this they found would be an expensive proceeding; there were no railroads in those days. They asked Fox himself to give bail for his appearance in London, which he refused to do. In the end, they adopted a proceeding so extraordinary as to be, probably, without parallel in the whole annals of criminal jurisdiction.

They sent him to London, on his pledging his word that, "if God did permit," he should appear before the judges on a certain day. Fox gave the word, and honorably kept it. He appeared, and was told to come again on another day. At his second appearance, the indictment set forth that he and his friends were embroiling the nation in blood. Fox told them that he was the man against whom such a charge was laid, and related to them the circumstances under which he had come up to appear before them. Seeing his hat on his head, they asked him "why he stood before them with his head covered." He told them that he did not retain it out of any contempt to them. They commanded it to be removed; and, calling for the marshal of the King's Bench, they commanded him to secure Fox. The marshal declared that the house was quite full. Judge Foster then said, "Will you appear to-morrow about ten o'clock at the King's Bench bar, in Westminster Hall?" "Yes," said he, "if the Lord give me strength." Upon which the judge said to his co-assessor, "If he says yes, and promises it, ye may take his word."

On the next day, Fox appeared accordingly once more. The charge of bloody practices was repeated. "I am the man," said Fox, "against whom this charge is laid; but I am as innocent as a child concerning the charge, and have never learned any war postures. Do you think that, if I and my friends had been such men as this charge declares, I would have brought it up against myself, or that I should have been suffered to come up with only one or two of my friends with me?" The result was, that for this time the courageous martyr was set at liberty by royal warrant.

But this was not the only imprisonment undergone by Fox in Lancaster jail. In the year 1663 he was seized again, and in the same house as before. He was brought at this time before several justices, and underwent a long examination. "You deny God," said Middleton, one of the number, "and the church, and the faith." "Nay," replied George Fox, "I own God, and the true church, and the true faith; but," said he (having understood Middleton to be a papist), "what church dost thou own?" The other, instead of answering this question, said, "You are a rebel and a traitor." Fox asked him whom he spoke to, or whom he called rebel. The other, having been silent a while, said, at last, "I spoke to you." Fox, then striking his hand on the table, told him, "I have suffered more than twenty such as thou, or any that are here; for I have been cast into Derby dungeon for six months together, and have suffered much, because I would not take up arms against the king before Worcester fight; and I have been sent up prisoner out of my own country, by Colonel Hacker, to O. Cromwell, as a plotter to bring in King Charles. Ye talk of the king, a company of you; but where were ye in Oliver's days, and what did ye do then for the king? But I have more love to him, for his eternal good and welfare, than any of you have."

After some more debate of this kind, Middleton said, "Bring the book, and put the oath of allegiance and supremacy to him!" But Fox, knowing him to be a papist, asked him whether he, who was a swearer, had taken the oath of supremacy; for this oath, tending to reject the pope's power in England, was a kind of test to try people whether they were papists, or no. "But as for us," said Fox, "we cannot swear at all, because Christ and his apostles have forbidden it!"

"Now, some of those that sat there, seeing Middleton thus pinched, would not have had the oath put to G. Fox; but others would, because this was their last snare, and they had no other way to get him into prison. So they tendered Fox the oath, and he refusing to take it, they consulted together about sending him to jail; but all not agreeing, he was only engaged to appear at the sessions; and so for that time they dismissed him."*

Fox appeared at the Lancaster sessions, and was accused of being concerned in the popish plot. As, however, it was impossible to substantiate this charge, he was required to take the oaths; which, now as always, he refused to do. He was, therefore, committed to prison.

* Sewell's Hist. of Quakers, vol. II., pp. 63, 64.

The room in which Fox was incarcerated is still visible. He who penetrates within the enclosure of the castle will wonder at the kind of life which kings and princes must have led in the days of its erection. Here are the same rooms of John of Gaunt, visited sometimes by his father, Edward the Third, — small, stately, strong apartments, having few windows in the exterior, and those narrowed to the smallest possible dimensions, — well fitted to serve as the prisons they have since become. Fox's room was in the donjon, and the window of what was his residence during many long, dreary months, is conspicuous over the greater part of the ancient town. It was evidently at one period a room of considerable size, but in Fox's day it was old and ruinous. He could scarcely walk across his apartment, because of the dilapidated state of the floor. The smoke which came from the other prisons was so dense, that sometimes a burning candle was scarcely visible, and he was in imminent danger of being choked; and the turnkey was with difficulty persuaded to unlock one of the upper doors, in order to let out the smoke. In wet weather it rained upon his bed. The inconveniences of his imprisonment affected Fox to such a degree, during a cold and prolonged winter, that his body became swollen, and his limbs benumbed. When he was brought up at the March assizes, 1665, he was so weak that he could scarcely stand or move. Although, upon many occasions during this incarceration, Fox demonstrated the absurdity of the charge brought against him, and even showed that the indictment on which he was accused was bad, he was readily silenced and sent back to prison, on his refusal to take the oaths of allegiance and supremacy. At length, he was conveyed on horseback to York, and thence to Scarborough Castle, where he underwent even greater hardships.

In 1674 Fox was again in prison, under an accusation of *præmunire*, passed against him at Worcester sessions, and clandestinely recorded in his absence. Here he was seized with a violen- sickness, which endangered his life. His wife came from the north to attend on him. She afterwards visited London, and solicited from the king his discharge. Charles granted a pardon, which Fox, however, refused to accept, saying "he had rather lie in a prison all his days, than come out in any way dishonorable to the truth he made profession of." He demanded a fair trial upon *habeas corpus*, and succeeded in quashing the indictment. When, afterwards, an effort was made to induce Sir M. Hale to put the oaths to him, on the plea that he was a dangerous man to be at liberty, that upright judge refused, saying that he had, indeed, heard some unfavorable reports regarding him, but he had also heard more good reports respecting him. In the course of a subsequent trial of this martyr, respecting tithes levied on his and his wife's estate, a document was produced under his hand and seal, constituting an engagement that he would never touch his wife's property, — an instance of disinterestedness which excited the applause of the judges. The suit was, in great part, baffled.

Nor were Fox's friends in this neighborhood allowed to escape. Many of his followers, and amongst them Margaret Fell, at whose house he had been apprehended, were also confined in the castle, where an apartment exists still called the quakers' room, because it was the scene of the sufferings of many of these oppressed and unresisting Christians. It is not possible for us to give in this chapter a comprehensive view of the various trials and inflictions undergone by this persecuted body. It may be sufficient to remark, that Carlisle Castle, as well as Lancaster Castle, was a celebrated scene of quaker imprisonments.

CARLISLE CASTLE.

Here, where the guilty and unfortunate Mary Queen of Scots was confined, and where, at a subsequent period, the heads and disfigured limbs of those who had espoused the cause of the young pretender were set up in ghastly array, — within the walls, which still bear the rude sculptures made by the hands of prisoners during the wars of the Roses, — multitudes of the early quakers were confined.

Their patience, magnanimity, and quiet endurance of untold hardships, remain as lessons of Christian principles; whilst the history of their hardships, and the survival of their tenets among a body preëminently devoted to the cause of benevolence and the quiet assertion of religious liberty, demonstrates how ineffective is the civil arm before the might of religious earnestness.

No proceedings at this period excited greater attention, or led to more important consequences, than the trial of William Penn and William Mead, at the Old Bailey, in the month of September, 1670. The charge against them was, "that William Penn and William Mead, with divers other persons to the number of three hundred, at Grace-church-street in London, on the 15th August, with force and arms had tumultuously assembled together; and that William Penn, by agreement between him and William Mead, had preached in the public street, whereby was caused a great concourse and tumult of the people," &c. The facts of the case were these: A guard had been placed to hinder the Friends from approaching their meeting-house, whereby a concourse was occasioned in the street; but no arms were employed, as it was contrary to the principles of the quakers that they should be. Before the commencement of the trial, the prisoners were kept five hours waiting whilst other criminal cases were disposed of. When the indictment against Penn and Mead was read, the attendants of the court removed the prisoners' hats. The lord mayor ordered them to be replaced; and when this was done, the recorder, Sir John Howel, complained that they had not showed due respect to the court by removing their hats, and fined them in a sum of forty marks each for the neglect. As the trial proceeded, Penn declared that he held it to be an indispensable duty to meet for purposes of public worship, and desired to know upon what law he was prosecuted. The recorder replied, "Upon the common law." Penn demanded to be shown the law, and refused to plead to an indictment that had no legal foundation.

Recorder. You are an impertinent fellow. Will you teach the court what law is? It's *lex non scripta*, that which many have studied thirty or forty years to know; and would you have me to tell you in a moment?

Penn. Certainly, if the common law be so hard to be understood, it's far from being very common; but if the Lord Coke in his Institutes be of any consideration, he tells us that common law is common right, and that common right is the great charter privileges confirmed by 9 Hen. III.; 25 Edw. I.; 2 Edw. III.; Coke's Institutes 2.

Rec. Sir, you are a troublesome fellow, and it is not for the honor of the court to suffer you to go on.

Penn. I have asked but one question, and you have not answered me, though the rights and privileges of every Englishman be concerned in it.

Rec. If I should suffer you to ask questions till to-morrow morning, you will never be the wiser.

Penn. That is according as the answers are!

Rec. Sir, we must not stand to hear you talk all night.

Penn. I desire no affront to the court, but to be heard in my just plea; and I must plainly tell you, that if you will deny me *oyer* of that law which you suggest I have broken, you do at once deny me an acknowledged right, and evidence to the whole world your resolution to sacrifice the privileges of Englishmen to your sinister and arbitrary designs.

Rec. Take him away! My lord, if you take not some course with this pestilent fellow, to stop his mouth, we shall not be able to do anything to-night.

Mayor. Take him away, — take him away, — turn him into the bail dock!

Penn. These are but so many vain exclamations. Is this justice or true judgment? Must I, therefore, be taken away, because I plead for the fundamental laws of England? However, this I leave on your consciences who are of the jury, — and my sole judges, — that if those ancient fundamental laws which relate to liberty and property, — and are not limited to particular persuasions in matters of religion, — must not be indispensably maintained and observed, who can say he hath right to the coat on his back? Certainly, our liberties are openly to be invaded, our wives to be ravished, our children slaved, our families ruined, and our estates led away in triumph by every sturdy beggar and malicious informer, as their trophies, but our pretended forfeits for conscience' sake; the Lord of heaven and earth will be judge between us in this matter!

Rec. Be silent, there!

Penn. I am not to be silent in a cause wherein I am so much concerned; and not only myself, but many ten thousand families besides.

It was now Mead's turn, who defended himself no less manfully. He defined a riot, and showed that his conduct had borne no relation to that offence. He was interrupted by the recorder, who, contemptuously pulling off his hat, said, "I thank you, sir, that you will tell me what the law is. You deserve to have your tongue cut out." He, too, was ordered to the bail dock.

The judge then proceeded to charge the jury. As Penn, however, was not out of hearing, he protested, with raised voice, against so illegal an act as that of charging the jury in the absence of the prisoner. The recorder, in a state of violent excitement, cried out, "Take him away into the hole! To hear them talk thus does not become the honor of the court."

After an hour and a half, eight of the jury came down, — the court sent an officer for the other four. After much menacing language, they were sent back to agree upon a verdict. At length they returned.

Clerk. Look upon the prisoners at the bar. How say you?

Is William Penn guilty of the matter whereof he stands indicted, in matter and form, or not guilty?

Foreman. Guilty of speaking in Gracious-street.

Court. Is that all?

Foreman. That is all I have in commission.

Rec. You had as good say nothing.

Mayor. Was it not an unlawful assembly? You mean he was speaking to a tumult of people there?

Foreman. My lord, this was all I had in commission.

After much scurrilous browbeating, the jury requested to give in their verdict in writing, which they did, finding still Penn guilty of speaking, and acquitting Mead. Still the court threatened and reviled. But Penn boldly required the clerk to record it, and turning to the jury said, "You are Englishmen; mind your privilege; give not away your right."

Several persons were sworn to keep the jury all night in seclusion, without meat, drink, fire, or any ordinary conveniences. But again they repeated their verdict. "I knew," said one on the bench, "that Mr. Bushell would not yield."

Bush. I have done according to my conscience.

Mayor. That conscience of yours would cut my throat.

Bush. No, my lord; it never shall.

Mayor. But I will cut yours so soon as I can.

After more threatening and bullying, silence was proclaimed, and the question deliberately put to the jury once more.

Clerk. What say you? Is William Penn guilty of the matter whereof he stands indicted, in matter and form aforesaid, or not guilty?

Foreman. Guilty of speaking in Grace-church-street.

Once more the court bullied; once more Penn remonstrated, on behalf of his jury.

Rec. My lord, you must take a course with that same fellow.

Mayor. Stop his mouth! Jailer, bring fetters, and stake him to the ground.

Penn. Do your pleasure. I matter not your fetters.

Rec. Till now I never understood the policy and prudence of the Spaniards in suffering the inquisition among them; and certainly it never will be well with us till something like unto the Spanish inquisition be in England. After more objurgation, the recorder said, "Draw up another verdict, that they may bring it in special." The clerk said that he knew not how to do it. The recorder declared he would have another verdict, or that they should starve. The jury was remanded once more, till seven o'clock the next morning. Then the question was again put: "Is William Penn guilty or not guilty?"

Foreman. Not guilty.

Clerk. Is William Mead guilty or not guilty?

Foreman. Not guilty.

The assembly showed their satisfaction, but the recorder demanded that each separate juror should declare for himself the verdict. It was done. Penn then demanded his liberty, but it was denied him, because his fines were not paid. In the issue, Penn, Mead and the jury, were consigned to Newgate. How they recovered their liberty is unknown.*

The trials undergone by the quakers under the six oppressive acts of Charles II. were very severe. On the accession of the king they had enjoyed a momentary respite, and had been delivered from the confinement in which they were held. Their bold and unflinching testimony had been, however, of the greatest service in advancing the recognition of the principles of religious liberty, and none more warmly recognized their services than the baptists, themselves very prominent sufferers in the sacred cause. The interval was a brief one. Like other dissenters, they became, after the restoration, the prey of unprincipled informers, and were harassed by all the variety of penal enactments, by fines, distraints, imprisonment. In 1683 there were, it was computed, seven hundred members of their society in the different prisons of England.

* This whole trial may be found in "Phœnix; or, a Revival of Scarce and Valuable Pieces. London, 1707." Its effect on the cause of liberty was prodigious.

CHAPTER IX.

"CHRIST'S CROWN AND COVENANT."

"Tyrants! could not misfortune teach
That man has rights beyond your reach?
Thought ye the torture and the stake
Could that intrepid spirit break,
Which even in woman's breast withstood
The terrors of the fire and blood?" — SCOTT.

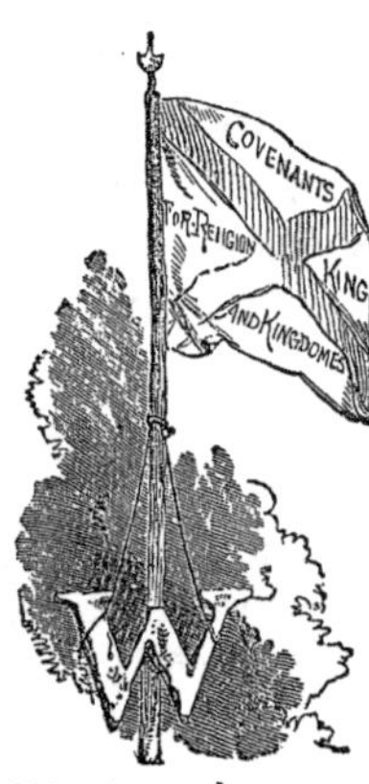

COVENANTERS' BANNER.

WHICH is the way to Bothwell-bridge?" was my question, as, alighting from one of the Glasgow railroads near the village of Uddingstone, I sought my course onwards. "There is a regular road to it, sir; turn to your left, and you 'll be there." No course could be more agreeable than that to which my informant just pointed. It was what it became a road to be which passed through the estates of the Douglases and Hamiltons, broad, trim, well-sheltered by trees, and affording plentiful accommodation for the foot-passenger. The country around was bold and charming; smiling, luxuriant, open scenery, never rugged and precipitous, made up of recurrent "lines of beauty." I know of no sensations more agreeable than those which attend a fine day in a rich country; especially if, with an unexhausted body, one treads over ground which has been the seat of ancient story, expecting, at each turn or ascent, some characteristic view, or some object of historical interest. It was in this mood that, under the shadow of the park-wall of Lord Douglas, I drew near to the pleasant but very modern village of Bothwell, or Both'll as it is called by the natives, encountering in my way, however, very little of that which I sought, though the graceful Free Church, and the imposing tower of the Established one, might have claimed, at another time, some passing admiration. But I knew that I was within reach of scenes which, slowly as they might develop themselves, are attractive to the tourist, and full of interest to the eager antiquary. Somewhere to my right, though I could not yet see it, was the ruin of the ancient castle of Bothwell, associated with the memories of Wallace, Edward I., Bruce, and the dark and desperate husband of Mary Queen of Scots. I knew that I was not far distant from the ruins of Blantyre Priory, founded by Alexander II., and from "Bothwell banks, that bloom so fair," situated upon its opposite side. Each eminence I climbed might, for aught I knew, bring into view the palace and park of the Duke of Hamilton; might open a prospect which would comprehend the estate whence the injured and revengeful assassin of the Regent Murray derived his title; or introduce me to the remnants of the ancient Caledonian forest, once famous for its breed of wild cattle, now almost extinct; or to the ruins of the fortress of Craignethan, better known under the name of Tillietudlem. Such, at least, are the localities which solicit, in this neighborhood, the regards of the passing traveller. I was not far, moreover, from the historical town of Hamilton, which I afterwards visited, and found to resemble, in its better parts, a slip-shod damsel caught in her slovenliest *déshabille* upon a washing-day; and in its worst, nothing to which an Englishman's notion of a country town could, for filth and wretchedness, furnish a comparison; and this, too, though lying in the immediate adjacency of the duke's "peelace" itself. Some one has said that, were he a monarch, the first thing he would do would be to run away with his crown. Methinks, were I the Duke of Hamilton, my first measure would be to annihilate, if I could not reform, the town which gave me my title. But this is an anticipation.

Passing through the village of Bothwell, one descends, by a gentle slope, to the banks of the Clyde. But it is not till you have just reached the spot, that you obtain a sight of the transfluvial erection which bears the name of Bothwell-bridge. It is well to cavil at antiquarian tastes, and to complain that they would willingly reduce the world to a heap of ruins; but it is impossible to repress a feeling of disappointment, when modern improvement has erased so many vestiges of ancient association. The history

BOTHWELL-BRIDGE.

of the covenanters represents this celebrated bridge as about twelve feet in breadth; it is now thirty-two. A main feature of the romantic story is connected with an embattled gateway, which stood on its south-east end; it has been long entirely removed. Instead of the sharp acclivity which rose up to a point from each side of the river, the road over the Clyde is now as level as that of Waterloo-bridge in London. On the further side, too, where the body of the insurgents were once mustered, "grove" now "nods on grove," round the beautiful entrance to Hamilton-park, in all the plentifulness of ornamental plantations. But I checked myself by remembering the Frenchman's definition of a tory, that he was one who, if he had been living at the creation, would have said, "Let chaos be," and I endeavored to discover what might render these egregious improvements less distressing. When I expressed my disappointment to the toll-keeper, he forthwith took me to a point whence I perceived that, though on one side the bridge was much changed, the other side was yet unaltered. One looks with deep interest on those buttresses, now gray with age, and partially overgrown with grass and low shrubs, as one thinks that they were the very objects on which the eyes of the covenanters and their persecutors had alike rested; that Hamilton, Burley and Hackstone, on the one side, and Monmouth, Dalzell and Claverhouse, on the other, had manœuvred in view of them; that here the deadly battle had raged; and that the river which flowed beneath that bridge in 1679 poured its tide along as deep and rapid as it does to-day, though then it bore with it gallant bodies, and ran red with the blood of the slain.

It was the distinguishing characteristic of all the Stuarts, that, ignorant alike of true liberty and spiritual religion, they had no other notions of the right and the true than those which were forced upon them by the groans and rebellion of their outraged subjects. The example of Mary Queen of Scots might have taught a son ordinarily constituted some lessons on the evil of misrule; it left James I. not a whit the wiser. Instead of deriving benefit from the experience of his father, Charles I. surpassed him in miscalculation. The son of that monarch who had lost his head on a scaffold for not respecting the people's rights was no sooner seated in power, than he trod the very path of his more determined father; transmitting to his brother James, and after him to his sister, Queen Anne, precisely the same predilections. In the case of Charles II. there were some events which rendered his conduct peculiarly inexcusable. He was not ignorant of what he might deem the bigoted peculiarities of the Scottish character; he had resided among the people; had himself signed, voluntarily or involuntarily, the Scottish covenant; had professed to mourn over the sins of his father; and, though he had protested that "presbyterianism was no religion for a gentleman,"* he had been indebted to that very system for his reïnstatement on a throne, forfeited by his ancestors for their fondness for tyranny, and their recklessness of all laws, divine and human. If conscience could not bind him, at least policy and interest might be expected to exert some sway. But Charles II. was not to be bound. A libertine, and reproved as such by some of the Scottish ministers in his earlier days; a hard-hearted, ungrateful man, as was proved by his conduct to his former friends; † a traitor to his promises, some of which had specially regarded the security of the Church of Scotland; a man to whose carelessness and cold-blooded apathy sorrow and suffering were indifferent; — such are the hands into which the constitution of church and state provides that spiritual matters may be thrown; and such was the man whom, though they did not take the pains they might have done to know him well, a large party in both Scotland and England reïnstated on the throne as their covenanted king. They had their reward.

The observations already submitted to the reader on the course of policy adopted by the presbyterians, relative to the questions of religious liberty, will sufficiently exempt us from the charge of vindicating their course. But, whatever the inconsistency of their system, Charles was deeply pledged to support it. A letter from him, addressed to the presbyterian body in Edinburgh, to be transmitted by them to the other presbyteries, contained the assurance,

* "An anecdote is told of Mr. Robert Blair's civility to Charles, who visited him at his own house. Mr. Blair was minister at St. Andrew's, and 'famous for his familiar way.' When the king came in he was sitting on a chair, being at the time under a bodily infirmity, which kept him from rising, and excused it. When Mrs. Blair ran to fetch a seat to his majesty, he said, 'My heart, do not trouble yourself; he is a young man, and may draw in one to himself.'" — *Memoirs of Blackader.*

† The Act of Oblivion and Indemnity was called, sarcastically, "an act of oblivion for his friends and of indemnity for his enemies."

"We also resolve to protect and preserve the government of the Church of Scotland, as it is settled by law, without violation." There were two men about the court of Charles whom the Church of Scotland regarded as hostages for the performance of these promises. They were both covenanted presbyterians; one of them had sat as a Scottish commissioner in the assembly of divines, the other was a minister of the kirk itself. These men were Lord Lauderdale and James Sharp; men at that time trusted, but whose names now "fester in the infamy of years."*

* The following is Bishop Burnet's description of Lauderdale: — "I knew him very particularly; he made a very ill appearance. He was very big, his hair red, hanging oddly about him. His tongue was too big for his mouth, which made him bedew all that he talked to; and his whole manner was rough and boisterous, and very unfit for a court. He was very learned, not only in Latin, in which he was a master, but in Greek and Hebrew. He had read a great deal of divinity, and almost all the historians, ancient and modern, so that he had great materials. He had with these an extraordinary memory, and a copious, but unpolished expression. He was a man, as the Duke of Buckingham said to me, of a blundering understanding. He was haughty beyond expression, — abject to those he saw he must stoop to, but imperious to others. He had a violence of passion that carried him often to fits like madness, in which he had no temper. If he took a thing wrong, it was a vain thing to study to convince him. That would rather provoke him to swear he would never be of another mind. He was to be let alone, and perhaps he would have forgot what he said, and come about of his own accord. He was the coldest friend and the violentest enemy I ever knew. I felt it too much not to know it. He at first seemed to despise wealth; but he delivered himself up, afterwards, to luxury and sensuality; and by that means he ran into a vast expense, and stuck at nothing that was necessary to support it. In his long imprisonments (for the cause of the king, to which he had apostatized), he had great impressions of religion on his mind; but he wore these out so entirely, that scarce any trace of them was left. His great experience in affairs, his ready compliance with everything that he thought would please the king, and his bold offering of the most desperate counsels, gained him such an interest in the king, that no attempt against him, nor complaint of him, could ever shake it, till a decay of strength and understanding forced him to let go his hold. He was, in his principles, much against popery and arbitrary government; and yet, by a fatal train of passions and interests, he made way for the former, and had almost established the latter. And whereas some, by a smooth deportment, made the first beginnings of tyranny less discernible and unac-

Under their deceitful auspices it was easy to persuade the presbyterians that the dispositions of the king were such as to render all treaties unnecessary. Monk had pledged himself "that the welfare of the church should be a great part of his care." On the 23d of October, 1660, Lauderdale, then secretary of state for Scotland, wrote as follows: "As to the concerns of our Mother Kirk, I can only promise my faithful endeavors in what may be for her good; and, indeed, it is no small comfort to me, in serving my master, to find that his majestie is so fixt in his resolution not to alter anything in the government of that church; of this you may be confident, though I dare not answer but some would be willing to have it otherwise. * * *I dare answer for the king*, having of late had full contentment in discoursing with his majestie on that subject." Whatever the views of Lauderdale, or the intention of Charles on his first accession, however, the flame soon burst out. In the act which asserted the king's power in matters of peace or war, all treaties with other nations, not made by royal authority, were pronounced treasonable. The "covenanted king," therefore, had, by this act, provided against the covenant which set him on his throne. In the same year, the first of his reign, Charles, forgetful of his father's experience, and of his own pledges, permitted episcopacy to be reëstablished in Scotland. This was done mainly by two acts: one, "the Act of Supremacy," which constituted the king supreme judge in matters ecclesiastical; whilst the other, "the Act Rescissory," cancelled all the acts and proceedings of preceding parliaments between the years 1640 and 1648. Lauderdale is not to be blamed for this act, of which he strongly disapproved, nor even Charles himself; it was passed without his knowledge. It was proposed, according to Burnet, half in jest, by Primrose, the *quasi* master of the rolls, and carried through by the Scottish ministry after a drunken freak. By the Scottish parliament, held in May, 1662, it was required that all appoint-

ceptable, he, by the fury of his behavior, heightened the severity of his ministry, which was liker the cruelty of an inquisition than the legality of justice." — *Hist. of His Own Time*, vol. I., p. 102.

ments to Scottish benefices, since 1649, should be confirmed by their respective patrons, and also by the bishop of the diocese. Four hundred ministers refused to comply with these terms, and were summarily ejected. Sharp was promoted to the archiepiscopal see of St. Andrew's. At the same time, Dr. Leighton, son to the persecuted puritan, who had never liked presbytery, but had consistently adhered to the king, was appointed Bishop of Dunblane, which he chose because the diocese was the smallest. His piety was most eminent; but if, as Burnet says, he disliked presbyterianism because of its fury against those who differed from it, his judgment was considerably inferior to his piety, when he joined the most cruelly persecuting establishment that ever existed. He afterwards desired to resign his bishopric. These symptoms of the designs of the court justified the utmost distrust on the part of the presbyterians; and, in a letter to Lord Lauderdale, in the beginning of 1661, Baillie speaks out in a very uncompromising style: "What needed you do that disservice to the king, which all of you cannot recompense, — to grieve the hearts of all your gracious friends in Scotland, to whom the king was, is, and will be, I hope, after God, most dear, — with pulling down all our laws at once which concerned our church since 1633? Was this good advice, or will this thrive? Is it wisdom to bring back upon us the Canterburyian times? The same designs, the same practices, will they not at last bring upon us the same horrible effects, whatever fools dream? * * My lord, ye are the noblemen of the world I esteem most, and love best. * * If you have gone with your heart to forsake your covenant, to countenance the introduction of bishops and books, and strengthening the king by your advice in these things, I think you a prime transgressor, and liable among the first to answer to God for that great sin, and opening a door, which in haste will not be closed, for persecution of a multitude of the best persons and most loyal subjects that are in all the three dominions."* In another letter to a friend, the same writer says,

* Baillie, April 18, 1661.

"What ye desire me to write to Lauderdaill, I have done it already, as my testament to him, fully and sharply enough. * * I think, verily, if that wicked change come, it will hasten me to my grave."* It did; the next year the good, but in many respects mistaken man, died.

The king on resuming his throne had declared, presbytery being then the order of the day, that it was his intention to uphold the Church of Scotland as by law established. The miserable shift now was, that as all the laws upholding presbyterianism had been rescinded by parliament, in supporting episcopacy against presbyterianism, he was but redeeming his pledge. The careful observer will not fail to mark in this a peculiar condition of a law-church — that the power which makes is equally competent to unmake. But the whole course of proceedings in England and Scotland was a series of occurrences impossible to be believed, had not the facts demonstrated them to be too true.

A fierce, exterminating war was now carried on against the presbyterians, by the very men they had most trusted. The royalists avenged themselves for their wrongs, real and supposed, by every kind of reprisal. The Marquess of Argyll was brought to the block in requital for the part he had taken against Charles I., and in the execution of Montrose.† The hand of Lauderdale was early turned against his former companions. Among these Johnston of Warriston deserves to be commemorated.

* Baillie, June 24, 1661.

† Argyll pleaded the Act of Oblivion as to these offences, which, by intervention of the king, was allowed; and when, moreover, charged with taking office under Cromwell, said, "What could he think of that matter, after so eminent a man as the king's advocate had done the same?" on which that legal functionary called him "an impudent villain." Argyll was at last condemned on the testimony of some letters which he, in the days of their friendship, had written to Monk, and which Monk now sent to Scotland. He was found guilty of treason, and beheaded by "the maiden." Some of the noblest blood in Scotland perished by this prototype of the guillotine, of the invention of which so singular a story exists. The Earl of Argyll, who was beheaded in 1685, for his part in the insurrection of the Duke of Monmouth, said it was "the sweetest maiden he had ever kissed."

This man, uncle of Bishop Burnet, had held several offices of trust under the Scottish church, and had been appointed, together with Lauderdale and others, commissioner from the General Assembly to the Assembly of Divines. He was a thorough presbyterian. When that assembly was divided, in 1650, upon the question whether malignants should be taken into places of power and trust, he had asserted the negative, and had written and spoken against taking office under Cromwell; but had been, at length, after much importunity, prevailed upon to become clerk register, equivalent to master of the rolls, under the protectorate On the restoration, he was ordered to be seized, and, contriving to escape, was declared fugitive, and forfeiture was pronounced against him. It is said that, whilst in Hamburg, poison was administered to him by Dr. Bates, one of King Charles' physicians, who, moreover, caused him to be bled to such an extent that he narrowly escaped death; and that, in consequence of this treatment, he "so far lost his memory that he could not remember what had been said or done a quarter of an hour before, and continued so till the day of his martyrdom." He was, however, at length apprehended at Rouen, whilst engaged in his private devotions, and committed to the Tower of London, whence he was sent down to be executed at Edinburgh. He was so miserable a wreck of his former self, that, says Burnet, "it was a reproach to any government to proceed against him." His want of memory rendered him a pitiable spectacle in the eyes of all men, excepting Sharp and the bishops, who laughed at his infirmities. When the question arose respecting his execution, many were inclined to delay it; but Lauderdale interposed, and delivered "a most dreadful speech for his present execution." He was, accordingly, sentenced to be hung at the cross of Edinburgh, and his head placed at the Nether Bow. At length, having spent the short time allotted to him in the most devout and edifying religious exercises, he was taken from prison to undergo his sentence. As he advanced to the scaffold, he called out to the people, "Your prayers! your prayers!" Arrived at the place of his death, he said, "I entreat you, quiet yourselves a little, till this dying man deliver his last speech among you," — requesting them to bear with him that he made use of notes to refresh his memory, so impaired by long sickness and the cruelty of his physicians. In this speech he confessed his sins, bewailed his having taken part with the usurper, and declared his " adherence to the covenanted work of the reformation," disavowing any part in the late king's death, committing his soul to God, and occupying himself in conclusion in fervent prayers, though denied the presence of any minister. He was aided up the ladder by some of his friends, and when he reached the summit, he exhorted Christians to be ready to suffer in the name of religion, as he was. The executioner desired his forgiveness; to which he replied, "The Lord forgive thee, poor man!" and gave him money. Then, ejaculating, " O pray, pray! praise, praise, praise!" he was turned off.* His head was exposed with that of James Guthrie, † accused of conspiracy against Charles I.

At this period the solemn league and covenant, late the pride and glory of the presbyterians, was burnt by the common hangman, and those ministers who had refused to submit to the conditions by which alone their benefices could be retained were replaced by others. These successors were men who had little sympathy with vital religion; they were, by their very position, parasites; and they were frequently ignorant, and often grossly immoral. Under such a ministry, the churches, which now echoed weakly to the notes of passive obedience and non-resistance, became almost deserted. At the same time, the civil offices were filled by libertines, or by avaricious men, who availed themselves of every advantage for their own aggrandizement. The general assembly

* Howie's Scots Worthies, pp. 228—237.

† This Guthrie had been minister at Stirling at the time of Charles' residence there, and had often preached at his majesty, in a manner which, Burnet says, was "indecent and intolerable." He was cited before the king to answer for his sermons. He refused, saying that the king and council were not authorities in matters of doctrine. This irritated the king excessively, and was never forgotten.

was dissolved; presbyteries were forbidden; field-preaching was prohibited, as an act of sedition and contempt of the royal authority, exposing the offender to death and confiscation of property; whilst absentees from their parish churches were liable to the severest penalties. The deprived ministers were banished to a distance of six miles from any city or cathedral church, and three from any borough. At this period, also, was established a high commission court, where, without "accusation, evidence or defence," fines and imprisonment were extensively inflicted. Gentlemen and ladies of rank attending field-preachings were proscribed, prohibited from conversing with their nearest friends, or from receiving the necessaries of life. These persecuting laws were put into execution in a manner which renders it difficult to determine whether ferocity or cupidity were the most conspicuous. When Lauderdale received fines for attending conventicles, he said, "Now, gentlemen, you know the price of a conventicle, and shame fall them that tires first." And when a soldier, pursuing his severe exactions, was asked by his victim why he was so treated, he replied, "Because ye have gear, and I maun ha' a share o 't." A deputation waited on Lauderdale, to petition for liberty. "This put," says Burnet, "Duke Lauderdale in such a frenzy, that at the council table he made bare his arms above his elbows, and swore by Jehovah that he would make them enter into these bonds."

The military apostle of this persecution was Sir J. Turner, who, savage by nature, and usually half-drunk, swept like a whirlwind over Nithsdale and Galloway, at the head of his "lambs" (as in bitter irony they were termed), dragging people to church, devouring the substance of families, binding prisoners with iron chains, applying thumbscrews and instruments of torture, and carrying ruin and desolation in his train. "Sabbath was the day on which these extravagances were very often committed. The soldiers sat drinking and revelling in the nearest alehouse until public

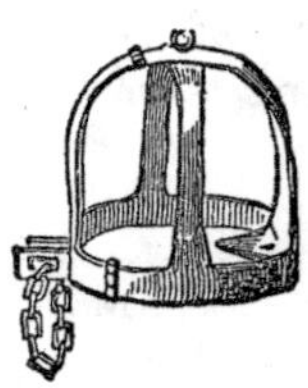

THE GAG.*

* An instrument of torture, extensively used at this period. It was employed in the burning of witches, to stifle their cries during execution.

worship drew to a close. The last psalm was the signal of attack; they sallied from their cups, surrounded the church-yard, and placed sentinels at the doors. The people were made to pass out one by one, and interrogated whether they belonged to that congregation. If they answered in the negative, they were fined upon the spot; generally, all the money they had was taken from them. Those who had none, or too little, were plundered of their coats, hoods, plaids and Bibles; and the soldiers, laden with their sacrilegious spoils, returned from the house of God as from the field of battle, or the pillage of a stormed city. In churches where a presbyterian officiated, they were not to be obstructed by doors or decency, but would rudely interrupt the divine service, entering in armed parties, wounding, and haling multitudes from devotion to imprisonment. After all this insolence and barbarity, to secure themselves from danger, they compelled the people to declare, by certificate, that they had been kindly dealt with, and bind themselves to make no complaints."* "They suffered extremities that tongue cannot describe, and which heart can scarcely conceive of, from the dismal circumstances of hunger, nakedness, and the severity of the climate; lying in damp caves, and in hollow clefts of the naked rocks, without shelter, covering, fire or food; none durst harbor, entertain, relieve, or speak to them, on pain of death. Many, for venturing to receive them, were forced to fly, and several put to death for no other offence; fathers were persecuted for supplying their children, and children for nourishing their parents; husbands for harboring their wives, and wives for cherishing their own husbands. The ties and obligations of the laws of nature were no defence, but it was made death to perform natural duties; and many suffered death for acts of piety and charity, in cases where human nature could not bear the thoughts of suffering it." "Such of them as escaped execution were transported, or rather sold as slaves, to people desolate and barbarous colonies; the price of a whig was fixed at five pounds, and sometimes they

* Memoirs of Blackader.

were given away in presents by their judges." * Many were "indicted, tried and executed, on the same day, and intercessions on their behalf met with the reply that 'they should have no time to prepare for heaven, for hell was too good for them.' Drums were ordered to be beat at the execution, to drown the dying words of the martyrs; and the least expression of sympathy in the crowd exposed the individual to be dragged to the scaffold."

A general convulsion followed. Maddened by the repetition of such outrages, many of the people rose against Turner, and over-estimating, as excited popular assemblies are apt to do, their real power, marched in a body to Edinburgh. They were met at the Pentland-hills by General Dalzell, and were routed in great confusion. But they were not yet subdued.

The ablest of hands has drawn the portrait — far too favorable — of one of the men most distinguished as a royalist in suppressing these insurrections, whose name first appears at the battle of the Pentland-hills — Graham of Claverhouse. Brave, imperious, unswerving, he was cruel, implacable, and fearfully revengeful. His commanding and handsome person might have been justly admired, had there not been a Medea-like ferocity discernible in that bold forehead, on those widely separated eyes, and on that curled lip, which he had in common with others of his class, — as, for instance, with the modern Murat. The most terrible superstitions attached themselves to his name. It was the age in which men believed much — often too much; and Claver'se, as he was called, was supposed to be closely in league with the author of all evil. There are some who still believe that, at the battle of Killiecrankie, in which he fell, fighting for the lost cause of James II., no bullet of lead would take effect on him, and that he was killed by a silver button, shot at him by his own servant.

Dalzell, associated with him in these cruel campaigns, was not less notorious. His portrait is characterized by a head of unusual size, which he had sworn never to shave after the death of Charles I. He had first learned war in Muscovy, where he was charged

* M'Crie's Vindication of Scottish Covenanters.

with roasting men alive. His cruelties were enormous. He struck one prisoner before the privy-council with the pommel of his sword "on the face, till the blood sprung." He imprisoned another poor victim, who suffered a man, pursued by his soldiers, to run through her house, in the thieves' hole at Kilmarnock, "among toads, and other venomous creatures," as the relator tells us, "where her shrieks were heard at a distance, but none durst help her." When one of his victims pleaded his age as a reason why he should not suffer banishment, he savagely told him that he was not too old to hang — "he would hang well enough." He was a ferocious ruffian, worse, in some respects, if that were possible, than Claverhouse himself.

But the man who was suspected of being the real instigator of these unmanly outrages was James Sharp. We have said that he received the archiepiscopal see of St. Andrew's as the price of his treachery. He was a fellow-student at St. Andrew's with Guthrie, of whom we have spoken, and who wrote upon him the following distich, which marks the early character of the man:

> "If thou, Sharp, die the common death of men,
> I'll burn my bill and throw away my pen."

He was charged, when young, with murdering his own infant, and burying its dead body beneath the hearth-stone. As, however, he avowed his repentance for the act, it did not prevent his becoming, afterwards, minister of Craill. He had been, on more than one occasion, chosen by the Assembly of the Church of Scotland as its confidential agent. But when the restoration took place, the part he took was characterized by the most treacherous duplicity. It was he who persuaded the presbyterians that there was no need to make terms with the king, and who asserted that the rumored intention of Charles to set up prelacy was "a malicious lie." It was, however, most probable that the restoration of prelacy took place at his suggestion. When he had received the archbishopric of St. Andrew's and the primacy of Scotland, he became an unrelenting persecutor of his former friends, continually stimulating the privy-council to fresh acts of severity, and even exceeding those remorseless inquisitors in his love of cruelty and thirst for blood. He encouraged the clergy to supply him with informations, and proceeded against the accused with the most incredible rigor. The consequences were such as might have been almost foreseen, in a day when religion often took a form of passionate enthusiasm, and loved to array itself in the habiliments of an ancient and semi-civilized antiquity. Stung to madness by the inquisitorial injuries inflicted by the archbishop, and justifying their savage proceedings by Jewish precedent, nine men conspired to waylay and murder the spy of Sharp — one Carmichael. Among these associates was Hackston of Rathillet, his brother-in-law, Burley of Kinlock, or Balfour, and Robert Hamilton. As they searched for the informer on Magus Moor, near St. Andrew's, they were informed of the vicinity of the archbishop himself. The primate was in his carriage, with his daughter by his side. Perceiving their approach, he urged his attendants to put the horses to their utmost speed. It was in vain. One of the pursuers, better mounted than the rest, cut the traces of the horses and wounded the postilion, and the whole party was soon upon the spot. Then Burley, exclaiming "Judas, be taken!" fired a pistol into the carriage, from so short distance as to set the archbishop's lawn sleeves on fire. He was then dragged out of his carriage, whilst the rest of the party fired their pistols at him in a volley. Imagining they had completed the dreadful deed, they were riding off, when one of them overheard the lady saying to the postilion that her father was not yet dead. On this, Burley returned, and kicking off the prelate's hat with his foot, cleft his skull with his sabre.

Far be it from us, whatever the provocation, to justify such a deed of cold-blooded assassination. It has been often exhibited in its terrors to the disadvantage of the religious men of that day, and by none more forcibly than by the late Sir Walter Scott. It was a deed which, under any circumstances of aggravation, Christianity scorns even to palliate. But, because Balfour and his party were bloody assassins, it does not follow that the Archbishop of St. Andrew's was a saint.*

Chambers, in his "Picture of Scotland," relates the following anecdote, which, he says, "we received from the grandson of the person who witnessed it:"

"Between ninety and a hundred years ago, an aged man, of a forlorn and wretched appearance, applied for lodging at a small public-house in the suburb of Edinbro', called Portsburgh. He seemed to have just terminated a long and painful journey, and, from his lodging at this part of the town, was supposed to be a west-country-man. During the night he alarmed and attracted the people of the house by sounds which betokened great bodily pain. A light being brought forward to his wretched pallet, he was found to be in the *deid thraws*, his body convulsed, his eye glazed, and teeth set. In a little time, collecting the remnants of his strength, he raised his right hand above his head, and exclaimed, in a voice that indicated extreme remorse, 'There's the hand that slaughtered Bishop Sharp; is there ony blude on 't, think ye?' Having uttered this, he expired. The body was buried among the strangers in the Greyfriars' church-yard."

This deed instigated the privy council to new acts of severity. The act was really that of a party only, but it was made the pretext for new harassments and persecutions. One of the first

* Every Christian man, well read in history, cannot fail to regard the influence of the Waverley Novels with the utmost jealousy. The author's love for history is that of an antiquarian, not that of a moralist. He is usually true to scenery, costume, and to the great incidents he professes to record. But, though it is sometimes difficult to lay one's finger on the precise passage one would dispute, the tendencies of the whole are, usually, where religion is concerned, most false. The worst evils of the anti-religious party are smoothed or totally suppressed; the severity and errors of the nonconformists tortured into the ridiculous, or exaggerated into the wildest enthusiasm. Much of this falsification is effected by the introduction of fictitious personages, placed in situations so ridiculous, or unfavorable, as to deprive the reader of all sympathy with their opinions. Party had something to do with this misrepresentation; a love of military glory still more; Jacobinical propensities even more yet; and, it is to be feared, a dislike of spiritual religion most of all.

questions hereafter put to the suspected was, whether they thought the death of the archbishop a justifiable act? It will be readily imagined that many, who would have revolted from that deed with horror and indignation, had its perpetration been proposed to themselves, would be slow, under the common persecution which involved them all, to sacrifice their criminal brethren. Fresh orders were given to proceed against all who were found attending field-meetings, as traitors; and as an act to this effect was the last to which Sharp had set his hand, the severe measure was entitled "the bishop's legacy."

Under the command of Robert Hamilton, brother to Sir W. Hamilton, of Preston, a Cameronian of the severest order, the persecuted presbyterians flew to arms. Marching in a body to Rutherglen, where illuminations were taking place in honor of the restoration, they extinguished the bonfires, burned at the market-cross copies of the several edicts by which they were oppressed, and retired, leaving behind them a statement of the causes which had led them to take up arms against the government.

Claverhouse now took the field, and having understood that an open-air meeting was to be held at Loudon Hill, about twelve miles from Hamilton, resolved to disperse it. But his forces, having been suddenly called into action, were weak, amounting only to about a hundred and fifty foot soldiers, besides a few horse, and neither well armed. He had full powers to kill all whom he found in a posture of rebellion. But the ground on which he found the covenanters encamped had been skilfully chosen, with a morass in their front. Claverhouse was routed for the only time during his life, and compelled to retreat on a horse that was frightfully mutilated. The general retired to Glasgow, whither he was pursued by the insurgents; though, when they ventured to attack that city, they were repulsed. Deeming his position, however, not a strong one, Claverhouse retreated from Glasgow to the main army at Sterling.

In the mean time, the covenanters took up a position near to Bothwell-bridge, where they were numerously joined by those who were terrified by the recent proclamations. The insurgent body now consisted of two parties: the Cameronians — so called from Richard Cameron, a bold protester against all compliances — and the Erastians — as they were scornfully termed by their brethren, who held the lawfulness of the interference of the civil magistrate in matters of religion. Hamilton was the leader of the former party; John Walsh, a presbyterian minister, of the other. Unhappily, the most serious differences prevailed between these factions; and, at a time when the utmost concentration of their forces was necessary, the insurgents spent their time in debate and discord amongst themselves.

This historical summary, necessary to put the reader in possession of the facts which give interest to the scene, ought to be in the mind of every tourist who visits "Bothwell-brigg."

The court of London had sent down the Duke of Monmouth, Charles' natural son, and one who, among the royalists of that day, had some touch of pity in his breast, to take command of the king's forces against the insurgents. This measure, extremely distasteful to the privy council of Scotland, may be regarded as an indication that the king was growing somewhat weary of the internecine strife, and was desirous of being, according to his own phrase, monarch of the whole nation, and not of a mere party. The Scottish ministers of state contrived, however, to get Dalzell appointed as the duke's lieutenant, that he might check the movements they could not openly oppose. On the 18th of June, 1679, Monmouth arrived at Edinburgh, whence he marched slowly towards Hamilton. His tardiness was occasioned by his desire to receive overtures of peace from the insurgents. Two days after he left Edinburgh, an order reached the duke to proceed instantly with all the extremities of war. On Sunday, the 22d, the opposing forces were almost within view of each other; the advanced guards of the duke being at Bothwell, and the insurgents on Hamilton Moor, with a detachment posted at Bothwell-bridge. The insurgents had resolved, after a stormy discussion, to send a statement of their grievances to Monmouth. But this resolution had not been arrived at without a strenuous opposition; and so violent had been the dispute, that Hamilton, their general, with several of his supporters, had altogether withdrawn themselves from the deliberations. The petition, begging for the free exercise of their religion, and for the speedy summoning of the General Assembly, was presented to the duke, who replied by requiring, as a preliminary condition, that they should lay down their arms, — on doing which, he promised that he would intercede with the king in their favor. Half an hour was allowed for the fulfilment of the condition. The messengers returned to the insurgents; but the only result was the renewal of the former altercations.

The river Clyde, at Bothwell, runs between considerably sloping banks, more steep on the side of the village of Bothwell than on the opposite side, on which the insurgent army was posted. The stream is here so deep and broad as to forbid the advance of troops in the teeth of an armed force, except by means of the bridge itself. The king's army posted themselves on the heights of Bothwell, and thus held a commanding position. They were, besides, greatly superior in the force of their artillery. They first made an attack on the bridge, which was at that time crowned by a gateway, barricaded by stones and timber, and vigorously defended by Hackstone of Rathillet. But the insurgents were deficient in ammunition, and the supply they had was soon exhausted. They sent to the main army a demand for more; but, instead of receiving a supply, were ordered by Hamilton to retire. This was wantonly sacrificing the only point at which a defence could be sustained. Before they yielded to this suicidal command, they swept their enemies from the bridge, as if to demonstrate that, had means and appliances been left to them, they would yet have maintained their post. But retirement became inevitable, and they were soon compelled to join the main body of the insurgent forces. This ended the defence; the royal troops, unresisted, slowly crossed the bridge, and defiled before their stupefied and now resistless victims. In a moment more, the rout was universal: Claverhouse and his soldiers attacked the insurgents like demons. Everywhere was disaster and dismay. The carnage was fearful. Four hundred men were killed, almost in cold blood. Twelve hundred were taken prisoners. These were disarmed and stripped, commanded to lie flat on the ground, and forbidden to change their posture. He who raised his head, even for an instant, was shot dead. A person named William Gordon, who was ignorant of the disasters of his party, while hastening to join them, was slain on the spot. Others, who had sought the camp in the hope of hearing a sermon, were killed. A man, because he was found reading the Bible, was cloven through the skull. The surviving prisoners were marched to Edinburgh, where they were imprisoned in the inner Greyfriars church-yard, lying at night on the ground, and standing during the day, for a period of five months. If, in the course of the night, a prisoner lifted his head, he was instantly fired upon. Provisions were obtained with extreme difficulty; and the women suffered all kinds of insult from the soldiers, by whom they were continually guarded. After they had thus occupied this church-yard for nearly five months, a few rough deal boards were erected for their accommodation, which was regarded as a special favor. Some of these prisoners were liberated, on a promise not to take arms without the king's leave. But two hundred and fifty, who refused to take the bond, were ordered to be transported to Barbadoes, and sold as slaves. The vessel was wrecked on the Orkney Islands, and most of them perished.*

The insurgents who escaped the furious onslaught of Claverhouse at Bothwell were immediately proclaimed rebels; and, though the Duke of Monmouth published a promise of amnesty to those tenants and sub-tenants who should lay down their arms by a prescribed day, few dared to trust themselves in the hands of the magistrates. Claverhouse now began a course of proscription and extermination. Marching into Galloway, he tracked all who had

* Memoirs of Rev. J. Blackader.

been, or might have been, at Bothwell-bridge, seizing their horses, plundering their persons, and committing himself, as well as tolerating in his soldiers, every kind of outrage and debauchery.

Even Claverhouse's mind, hardened as it was, was not unsusceptible of remorse. He confessed to some of his friends that the dying prayer of some of his victims often rose up before his thoughts; and this was, perhaps, the cause of his being more slow than usual in committing a similar murder about ten days after. "In one of his expeditions he seized Andrew Hislop, and carried him prisoner along with him to the house of Sir James Johnston of Wester-raw, without any design, as it would appear, to put him to death. As Hislop was taken on his lands, Wester-raw insisted on passing sentence of death on him. Claverhouse opposed this, and pressed a delay of the execution; but his host urging him, he yielded, saying, 'The blood of this poor man be on you, Wester-raw; I am free of it." A Highland gentleman, who was traversing the country, having come that way with a company of soldiers, Claverhouse meanly endeavored to make him the executioner of Wester-raw's sentence; but that gentleman, having more humanity and a higher sense of honor, drew off his men to some distance, and swore that he would fight Colonel Graham sooner than perform such an office. Upon this, Claverhouse ordered three of his own soldiers to do it. When they were ready to fire, they desired Hislop to draw his bonnet over his face; but he refused, telling them that he had done nothing of which he had reason to be ashamed, and could look them in the face without fear; — and, holding up his Bible in one of his hands, and reminding them of the account which they had to render, he received the contents of their muskets in his body." *

It is said that Claverhouse, in his expeditions up and down the country, subsequently to the battle of Bothwell-bridge, killed nearly a hundred persons in cold blood, amidst varied circumstances of licentiousness and atrocity. For such services he was

* M'Crie's Covenanters.

created Viscount Dundee, and made a privy-councillor. He was ardent in the cause of James II. till he met with his death at the battle of Killiecrankie. He fell with a violent imprecation on his lips.

Every tourist in Scotland is familiar with the wide estuary called the Frith of Froth, which constitutes the ocean highway to Edinburgh and the heart of Scotland. The most cursory view of the shores must have made him acquainted with a steep, abrupt mountain, which rises up at its entrance, like some huge natural pyramid, and which bears the name of Berwick-law, because offenders were anciently executed upon its summit. About three miles to the east stand the massive towers of the ancient castle of Tantallon, on the edge of a promontory inaccessible on the sea-side, and only united to the land by a narrow isthmus, once the seat of "the noble Lord of Douglas blood," but destroyed for its adherence to the royal cause in the days of Charles I. The poem "Marmion" contains its best description :

"I said Tantallon's dizzy steep
Hung o'er the margin of the deep,
And many a tower and rampart there
Repelled the insult of the air ;
Which, when the tempest vexed the sky,
Half breeze, half spray, came whistling by.
* * * *
Above the booming ocean leant
The far-projecting battlement ;
The billows burst in ceaseless flow
Deep on the precipice below ;
And steepy rock and frantic tide
Approach of human step defied."

But the object of my principal attention, when I last visited the spot, was neither Berwick-law nor Tantallon Castle. Some of those misadventures to which railway travellers are subject had caused me to leave my route, and to walk across from Linton to North Berwick. It was a very wet and altogether unpropitious morning; and, as is usual in such cases, it seemed as if the desired point would never be attained. At length, from the distance I had walked, I hoped I was nearing the end of my journey, when I happily met a passenger, — almost the only one whom, on that morning, it had been my good fortune to encounter. "How far is it to North Berwick?" "How far is it? I cannot justly tell ye, — ye 'll be near aboot half waa." The best consolation under the disappointment was, that the rain was now beginning to abate, and there was the hope that, by the time the rest of the journey was traversed, I might obtain a favorable view of that which I had travelled so far to see. So, in view of hard rocks, but with feet upon the softest roads conceivable, I trudged on over a country in the highest degree uninteresting, near to the sea; which was, however, from no point visible, though now and then a few sea-gulls saluted me with their unfamiliar screams. At length the sun caught the top of Berwick-law, and the scene began to brighten, especially when, soon after, I became aware of the vicinity of the object of which I was in search.

The ascent of the hill speedily rewarded my expectations. From its summit a lovely scene presented itself. On my right, constituting a huge foreground, was Berwick-law, a spot celebrated, in the annals of witchcraft, for the executions which took place upon it. On the left was the ancient and English-looking village of North Berwick, snugly shut in by cliffs and hills. Before me was a considerable expanse of cultivated land; and beyond, at some little distance out at sea, surrounded on all sides by the magnificent ocean, was the Bass rock, deriving its name probably from a bass or hassock, — what in Yorkshire would be termed a buffet, to which it bears considerable resemblance, — a huge mass rising suddenly from the waters, and thrown up evidently in one of nature's most heaving convulsions. This little but very remarkable natural phenomenon has a history; and it is one of unusual interest. During the wars between the Scots and Picts it was inhabited by one of the crowd of ancient saints, who was called St. Baldred. He is said to have been a successor of

St. Mungo, and was, perhaps, a Culdee presbyter, residing here for safety from persecution. It is even reported that he miraculously caused this remarkable rock to rise up from the waves. The tradition is, at least, as good as many others of a much later period, and quite as authentic as many of the tales told of the puritans about the time of which we are now writing. To the honor of this somewhat apocryphal saint a chapel was at a later period erected by Cardinal Beaton, which was occasionally used as a place of prayer till the Reformation. The rock afforded a temporary protection to Robert III., before his captivity by the English. Walter Stewart, son of the Duke of Albany, was imprisoned here. James VI. paid a visit to it in 1581, and the accounts of his treasurer include the following item: "To Alexander Young, his hienes servitour for his grace's extraordinar expenses in his jornay towardis the Bass, conforme to his hienes precept, as the samin with his acquittance producit upon compt proportis XL. li." (Forty pounds).* James even desired, it appears, to purchase it of its then possessor, — one of the Lauders, — offering him whatever he pleased to ask for it. Lauder replied, "Your majesty must e'en resign it to me, for I 'll have the auld crag back again." Charles I. claimed it, on what ground does not appear, nor does the claim seem to have been successful. When Cromwell invaded Scotland, in 1650, the public records of the Church of Scotland were consigned to this fastness, which, however, soon after fell into the hands of that victorious general, who conveyed them in casks to London. At the restoration, they were ordered to be returned. But Lauderdale, believing that the covenant and other papers signed by the king were among the documents, detained them till search should be made. Not being found, fifty hogsheads were charged with them, and they were sent back to Scotland. But so much time had been lost, that the season became stormy before they could be transported. The ship was cast away at Berwick, and the papers were most of them lost.† After a second removal,

* "The Bass Rock." Edinburgh, 1848.
† Burnet's Own Times, vol. I., p. 110.

the remnants were again brought to London, on the occasion of the recent disruption of the Scottish church; but only to be consumed by fire in the House of Commons, in 1834.

When, after the restoration, the jails of Scotland were crowded with the victims of the sanguinary persecutions which preceded and followed the battle of Bothwell-bridge, the Bass rock was purchased by Lord Lauderdale, on behalf of the government, at the price of four thousand pounds, as a state-prison; himself being appointed to the undying disgrace of governor of the Bass, with a salary of one hundred pounds per annum. It was now made a prison for presbyterian ministers, and underwent such changes as were necessary to fit it for its new destination.

It is a beautiful walk which leads along the shores of the Frith of Forth, from the town of North Berwick to that part of the coast which lies opposite to this singular rock. Were the charms of the scene better known to English tourists, it would certainly be more frequently visited. A wide expanse of sand, of the whitest and firmest kind, spotted here and there with beautiful limpet shells, constitutes a level esplanade, of about a mile in length, on the eastern side of the town; whilst within view are the broad waters of the Forth, bearing numerous vessels on their bosom; and, on the opposite side, the coasts of Fife, diminishing away in the distance as the estuary grows wider, till the observer scarcely knows whether his eye can discern the distant shore or not. Beyond this esplanade the rocks rise more precipitously, commanding a majestic view of the wide German ocean, heaving its faint blue tide, as if with the pulses which carry life and health through the terraqueous system. Then, after a short distance, the rocks subside again into a beautiful and quiet inlet, called Canty Bay, and immediately opposite stands the hoary rock itself, not near enough to the land to be discernible as to its minuter features, but leaving sufficiently evident to the eye the remnants of its ancient and time-worn structures. Strange is the appearance of this crimeless prison! The steep slope of its upper surface gives a sensation of the uncomfortable, as if it were impossible that a living being could find a secure footing upon so shelving a surface. Its distance from the shore renders escape almost hopeless. It is not possible to reach the spot in a storm. There is but one place of landing; and of any herbage, besides the grass which grows on its top, there is now no vestige remaining. Nowhere else can the spectator realize a more vivid conception of utter solitude!

BASS ROCK, FROM CANTY BAY.

A more miserable and forlorn prison-house than this of the Bass rock it is impossible to conceive. With no fresh water, — for the water to be found on the island was often corrupted, and the prisoners were obliged to mix it with oat-meal before it could be drunk, — washed at times by the spray from the boiling ocean below, and exposed to the damps which arose from the water drizzling down from the pent-house surface above; in narrow and inconvenient rooms, some of them lighted by slits far above their heads; liable, from the situation of the prisons, to have their movements watched, their sufferings insulted, and their conversation overheard; the rooms ordinarily so full of smoke as to compel them sometimes to put their head and shoulders out of the window, in order to draw fresh air; exposed to the fierceness of every wind that blew; often in want of provisions, which, in stormy weather, could not be landed; far from friends and home, — more than forty poor sufferers were incarcerated, some for a period of six years. Some miserable consolation might be derived from beholding — when they were permitted to behold it — the glorious scene of nature's loveliness which spread itself on every hand around them. The "highway of nations" around, or the bright heavens above, — the changes of atmosphere, the glorious sunrise or sunset, the darkening storm, — all would have their attractions in such a Patmos. They could look at Tantallon, but in the tales of its wild chivalry and fierce warfare there was little to touch their sympathies. Berwick-law rose up near them, but naked, stern and forbidding, presenting to them no idea of sympathetic life. The eye could wander on to the huge crags which marked the distant Arthur's Seat, perhaps to think that, within the privy-council chamber, at the base of those hills, some poor victim whom they knew was at that moment undergoing the torture so dreadfully familiar to themselves; the more smiling coast of Fife presented its singular and picturesque undulations to their view, but far, far away; many of them could look from that prison fastness upon the locality of their homes and their ministry, only to lament a denounced religion and an outraged covenant. What could comfort them? Nothing, but gospel truth and a good conscience.

> "He that hath light within his own pure breast
> Can sit i' the centre and enjoy bright day;
> But he who hides a dark breast and foul thoughts
> Benighted walks beneath the noon-day sun:
> Himself is his own dungeon." — MILTON, *Comus.*

The following is the testimony of one of the prisoners: — "Every day I read the Scriptures, exhorted and taught therefrom, and prayed with such of our society as our masters did permit to worship God together, and this two times a day. I studied Hebrew and Greek, and gained some knowledge in these oriental languages.

I likewise read some divinity, and wrote a treatise on faith, with other miscellanies, and wrote some letters to Christian friends and relations. Thus I spent my time, and not without some fruit." Another said, "I have the experience of that saying, '*Tanta est dulcedo celestis gaudii, ut si una guttula deflueret in infernum, totam amaritudinem inferni absorberet.*'" *

BASS ROCK, NEAR VIEW.

So long as time shall endure, the Bass rock will remain an imperishable monument to John Earl of Lauderdale.†

Here was imprisoned Robert Gillespie, who had opened a conventicle and preached without license and without lawful ordination. He was kept for a time totally secluded from all intercourse with his friends, though, latterly, the injunction was relaxed. Here, too, was found Alexander Peden, once minister of Glenluce, in Galloway, but prohibited by the Scottish act of parliament from exercising his ministerial functions. He joined the covenanters,

* Such is the sweetness of the joy of heaven, that if the least drop of it were to flow into hell, it would absorb all its bitterness.

† "Quod non imber edax, non aquilo impotens
Possit diruere, aut innumerabilis
Annorum series, et fuga temporum." — *Hor. Car.* l. iii.

and although he parted from them before they proceeded to the fight of the Pentland-hills, was yet proceeded against as if he had been actually present at that battle. He was probably confined in this prison during four years. A singular circumstance marked his history in this spot. One day, a soldier passing by him cried out, "The devil take him!" Peden, who spoke with authority, said, "Poor man! thou knowest not what thou art saying; but thou wilt repent that!" The soldier was terrified, and sent for Peden to pray with him. When next it was his turn to relieve guard, he said, "I will lift no arms against Jesus Christ's cause, nor persecute his people; I have done that too long." He was threatened with death; but he persisted in his refusal. The garrison were compelled to send him on shore. He afterwards became an exemplary Christian. Even this prison was no security against such influences. The history of Peden's future career was full of remarkable incidents, which we must not stay to relate. Within these walls was also found James Mitchell, who made an unsuccessful attempt upon the life of Archbishop Sharp, which he justified by passages of Old Testament history. He was apprehended by the brother of the primate. In order to extort a confession from him, Sharp swore "with uplifted hands, by the living God, that no harm should befall him if he made a full discovery." By authority of Lauderdale, also, his life was promised him on a similar condition. He confessed, and subscribed the confession, and was sentenced to have his right hand cut off. But, as he refused to repeat this acknowledgment before the court of justiciary, which was necessary to his punishment, the prosecutors pleaded that they were exempt from their promise. He was sentenced, therefore, to be examined by torture. The horrible instrument called the "boots" was brought forward. This consisted of several pieces of wood firmly fixed together, leaving an aperture for the reception of the leg of the accused. When it was thus fitted on, wedges were violently driven with a mallet between the boot and the leg, which, compressing the shin-bone, caused the most exquisite suffering. He was bound in an arm-chair, and asked which leg should be taken, The executioner was commanded to take either, and the left leg was inserted. But Mitchell lifted it out, and said, "Since the judges have not determined it, take the best of the two, for I freely bestow it in the cause," and he put in the other leg. As stroke after stroke descended, questions were put to the prisoner, and the answers written down. But nothing satisfactory was elicited. At last, the prisoner fainted, and was borne off. It was proposed to proceed with the other leg, but the intention was abandoned, through the fears of Sharp that he should have a shot from a steadier hand. At length, after much imprisonment, — partly on the Bass rock, — he was tried for the attempted assassination. The principal evidence was derived from his own confession, made four years previously. In vain did Mitchell plead the promise under which that confession had been made. It was solemnly denied, even by Lord Lauderdale and Sharp. When, on his trial, Mitchell's counsel asked for the production of the minutes which contained the promise under which the confession had been made, the request was denied, upon the plea, which Lauderdale was not ashamed to urge, that the books of the council were the king's secret! Mitchell was sentenced to be hanged at the Grass-market. When the court broke up, the lords of the privy-council referred to the records, and there found the promise made to Mitchell which they had just denied. For a moment Lauderdale wavered, and seemed inclined to grant a reprieve. But Sharp was resolute. "Then," said Lauderdale, "let Mitchell glorify God in the Grass-market!" Bishop Burnet gives the unexceptionable authority of Primrose, the clerk-register, for this statement. It was this conduct of Sharp which, probably, led to his death, two years after, as we have related. Mitchell was executed, and died with the heroism of a martyr. This attempted assassination exhibits the stern ferocity engendered by the Scottish covenant, and the inflexible firmness of some who were bound by its provisions. We honor conscience; but conscience and law are not identical. The men acted as they believed; but their belief was not founded upon what was written. Mitchell originally deserved to die; but no words can express the sentiments due to the treachery, barbarity and infamy, of those who condemned him.*

The close of Blackader's labors bore a singular relation to the scene of his imprisonment. Ten days before his apprehension he had preached on a hill opposite to the Bass rock, and had prayed with special energy for those who were imprisoned in that desolate fortress. Soon after he was seized in Edinburgh, and himself received a similar sentence. Here he died, aged seventy. His prison is still to be seen, and a tombstone in the church-yard of North Berwick marks the spot of his interment.†

The account given in this chapter of the martyrs of the covenant has been brief and imperfect. The reader may find the whole series of transactions in Burnet's History of his Own Time, the volume entitled "The Bass Rock," &c.

None can fail to regard the league and covenant with solemnity, when he recalls the events of its dismal history. But as a matter of legislation it was "a mockery, a delusion, and a snare." If it were lawful for presbyterians to sharpen swords against prelacy, it was by the same rule lawful for the adherents of prelacy to turn the sword so sharpened against those who had prepared it. The principle announced by Castalio, whom Calvin bitterly opposed, is clear and intelligible: — "Let us obey the righteous

* Yet on Sharp's monument is this inscription: — "Pietatis exemplum; pacis angelum; sapientiæ oraculum; gravitatis imaginem; boni et fidelis subditi, impietatis, perduellonis, et schismaticis hostem acerrimum," &c. It is well that marble cannot blush. The latter clause is all of the inscription which is true. When this monument was opened, a few years since, it was found empty. It is conjectured that it was opened in search of treasure.

† The Bass rock is now abandoned to Solan geese, which it harbors in great abundance, and to a few sheep, the flesh of which is in great request; some butchers have been known to boast of selling five times as much Bass wether mutton as the rock can by possibility sustain. Of the former, Defoe says, "Their laying but one egg, which sticks to the rock, and will not fall off unless pulled off by force, and then not to be stuck on again, though we thought them fictions, yet, being there at the season, we found true, as also their hatching upholding the egg fast by the foot." Whatever the means Defoe might have taken to verify the reports, they are only fictions.

Judge, and leave the tares till the harvest, lest, perchance (whilst we seek to be wiser than the Master), we root up the wheat. For neither is it yet the end of the world, nor are we angels to whom this office has been intrusted." * Good men as they were, Gillespie, Henderson, Baillie, and the numerous ministers of London, Lancashire and Chester, who swore by the directory, were scarcely angels; nor were they prone to think that name deserved by Cromwell, Milton, Goodwin, Owen, and the host of sectaries. And deeply did they feel, under the terrible retribution which followed, that Charles II., Monk, Sharp, Lauderdale, Middleton, were no angels!

* Bib. Sac., pp. xi., xii.

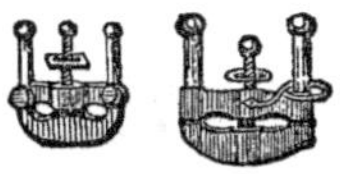

THUMBSCREWS.

CHAPTER X.

APPEARING IN TRUE COLORS.

"Were I now to preach before a great magistrate that had the power in his hands, I would say, My lord, you bear not the sword in vain. Let them be fined and imprisoned, — nay, hanged, my lord. Now, if my lord should say, Do you endeavor to refute and convince them of their errors by sound doctrine and good example of life; then would I say, No, my lord, they will never be convinced by us, for we have not wit or learning enough to do it, neither can we take so much pains. It is easier to talk an hour about state affairs than to preach convincing and sound doctrine. The fanatics, therefore, must be confuted by bolts and shackles; by fines and imprisonments; by excommunications and exterminations; and, therefore, my lord, let them be scourged out of the temple: let them be whipped out of the nation." — *Speculum Crape-gownorum*,* by D. DEFOE.

ELSTOW CHURCH.

HERE are few more interesting chapters in the miscellaneous volume of human life than those which describe the manner in which some men have "achieved greatness." The case of a single individual whom we desire to recall to the mind of the reader may stand as an illustration of some of these phenomena. Let us imagine, in a secluded village, in a flat midland county, a cottage — none of the best — built in the antique style of wood and plaster, with a steep roof and narrow windows, some of them very parsimonious of light and air, a poor but honest family, deriving their daily sustenance from

* Crape gowns were at this time the clerical fashion; a fashion, however, which this pamphlet of Defoe's rendered obsolete.

the mean occupation of mending pans and kettles, mainly desirous that their son — destined, perhaps, to pursue the same occupation as themselves — should possess the rudiments of a decent education, and be taught — what few of their class then possessed — the art of reading, and even of writing. Let it be supposed that this boy, chubby, red-haired, and burly in person, gives, as he advances in years, no little trouble to his ignorant but well-meaning parents. Strong, masculine, self-willed, mischief delights him. His passions, even in early life, are strong — often ungovernable. He is riotous and unruly; a very roysterer among his young acquaintance, who are, nevertheless, attracted to him by some indefinable charm, and delight in his humor, and in those massive or barbed phrases which distinguished his very vulgarity. Yet there are times in which this prevalent course of his life becomes interrupted; when he breaks away from his companions and plunges into solitude; when some unexplained sadness seems to bow down his mind; when his sleep is often broken, and those who watch his couch can observe writhings and shudderings, as if he were possessed by some infernal spirit. He grows up a tall and powerful lad; and, as he grows, he becomes less sad and more jovial; a despiser of all which calls itself religion; a captain among the gay and careless; daring beyond all ordinary precedent; remarkable for the breadth of his vulgarity and the emphasis of his oaths.

Such a disposition naturally impels him into all kinds of dangers; yet his preservations are all but miraculous. His companions tell of his hair-breadth escapes from drowning in the sea and in the river; how with his naked hand he once plucked out the forked tongue of an adder, and escaped unhurt; how he afterwards enlisted in the civil wars, and changed places with a fellow-soldier, who was killed in his stead. When in a state of extreme poverty, — a poverty greatly increased by the unsettled life he had led, — he marries, though destitute alike of money and of furniture, with not even a dish or a spoon which he could call his own, whilst all the fortune of his wife consists in two books left her by her father.

By dint of reading these, he is seized with a sudden impulse; bows at altars, worship priests, believes in apostolical succession, becomes religious just as a machine might be, whilst his soul lies torpid and frozen within. It is, however, but the fashion of a moment, and the wound-up spring speedily recovers its original shape. On the village-green, or at the street corner, wherever the idle love to congregate, there is he to be found; sometimes prompting their mirth; sometimes engaging with them in their games of pitch-halfpenny or quoits, or cat; not despising the public house, and foremost in the triple-bob major of the village belfry. Yet his companions think him somewhat odd; perhaps half-deranged. A sudden spasm will sometimes seize him in the midst of a game; he will stop, and seem as if he heard strange voices, and then resume his sport as if possessed with a demon of desperation. Then his frolics will become more boisterous, his oaths more fearful, till even the irreligious become disgusted with his enormous profanity.

Another change comes over him. He is grave again. He stands at the outer door of the church-tower, but no amount of persuasion can induce him to enter. The dance loses its charm; he ceases to swear; he becomes self-absorbed and dissatisfied. During a short period he gains more composure, and his countenance puts on a smirk of self-satisfaction. But it is transient, and he appears more than ever gloomy, anxious, haggard. Is he becoming a puritan? — for he seeks the conversation of the fanatics, and it is reported that he has been closeted with Gifford, the baptist preacher! He even remonstrates with some of his former acquaintance as to the impiety of their course. He has visions; reads his Bible; is alternately calm and gloomy; undergoes a whole campaign of conflicts, inconceivable to all except himself. Sometimes he thinks himself abandoned by hope; sometimes that the whole universe is leagued for his destruction. Now he attempts miracles; then he thinks himself possessed by the evil one. But, whatever the process through which he passes, all is as vivid as if actually within the range of his senses. He walks through the wilderness of this world, and dreams as he goes. Such was the process by which a poor tinker became a Christian; and such the materials out of which was formed, in due time, the Pilgrim's Progress!

Who has ever visited Bedford, — that pretty, well-arranged, compact town, — who has ever stood on the top of that beautiful Grecian bridge which now spans the river, and looked down that rich watery avenue, overshadowed with thick foliage on either side, towards the point where once stood the ancient castle, and not remembered John Bunyan? Simple, enchanting, noble man! What does not the world owe to thee, and to the great Being who could produce such as thee? Teacher alike of the infant and of the aged; who canst direct the first thought and comfort the last doubt of man; property alike of the peasant and the prince; welcomed by the ignorant and honored by the wise, — thou hast translated Christianity into a new language, and that a universal one! Thou art the prose-poet of all time!

In the year 1655 John Bunyan was admitted a member of the baptist church at Bedford, then worshipping under the ministry of John Gifford, who had been major in the army of Charles I. He had not long joined himself to this society, when he began to preach; and it may be readily supposed that the style of such a man as the author of the "Pilgrim's Progress" would render him uncommonly popular. The preaching of a baptist, however, was not without its dangers, even in the commonwealth; and Bunyan was indicted for the offence, probably by the presbyterian party. It appears, however, that, owing to the interference of the protector, the indictment was set aside. Soon after the restoration, his persecution began in earnest, and he was sentenced to perpetual banishment, for neglecting to come to church, and for holding unlawful meetings. This sentence was, however, commuted into imprisonment; and the county jail, which then stood on the top of Bedford Bridge, was the scene of his residence for more than twelve years. One is almost inclined to think of that building as the veritable "hospital of St. John the Baptist," which Bedford contains.

Sixty other dissenters and two ministers were imprisoned together with Bunyan. Whilst thus confined, he supported himself by making tagged laces. In the last year of his imprisonment, A. D. 1671, when the severity of his incarceration was considerably abated, he was elected pastor of the church at Bedford; and whilst in this prison, assisted by no books beyond his Bible and Fox's Martyrology, he wrote the Pilgrim's Progress. Bunyan gives an affecting account of the mental trials he endured when he was first imprisoned:

"I find myself a man encompassed with infirmities. The parting with my wife and four children hath often been to me, in this place, as the peeling the flesh from the bone; and that, not only because I am somewhat too fond of these great mercies, but also because I should have often brought to my mind the many hardships, miseries and wants, that my poor family was like to meet with, should I be taken from them; especially my poor blind child, who lay nearer to my heart than all beside. O! the thought of the hardships I thought my poor blind child might go under would break my heart to pieces! Poor child! thought I, what sorrows art thou like to have for thy portion in this world! Thou must be beaten, must beg, suffer hunger, cold, nakedness and a thousand calamities, though I cannot now endure the wind to blow upon thee. But yet, recalling myself, thought I, I must venture all with God, though it goeth to the quick to leave you." Bunyan was at length released from his prison by the interposition of Bishop Barlow, though he himself afterwards urged the rigorous execution of laws against nonconformists.

Bunyan had recovered his liberty when James II. ascended the throne. This incarnation of despotism — this concentrated essence of Stuart blood — began his reign by directing all his energies against the nonconformists. They being removed, he thought little difficulty would be found in uniting high churchmen and Romanists into one compact body. But he did not calculate what resistance those who were in power would make, when it was proposed to let in another power above their own. If James was a catholic, so was Charles before him, — at least, so far as he was anything; for religion with him was a mere turnstile, to be moved about as convenience might dictate. Monk, it is said, once caught him at mass, and told him "that if he played these pranks, though he had interest enough to bring him in, he had not sufficient to keep him there." Therefore Charles temporized. But James, from the beginning of his reign, proclaimed himself a catholic and a tyrant. His early declaration to the Scotch gave a sample of the kind of liberty they must expect: "I am resolved to maintain my power in its greatest lustre, that I may be the better able to defend your religion against fanatics."

Informers again abounded; meeting-houses were disturbed; ministers were searched for with the utmost rigor; tradesmen were separated by imprisonment from their business; families were painfully dislocated, fines heavily enforced, and spiritual courts loaded with business.

The infamous Jeffreys was a worthy agent of James in this new crusade against liberty of conscience. The old high commission court was restored, and this man, now chancellor, was its chief commissioner, aided by Crewe, Bishop of Durham, and Sprat, Bishop of Rochester. One of the first victims of this new confederation was Richard Baxter, who, at the instigation of Sir Roger L'Estrange, aided by Dr. Sherlock, was cited for portions of his paraphrase of the New Testament referring to diocesan bishops and the lawfulness of resisting the civil power. The whole transaction was a matchless specimen of effrontery and tyranny. When he appeared in Westminster Hall, it was moved on his behalf, as he was extremely ill, that the trial should be delayed. Jeffreys, in a passion, shouted out, "We have had to do with other sorts of persons, but now we have a saint to deal with, and I know how to deal with saints as well as sinners. Yonder stands Oates in the pillory" (he was actually there at the moment, for his evidence respecting the popish plot, and richly deserved his punishment), "and he says he suffers for the truth, and so says Baxter; but if Baxter did but stand on the other side of the pillory with him, I would say, 'Two of the greatest rogues and scoundrels in the kingdom stood there.'" The rest of the trial was in perfect accordance with this commencement. Baxter was defended by Pollexfen, who became, in the course of the trial, the object of Jeffreys' fury. Jeffreys told him, "You cant to the jury beforehand. Come, then," said he, "what do you say to this count?" quoting a portion of the paraphrase; "is he not an old knave to interpret this as belonging to liturgies?" "So do others," replied Pollexfen, "of the Church of England, who would be loth so to wrong the cause of liturgies as to make them a novel invention, or not to be able to date them as early as the Scribes and Pharisees." "No, no, Mr. Pollexfen," said the judge; "they were long-winded, extensive prayers, such as they used to say when they appropriated God to themselves: 'Lord, we are thy people, thy peculiar people, thy dear people.'" And then he snorted, and squeaked through his nose, and clenched his hands, and lifted up his eyes, mimicking their manner, and running on furiously, as he said they used to pray; but old Pollexfen gave him a bite now and then, though he could hardly get in a word. "Why, my lord," said he, "some will think it's hard measure to stop these men's mouths, and not let them speak through their noses." "Pollexfen," said Jeffreys, "I know you well; I will set a mark upon you; you're the patron of the faction. * * Don't we know how he preached formerly; he used to encourage all the women and maids to bring their bodkins and thimbles, to carry on the war against the king, of ever blessed memory, — an old schismatical knave, a hypocritical villain! * * What ailed the old blockhead, the unthankful villain, that he would not conform? Was he wiser or better than other men? * * A conceited, stubborn, fanatical dog, — hang him! This one old fellow hath cast more reproach upon the constitution and discipline of our church than will be wiped off these hundred years. But I'll handle him for it; for, by G——, he deserves to be whipped through the city!"

The jury found Baxter guilty, and Jeffreys told him that there was n't an honest man in England but what took him for a great knave. The sentence was, that he should be fined five hundred marks; be imprisoned till it was paid; and enter into recognizances to keep the peace for seven years. Jeffreys proposed the addition of a whipping through the city, but in this he was overruled. Being unable to pay the fine, Baxter was imprisoned for two years, till a change of measures set him at liberty. During his imprisonment, he was visited by Matthew Henry, who relates the conversation which took place during the interview.

The unsuccessful attempt of the Duke of Monmouth gave Jeffreys many opportunities of sating his bloodthirsty hostility to nonconformists. Among others, Lady Lisle was beheaded, and Mrs. Grant burnt alive, for admitting proscribed persons into their houses. Such cruelties, while they led some dissenters to abandon their profession, induced others to suspect the validity of the episcopal system itself, and to quit its communion.

"The dissenters continued to take the most prudent measures to cover their private meetings from their adversaries. They assembled in small numbers; they frequently shifted their places of worship, and met together late in the evenings, or early in the mornings. There were friends without-doors, always on the watch to give notice of approaching danger; where the dwellings of dissenters joined, they made windows, or holes, in the walls, that the preacher's voice might be heard in two or three houses; they had sometimes private passages from one house to another; and trap-doors for the escape of the minister, who always went in disguise, except when he was discharging his office. In country towns and villages, they were admitted through back yards and gardens into the house, to avoid the observation of neighbors and passengers. For the same reason, they never sung psalms, and the minister was placed in such an inward part of the house that his voice might not be heard in the streets; the doors were always locked, and a sentinel placed near them to give the alarm, that the preacher might escape by some private passage." *

In illustration, it may be observed that John Bunyan was usually in the habit of going to preach in the disguise of a carter, with a long whip upon his shoulder.

The oppressive conduct of James, which was so little disguised as to show that he was more weak than wicked, was next turned against the prelates. This roused the clergy, who now employed their pulpits to denounce his course. As if by some sudden wind, all the statements which they had so profusely made, in favor of non-resistance † and the royal prerogative, like the sentences of the Cumæan sibyl, were whirled away in an instant. The word of a king had been pronounced by Archbishop Sharp to be as sacred as his text; but when the English hierarchy was threatened, the doctrine became naught. In an instant they threw themselves into the position in which the reviled puritans of the commonwealth had stood before them. Even Oxford, which had described resistance as "impious, seditious and damnable," refused compliance with James' new commission court, and drew from him the sarcasm, "Is this your Church of England loyalty?"

To promote still further his design of bringing the whole nation under the influence of the Church of Rome, James now attempted a general toleration, endeavoring to make common cause with dissenters, and to outmatch the Church of England. Despairing,

* Neal, vol. v., chap. i.

† This doctrine was maintained by Jeremy Taylor, Usher, Bramhall, Saunderson, and most of the dignified clergy. Defoe declares that he had heard from the pulpit, "that if the king commanded my head, and sent his message to fetch it, I was bound to submit, and stand still while it was cut off." Cartwright, Bishop of Chester, said, "Though the king should not please or humor us, though he rend off the mantle from our bodies, * * nay, though he sentence us to death, * * yet if we are living members of the Church of England, we must neither open our mouths, * * nor must we ask our prince why he governs us otherwise than we please to be governed ourselves; we must neither call him to account for his religion, nor question his policy in civil matters; for he is made our king by God's law, of which the law of the land is only declarative." — *Somers' Tracts*, vol. ix., p. 129.

however, of gaining this point by act of parliament, and not unwilling to stretch his own prerogative, James proceeded to claim on behalf of the monarch a dispensing power as it regarded penal enactments made by act of parliament, and, with the concurrence of his judges, declared the authority of the crown to be absolute.

Religious liberty was thus held out to dissenters, at the expense of constitutional freedom. The dilemma was a difficult one; so difficult, as to make us cease to wonder that men should have taken opposite views on the subject. Some rejoiced in their actual freedom, however gained; whilst others saw that dissenters were only protected in order to divide them from the church, and that the end would be the bringing in of a popery which would crush them both. Bunyan, among the rest, detected the motive which prompted the new measures. Whilst addresses went up to the king from various bodies of dissenters, the principal men kept silence. Defoe says, "I told the dissenters I had rather the Church of England should pull off our clothes by fines and forfeitures, than that the papists should fall both upon the church and the dissenters, and pull our skins off by fire and fagot." * The truth, however, was, that the dissenters were afraid of toleration in the abstract. "The shell," to use Bunyan's simile, was yet "on their head." They hated popery; their feelings regarding it were the extreme of intolerance. Their own and their fathers' sufferings had been so great, that they were distrustful and timorous as to any decided action.

It was scarcely surprising. The havoc committed among them, during the recent execution of the penal laws, was frightful. Twenty thousand presbyterians suffered martyrdom in Scotland, during the reigns of Charles II. and James II.† The quakers complained that fifteen hundred of their body were in prison; of whom three hundred and fifty had died since 1660. Eight hundred and forty-one were transported to the West Indies, many of whom died in the passage, and some were sold as slaves. Eight thousand

* Defoe's Appeal to Honor and Justice, p. 52.

† M'Crie's Covenanters.

dissenters are said to have perished in prison, during the reign of Charles I. alone. As a proof of the temper of the times, it may be mentioned, that Jeremiah White, who had been one of Cromwell's chaplains, had "prepared a list of ministers and others who had suffered imprisonment; distinguishing those who had died, or were starved in jail, with an account of the fines levied by execution on their estates." A large reward was offered by James' party for its publication, as that which would bring infamy on the Church of England. White, however, absolutely refused. "He scorned the temptation, rejected the rewards, and told them he would not so far assist to pull down the church. In short, he refused either to publish his memoranda, or to give them the least opportunity for doing so themselves; and this purely as he saw the design of the party, which, as fellow-protestant, as well as a dissenter, he had more sense, honor and Christianity, than to join in."* According to Oldmixon, White had collected a list containing sixty thousand, who suffered for their religious opinions, from the Restoration to the Revolution, five thousand of whom died in prison.

William and Benjamin Hewling, who were baptists, suffered at this time a cruel death. John Howe fled the country. The objects for which the civil war had been undertaken during the last reign were utterly, and, for the present, hopelessly defeated, amidst a series of scenes to which English history offers no parallel.

The meeting-house at Stepney, built in 1674, still exists, to show what were the circumstances under which dissenting worship was carried on in those days, and how the congregations screened themselves from notice.

The lower part of it was probably employed as a family mansion, and divided into rooms. This whole area is now sustained by two majestic pillars, sent over from Holland after the revolution, when Matthew Mead was pastor of the church. But the upper part of the building, then accessible by stairs and trap-doors, was

* Defoe's Review, vol. II., p. 488.

fitted up as a place of public worship, in such a manner as to afford some security against the intrusion of an informer. The whole

MEETING-HOUSE, STEPNEY.

building is now one of the most venerable memorials of nonconformist history.

How James II. fulfilled the evil destinies of his notorious family, and, whilst deaf to all friendly warning, rushed madly on the catastrophe which ended his dynasty; — how the king, diverted from the powerless nonconformists, provoked a party able to avenge its wrongs, — the prelatical party itself; — how the seven bishops refused to proclaim the indulgence illegally granted by the monarch, and how James' war upon them hastened and consummated his own ruin; — how William, Prince of Orange, was summoned by the voice of the nation to the forsaken throne; — how, wearied and exhausted by persecution, the nation consented to a form of toleration which, though essentially imperfect, was a large improvement on the terror of the preceding reigns; — and how dissent became an evil to be borne with, if it could not be cured, — absurd and contemptible as such a condition is, — the reader of ordinary history already knows. That the main evil, however, still remained, though it was somewhat palliated and disguised, will be apparent in the few pages which yet follow.

CHAPTER XI.

"HIGH CHURCH."

"Sir Richard Steele hit the mark when he thus distinguished the two principal churches in Christendom, the Church of Rome and the Church of England: that the former pretended to be infallible, and the latter to be always in the right." — *Whiston's Life*, p. 168.

We have introduced the reader to London, as London, or some part of it, appeared at the commencement of the seventeenth century. The present scene is laid in the heart of the city a hundred years later. The ruins of the great and devastating fire have been long since removed, and the metropolis puts on an altered air. The opportunity would have been a noble one for carrying into execution the magnificent plans of Sir Christopher Wren, and for reducing the ill-arranged streets to a scheme presenting both grandeur and unity. But private interests had prevailed over public convenience, and the city arose as it best could. It was, however, greatly improved in its reconstruction. New churches, of which no less than fifty-one within the city were from the designs of Wren himself, met the eye in every direction, many of them alike remarkable for their elegance and convenience. The thoroughfares were, however, still narrow and confined; booths protruded in front of many of the houses; footpaths were unknown, except in a few favored quarters; and though some imperfect attempts had been made at lighting the streets, the effort had not, as yet, been remarkable for its succees. The great Cathedral Church of St. Paul's, though ruined in the plan for its construction by the desire of James II. to have it adapted to a Roman Catholic ceremonial, was advancing to its completion under the inspection of its now aged architect. The crowds which fill the streets are remarkable in their attire. The full periwig, the broad-bottomed coat, the conspicuous shoe-buckle, the dependent queue, distinguish the gentlemen, as the wide-spread hoop, now for some time in fashion, marks the ladies; whilst the more sober citizen contents himself with his single-breasted coat of russet color, and the square cravat which hangs pendent beneath his chin. How different is the new city in its character and costume from the old one, which so much distinguished itself in the wars of the parliament! The naked tyranny of the sovereign is not now the theme of every crowd and coffee-house. Popish plots are no more. The succession to the throne is no longer disputed. Commerce, formerly disordered and disorganized, is prosperous. England, which a little while ago expatriated its own religious men, has become the haven for those who, driven from their homes by the revocation of the edict of Nantes, have taken refuge here, and have introduced their manufactures to the great benefit of the entire community. Has the nation, then, unlearned its old illiberalities? Has it arrived at the conclusion that the war of the civil power with conscience is unrighteous and monstrous? Has the magistrate dropped his sword where the rights of Cæsar end, and where those of God begin? We shall see.

We are opposite to the New Exchange, A. D. 1703. (The reader will remember that, at the date of which we speak, it faced, not as now the east, but the south.) A large crowd is collected before the pillory which has been placed there. It is hung with garlands, by hands which little sympathize with the purpose of its erection. It contains a sufferer,—a man of the middle size, about forty years of age, with hooked nose, a sharp chin, a dark-colored wig, and a countenance bearing evident traces of much wear and tear, and in which the grave is about equally mingled with the satirical. His advent to the pillory has been a kind of triumphal procession; and now he is fixed in it, the scoffs do not arise nor the missiles fly; the mob, on the contrary, drink his health. The careful spectator may see, in the merry twinkle of those gray eyes, the trenchant thoughts which he afterwards puts into verse, styled "A Hymn to the Pillory." The exhibition over, to be repeated in Cheapside, and at Temple-bar, on successive days, refreshments are handed to him, and he departs from a scene which is rather a triumph than a punishment.

Who is the criminal? A man of intelligible principles, though they were now out of fashion; the most versatile writer, perhaps, of our literature; a wit, a true lover of liberty, a conscientious dissenter, a brave and undaunted spirit; the author of works which will live long after the majority of his contemporary generation are forgotten; the future idol of youth, one of whose works will stand beside the Pilgrim's Progress, on every juvenile shelf.

"Fearlessly on high stands unabashed Defoe."

What has he done? The answer to that question will demand a little retrospection.

When, on the revolution, William and Mary gained the throne of Great Britain, one of the earliest measures prompted by the king was a remission of the penal laws against protestant nonconformity. William's sentiments regarding religion were liberal; he was himself a presbyterian. Yet neither he nor the dissenters who so warmly supported him had any definite notion beyond that of "making the rule of Christianity to be the rule of conformity." Locke, to his immortal honor, though almost alone, advocated the true principle: "The cure of souls cannot belong to the civil magistrate, because the whole of his power consists in outward force; but true and saving religion consists in the inward persuasion of the mind, without which nothing is acceptable to God. * * * Magistracy does not oblige him to put off either humanity or Christianity. But it is one thing to persuade, another to command; one thing to press with arguments, another with penalties." It had been moved by Hampden, grandson of the patriot, in the House of Commons, that the oath which pledged the king to maintain the Church of England should be so modified as to admit of his assenting to any forms and ceremonies which parliament should approve. But the effort was fruitless. It was next attempted to remove all impediments which prevented dissenters from exercising civic functions. This also was frustrated by a large majority; and an equally fruitless attempt was made to rescind the Test Act. All that could be gained was the Toleration Act; an imperfect and insulting measure, since it gave what it conferred as an act of grace, and involved in its very name the right to withhold. It made no provision for free education; it was only available to those who avowed the doctrinal articles of the Church of England; and it excluded from its benefits all Roman Catholics. It was, in fact, the old enemy, but in a more decorous dress.

Such as it was, however, it was extremely distasteful to the high church section; and Bishop Burnet lost great favor with his prelatical friends for the part he took in upholding it. He who would make himself acquainted with the opinions of those who opposed it has only to turn to the bitter and caustic diatribes of South. Such were the sentiments with which, in Queen Anne's time, Westminster Abbey and the royal chapels resounded!

Before the death of William, but after that of Queen Mary, a controversy had arisen which assumes considerable importance in the ecclesiastical history of the times. When so large a number of the citizens were dissenters, it was impossible that municipal offices should not often invite their acceptance; and it was customary for dissenters, in order to comply with the requisitions of the Test Act, to receive the communion occasionally at church. On one occasion, Sir Humphrey Edwin, then lord mayor, carried the paraphernalia of his office to Pinner's Hall meeting-house. This daring act of "profanation" was like a spark thrown into a barrel of gunpowder. Rebuke, abuse and satire, were alike directed against the offence. Dr. Nichols complained that the lord mayor carried the sword with him to "a nasty conventicle, which was held in a hall belonging to one of the mean mechanical companies in the city." Swift, in his "Tale of a Tub," satirizes Sir Humphrey Edwin, by describing Jack getting upon a great horse, and eating custard, — custard being a standing dish at a lord mayor's feast. Defoe stepped in to this controversy. "There is a sort of truth," said he, "which all men owe to the principles they profess, and, generally speaking, all men pay it. None but protestants halt between God and Baal; Christians of an amphibious nature, that can believe one way of worship to be right, and yet serve God another. * * The prosperity of the church of Christ has been more fatal to it than all the persecution of its enemies. * * 'T is of absolute necessity that a man be of one side or the other; either the conformist will mar the dissenter, or the dissenter will mar the conformist. But to make the matter a gain to dodge religions, and go in the morning to church, and in the afternoon to meeting; to communicate in private with the Church of England to save a penalty, and then go back to the dissenters and communicate again there; this is such a retrograde devotion, that I can see no color of pretence for in all the sacred book."

On the death of King William, at the end of a reign favorable on the whole to religious liberty, high church principles were again in the ascendant, as might indeed have been expected from the reign of a granddaughter of the Earl of Clarendon. The tories were now triumphant; fanaticism was proclaimed dangerous to the welfare of the state. Dissenters were exposed to every kind of insult. Their meeting-houses were invaded by the mob, and ministers were insulted in the street. Almost all the May-poles in England were repaired, and drunkenness and revelling resumed their sway. To stem the tumult which threatened a revival of the old persecutions, the queen was compelled to issue a declaration, assuring dissenters of her intention to maintain the act of toleration. But, in the first parliament of the queen, a bill was introduced to interdict dissenters from the practice of occasional conformity, a custom which had been sanctioned by Bates, Howe, Baxter, and others of equal eminence. Sir Thomas Abney had revived the practice of Sir Humphrey Edwin, which led Defoe to address a letter to Howe, Sir Thomas' pastor, calling upon him either to vindicate or to denounce the practice. A correspondence of some warmth ensued. Defoe remarks, "Is it not very hard that the dissenters should be excluded from all places of profit and trust and honor, and at the same time should not be excused from those which are attended with charge, trouble and loss of time? That a dissenter shall be pressed as a sailor to fight at sea, listed as a soldier to fight on shore, and, let his merit be never so much above his fellows, shall never be capable of preferment so much as to carry a halbert? That we must maintain our own clergy and your clergy, our own poor and your poor, pay equal taxes and equal duties, and not to be thought worthy to be trusted to set a drunkard in the stocks? * * We wonder, gentlemen, you will accept our money to carry on your wars."

About this time, too, in the year 1702, Defoe published a pamphlet, entitled "The Shortest Way with the Dissenters; or, Proposals for the Establishment of the Church." In this pamphlet he had principally in view a sermon recently preached by Dr. Sacheverell, entitled "The Political Union," in which occurred this sentence, "that he could not be a true son of the Church of England who did not lift up the banner of the church against the dissenters." In a cuttingly ironical manner, Defoe exhorts the high-church party to proceed to severities against the dissenters. "Here is the opportunity, and the only one, perhaps, that ever the church had, to secure herself and destroy her enemies. If ever you will establish the best Christian church in the world; if ever you will suppress the spirit of enthusiasm; if ever you will free the nation from the viperous brood that have so long sucked the blood of their mother; if you will leave your posterity free from faction and rebellion, this is the time. This is the time to pull up this heretical weed of sedition, that has so long disturbed the peace of the church, and poisoned the good corn. But, says another hot and cold objector, 'This is renewing the fire and fagot; this will be cruelty in its nature, and barbarous to all the world.' I answer, it is cruel to kill a snake or a toad in cold blood; but the poison of their nature makes it a charity to our neighbors to destroy those creatures, not from any personal injury received, but for prevention; not for the evil they have done, but for the evil they may do. * * * * Some beasts are for sport, and the huntsmen give them the advantages of ground; but some are knocked on the head by all possible ways of violence and surprise. I do not prescribe fire and fagot, but, as Scipio said of Carthage, '*Delenda est Carthago*,' they are to be rooted out of this nation, if ever we will live in peace, serve God, or enjoy our own. * * * 'T is vain to trifle in this matter; the light foolish fondling of them by fines is their glory and advantage; if the gallows instead of the compter, and the galleys instead of the fines, were the reward of going to a conventicle, there would not be so many sufferers. The spirit of martyrdom is over; they that will go to church to be chosen sheriffs and mayors would go to forty churches rather than be hanged. * * * We hang men for trifles, and banish them for things not worth naming. But an offence against God and the church, against the welfare of the world and the dignity of religion, shall be bought off for five shillings. This is such a shame to a Christian government, that 't is with regret I transmit it to posterity."

So ingeniously was this production constructed, and so little did it transcend the expressed opinions of the high-church bigots, that in the first instance this pamphlet of Defoe's was received with enthusiasm. He himself tells us that he received thanks for it, and it was loudly praised by some who, when they ascertained the authorship, were enraged beyond measure.

It was for the publication of this pamphlet that Defoe was brought to trial at the Old Bailey, and, having submitted to the mercy of the court, was thus sentenced: — "That he pay a fine of two hundred marks to the queen, stand three times in the pillory, be imprisoned during the queen's pleasure, and find sureties for his good behavior during seven years."

The imprisonment in Newgate, which succeeded this trial, was ruinous to Defoe's circumstances; whilst his association in the prison with thieves and vagabonds severely injured his moral delicacy. During his incarceration he published several works, and led on the way to the Tatlers and Spectators of a subsequent day, by commencing his periodical "Review." When the high-church party were removed from power, and Harley became secretary of state, Defoe was released from his imprisonment.

The hall at Westminster, which has witnessed the inauguration of a long line of English monarchs, within which were tried Strafford, Laud and Charles I., and which, in modern times, was the scene of the indictment of Warren Hastings, witnessed, in the year 1709, a pompous ceremonial held over a very insignificant offender. We refer to the trial of Dr. Henry Sacheverell. This man, who was remarkable for nothing but his daring vehemence, whose first application for ordination was refused, and who, in one of his publications, spoke of "parallel lines meeting in a common centre," who had been an unsuccessful whig, and now brought his newly-gained toryism into the market for hire, had been by popular election inducted into the living of St. Saviour's, Southwark, and now derived from his boldness a notoriety entirely unmerited by his talents or his virtues. His manners were haughty, and his person, which he attired with the most sedulous care, agreeable and imposing. He had preached during this year two sermons; one before the judges at Derby, the other on the 5th of November, before the lord mayor, at St. Paul's, under the titles of "The Communications of Sin," and "The Perils of False Brethren, both in Church and State." Of the sort of doctrines delivered in these addresses it is almost unnecessary to select a specimen. We will, however, take the following. Referring to the Church of England, he says:

"If to assert separation from her communion to be no schism, or if it was, that schism is no damnable sin; * * If upon all occasions to comply with the dissenters, both in public and private affairs, as persons of tender conscience and piety; to promote their interest in elections, to sneak to them for places and preferment, to defend toleration and liberty of conscience, and under the pretence of moderation to excuse their separation, and lay the fault upon the true sons of the church for carrying matters too high;

If to court the fanatics in private, and to hear them with patience, if not with approbation, rail at and blaspheme the church, and upon occasion to justify the king's murder; If to flatter both the dead and the living in their vices, and to tell the world that if they have wit and money enough, they need no repentance; and that only fools and beggars can be damned, — if these, I say, are the modish and fashionable criterions of a true churchman, God deliver us from all such false brethren!"

Such were some of the means by which Sacheverell blew himself into popularity. In ordinary times, such a man might be left to his own insignificance. But when Sacheverell advanced, from abusing dissenters, to insinuate that the toleration act was unwarrantable and unjust, that the ministry of state tended to the destruction of the constitution, and that the means used to bring about the late revolution were odious and unjustifiable, the ministry, headed by Lord Godolphin, whom, under the name of Volpone, Sacheverell had especially attacked, brought against him a bill of impeachment.

The case excited the widest interest. During its progress business was almost at a stand. The summons of this hot-headed zealot to loosen from its scabbard the sword which the wiser policy of William of Orange had sheathed, was responded to by the multitude with acclamations of enthusiasm. The trial lasted three weeks, and excited the interest of the whole kingdom. Sacheverell was attended daily to Westminster Hall by an excited and furious mob. They compelled every person to pull off his hat to the high-church martyr as he passed; and each person endeavored to come near his person, and to kiss his hand. The queen, who attended the trial in her private capacity, was assailed by them with cries — "God bless your majesty and the church! we hope your majesty is for Dr. Sacheverell." The defence of this "high-church martyr" was a perfect *tour de force*. He denied none of the matters with which he was charged, but declared that King William, in arriving at the throne, had disclaimed the idea of resistance, — "As if," says Defoe, "the Prince of Orange had not brought with him an army to resist, but came with fourteen thousand men at his heels, to stand and look on while the English gentry and clergy, with prayers and tears, besought King James to run away and leave the throne vacant!" Sacheverell well knew that William III. had glozed over his movements by honeyed words. It was, moreover, pleaded, that the language held out by the doctor was sustained by the language of the church homilies — an argument not so easy for the church party to answer! He declared that, so far from bringing any charge against the queen, he held her person in the utmost respect and affection; and in answer to the accusation that he was an incendiary, quoted passages from his sermons, in which "he had invited the separatists to renounce their schism, and to come sincerely into the church." The occasion was distinguished by some parliamentary oratory of a high kind. Lieutenant-general Stanhope, especially, one of the managers, made a deep impression by his oratory.

The defence of the accused was written for him, it was said, by Atterbury. The result of the trial was that Sacheverell was declared guilty by a majority of eighty-two to sixty-nine. He was sentenced to be suspended for three years, and his books to be publicly burned. The issue was, in fact, a triumph for his party. The queen secretly favored him; the mob shouted for his cause; the high-church party stood by him, though they despised him in their hearts.

The result of the trial was, as might have been foreseen, an explosion of mob violence. The cavalcade which had waited on this inflated tool of a party on his way to and from Westminster Hall, after escorting Sacheverell to his house in the Temple, dispersed themselves over London, and proceeded to violence. They attacked seven meeting-houses; amongst the rest, Meeting-house Court, Blackfriars and Fetter-lane, demolishing pulpits, pews and galleries, and making bonfires of such materials in the streets, amidst huzzaing and cries of "High Church and Sacheverell!" They also attacked the houses of Mr. Burgess and Mr. Earle, and bore off or destroyed their furniture and books, and were with difficulty restrained from setting fire to one of the houses. Dissenters were insulted in the streets and in their dwellings. The houses of the leading whig partisans were also threatened.*

Nor did the consequences of this most injudicious impeachment stop here. Sacheverell made a triumphant progress through the kingdom, was everywhere hailed as a martyr, and almost worshipped as a demi-god. He dispensed his blessings with the air of the Vatican; became the toast at the dinner-table, and the idol of weak women; lived in immoderate luxury; and, when the immediate excitement had passed, fell into the contempt and oblivion he deserved. †

In Wrexham the effigies of the dissenting ministers were dressed up, paraded through the streets, and publicly burned. In the same place, Hoadly, who, though the champion of episcopacy, was the advocate of liberal principles, was represented in effigy, baptized with much ceremony, carried with a rope round his neck, scourged, pilloried, drowned.

MEETING HOUSE OF MATTHEW HENRY, CHESTER.

In the following election, the same tumults were repeated.

* Calamy's Life and Times, vol. II., p. 228.

† See Duchess of Marlborough's Correspondence, vol. II., p. 142.

Amongst other towns visited in this connection was Chester, the residence of one to whose character and writings the Christian world is inconceivably indebted — Matthew Henry. Henry well knew what intolerance meant. He was born in the year of the passing of the Act of Uniformity, and he saw its pressure upon his father during the first years of his life, and felt it himself during the latter. His ancient chapel, yet standing, demonstrates by its very position, shut in as it is from the street, with its windows well guarded by shutters, the tenure upon which dissenters at that time held their sanctuaries. Such precautions are very common in the sanctuaries of the old nonconformists.

In Chester, Sacheverell's mob was so furious, that Henry, though he gave his vote according to his conscience, durst not appear in public, and was compelled to forego his attendance on a funeral, and to omit the funeral sermon which was to have been preached on the occasion. The returned members were heralded in their procession by the figure of Dr. Sacheverell.

The feeling thus excited led to the dissolution of the whig ministry of the day. The contrast between the agitation of the country on this occasion, and the insignificance of the individual who caused it,

> "Resembles ocean into tempest tost,
> To waft a feather, or to drown a fly." *

In consequence of the trial of Sacheverell, high-church addresses flowed in upon the queen from all quarters, beginning with the city of London. Some of them asserted the doctrine of non-resistance in the most unqualified terms. On this Defoe asks, "Would any man that had seen the temper of the people, in the time of the late King James, believe it possible, without a judicial infatuation, that the same people should reässume their blindness, and rise up again for bondage? Never, since the children of Israel demanded to go back and make bricks without straw, and to feed on onions and garlic, was any nation in the world so sordid, and so unaccountably bewitched!" †

* Young. † Review, vol. VII., p. 107.

As the reign of Anne drew towards its close, the bill to forbid occasional conformity, and by this means to prevent dissenters from occupying civil offices, which had been three times refused by the lords, was passed almost without a murmur. Encouraged by the success of this movement, Bolingbroke and Atterbury instigated "the Schism Bill." This was a prohibition of collegiate and other dissenting institutions, under heavy penalties. "By virtue of this act, nonconformists teaching school were to be imprisoned three months. Each schoolmaster was to receive the sacrament, and take the oaths. If afterwards present at a conventicle, he was incapacitated, and liable to be imprisoned. He must teach only the Church Catechism. But offenders conforming were recapacitated; and schools for reading, writing and mathematics, were, after a warm debate, excepted." * The bill, in spite of great exertions on the part of the nonconformists, passed both houses, and received the royal assent. It was designed to follow it by another, declaring all dissenters in the kingdom unfit to vote in the election of members of parliament. But the queen's decease happily prevented this dangerous issue. She died on the very day that the Schism Act was to have taken effect. "O, that glorious first of August!" said Dr. Benson, in a sermon preached at Salter's Hall, "that most signal day, never to be forgot!" The queen's death prevented the further ascendency of Lord Bolingbroke, and rescued protestant dissenters!

* Calamy's Life and Times, vol. II., p. 283.

CHAPTER XII.

THE WILL MINUS THE POWER.

"Letting 'I dare not' wait upon 'I would.'" — SHAKSPEARE.

HE name of Dr. Doddridge is one on which all who have sympathy with the generous, the benevolent and the devout, will ever delight to linger. Though deeply engraven in the annals of protestant nonconformity, it is the exclusive property of no creed. Doddridge was no genius, in the ordinary acceptation of the word, and no one thing which he did transcended other things of a similar kind done by others. His learning has been often surpassed; his pulpit oratory was not resplendent; his poetry, though pleasing, bore no traces of inspiration; his power over the minds of others was not supreme. Yet there was in him such a combination of excellences as to lift him at once out of all vulgar mediocrity. Commencing with a youth which was fuller of a sportive playfulness than can be comprehended by the dull, and which exposed him to reproof from the cynical, though it was remote from vice and abhorrent from hypocrisy, the growth of his character was like the gradual ripening of a rich harvest, at length reaching the point of full maturity and ample abundance. The diligence of his self-cultivation, the integrity of his heart and frankness of his manners, the variety of his attainments, the judiciousness and pertinence of his conduct, and his unwearied industry, all united to fervor of devotion and an insatiable thirst for usefulness which have never been surpassed, give him a just claim to be regarded as belonging to the first rank among those whose nobility will be the most conspicuous, and whose honors the most enduring.

Such have been the thoughts of many, as they have looked upon the pleasant and well-built town of Northampton. Not a few have probably directed their first inquiries, on entering it, to the vestiges of the author of "The Family Expositor," and of "The Rise and Progress of Religion in the Soul."

Doddridge's meeting-house still stands on the Castle-hill, — a spot not to be visited without a crowd of historical reminiscences. Northampton is well known as one of our oldest fortified towns, dating from a period, at latest, soon after that of the Conquest. Compared with Windsor or with Nottingham, there is nothing in its appearance which would seem to claim eminence for it. It has no bold, projecting, almost inaccessible rock, and the river which flows through it is far from imposing. But the town is built upon very high ground, and the Castle-hill, which is a considerable elevation, overlooks a marshy tract, calculated to give great security to its ancient fortress. As we stand upon this hill, what crowds of varied historical associations rush upon the mind! Beauty and chivalry, conquest and defeat, tales of joy and sorrow, empires lost and won, have dated from this spot their all-varying fortunes. It was here that one of the most celebrated scenes occurred in the contest waged by Henry II. with the Roman hierarchy, when that king, under the constitutions of Clarendon, cited Thomas à Beckett to appear before a council of the states, and when the primate, blazing in all the splendors of his archiepiscopal pomp, refused to submit to the royal jurisdiction; and it was from this town that Beckett fled, in the disguise of a monk, to take refuge in Flanders. It was here that King John was besieged by his barons; and here that the same king met the papal nuncios, by whom, failing to make sufficient concessions, he was excommunicated. Here, also, Henry III. besieged his factious barons, under the conduct of the younger De Montfort. Here was held the splendid court of Edward I.; and through this town the king followed his beloved Eleanor. Here, too, a parliament was held, to consider the coronation and marriage of Edward II. Beneath these walls Henry VI. lost his kingdom in a battle with the Earl of Warwick. The poll-tax, which occasioned the insurrection of Wat Tyler, was passed by a parliament assembling in this town. It was in this castle that Richard III. determined to seize the crown of England from the infant hands of Edward V. Elizabeth, Charles I., Cromwell, Charles II., all have their memorials here. The castle was demolished in the year 1662; and though a few remains of the ancient building exist, its principal site is now occupied by edifices of a less imposing and more peaceful character.

"Time has seen, — that lifts the low,
And level lays the lofty brow, —
Has seen this broken pile complete,
Big with the vanities of state.
A little rule, a little sway,
A sunbeam in a winter's day,
Is all the proud and mighty have,
Between the cradle and the grave." *

We think with pleasure how the spot, once resounding with the histories of the great, is now consecrated by the memory of the good.

It was after a considerable conflict of opposite emotions, that Doddridge, then twenty-seven years of age, came, in the year 1729, to the conclusion that it was his duty to settle at Northampton; and it was within the walls of the Castle-street meeting-house that, during twenty-two years, he fulfilled the duties of a "good and faithful servant." His chapel, which would be deemed a large one for that period, is neat and commodious; and, though the lower part of it has been considerably renovated, the pulpit and the pewing of the galleries are still unchanged. A marble monument, in the most profuse style of mural decoration, bears an

* Prior.

inscription to the memory of Doddridge, more verbose than powerful.

But there is no part of this building altogether so interesting to the visitor as the vestry. Here are the chair in which Doddridge sat; the table at which he wrote his "Expositor;" the original invitation addressed to him to become the pastor of the church, with his reply; the drawing of the monument erected to his memory in the cemetery of Lisbon, where he died. These walls have been, doubtless, familiar with many of those communings of ardent devotion which rendered him so powerful in the pulpit and from the press; and here he often verified the sentiment, that "Solitude has nothing gloomy in it when the soul points upwards."

When Doddridge undertook — as he did immediately before his coming to Northampton — the formation of a dissenting academy, the course was not without its perils. This aspect of the case presented itself to the mind of Dr. Watts, who was consulted respecting the project. "Are the hands of enemies," writes Watts, "so effectually chained up from offering us any violence, that they cannot indict or persecute you, under the pretence that your academy is a school?" *

There were sufficient reasons for such a question. Since the Restoration, the nonconformists had been excluded from the benefit of the English universities, and their schools had been conducted in private, under the management of such individuals as were considered competent. One of the most eminent establishments was conducted by Mr. Morton, at Newington Green. At this school Defoe, Samuel Wesley, and many ministers, received their first training. Another was under the discipline of Mr. Kerr, of Bethnal Green. But these seminaries did not pass unmolested. Morton was exposed to perpetual annoyances from spies and informers; till, at length, worn out by vexations, he abandoned his country, and took refuge in New England. A little later, a still more eminent establishment was kept by Mr. Doolittle, who preached at Monkwell-street, and lived at Islington. Many men

* Doddridge's Correspondence, vol. II., p. 481.

of considerable nonconformist eminence received their education under his roof; amongst the rest, Matthew Henry and Dr. Calamy. But he was compelled also to break up his establishment at Islington, and to remove first to Battersea, and afterwards to Clerkenwell.* Indeed, no dissenter could at that time exercise the functions of a teacher without exposing himself to dangerous penalties. Roger Rosen, for teaching a few little children to read, was cited to Chester, excommunicated, and was in great danger of starvation.

In one of these academies, — that, namely, kept by Morton, — Samuel Wesley, father of the celebrated founder of Methodism, received, as we have said, his education. A book, bearing his name, but published probably without his consent or authority, was put forth, which contained severe strictures on the mode of education adopted by protestant dissenters. The work drew forth a reply, to which Wesley added a rejoinder, containing severe reflections on the nonconforming body. This was a cruel blow, especially at a time when dissenters with difficulty maintained a tolerated position. "When all is done, gentlemen," said Defoe, in his strictures on the work, "why do we erect private academies, and teach our children by themselves? Even for the same reason that we do not communicate with you, because you shut us out by imposing unreasonable terms. * * But while you shut our children out of your schools, never quarrel at our teaching them at those of our own, or sending them into foreign countries; since, wherever they are taught, they generally get a share of learning at least equal to yourselves, and, we hope, partake of as much honesty; — and, as to their performances, match them, and outpreach them, if you can. I wish that was the only strife between us."

The Schism Bill, as we have seen, gave new effect to this position of affairs. But, on the death of Queen Anne, the measure, though passed, sank into oblivion, as no lawyer, who hoped for favor from the court, would enforce its penalties. It was repealed by 5 Geo. 1. Severe, however, as the Schism Bill was, it had been far outdone by the measure promoted by the Long Parliament, which

* Calamy's Life and Times, vol. I., pp. 113—138.

provided that none but a protestant should educate the children of papists.

Even after the accession of the house of Hanover, occasional riots, stimulated by the party who were favorable to the Pretender, menaced the dissenters in various parts of the kingdom, and were stimulated by a celebrated sermon, preached March 31, 1717, by Bishop Hoadley, on the nature of the kingdom of Christ, in which he asserted "that Christ is the sole law-giver to his subjects, and the sole judge of their behavior in the affairs of conscience and eternal salvation;" and that, "to set up any other authority in his kingdom, to which his subjects are indispensably obliged to submit their consciences or conduct in what is properly called religion, evidently destroys the rule and authority of Jesus Christ as king." Sherlock charged Hoadley with endeavoring to prepare the way for the repeal of the Test Act; and the Convocation declared his sentiments subversive of all government and discipline in the church of Christ. This was the last *bonâ fide* sitting of this body. They have never been permitted to transact business since that period.

Such were the circumstances under which Doddridge first instituted, on his settlement at Northampton, his academy. He was, in many respects, in a favorable position for doing so. The dissenters were in high favor at court, and their adversaries in a position of declining influence. But they had, on many occasions, given great annoyance to Doddridge and his students, and at length they proceeded to systematic hostility. At a visitation in Northampton, in the year 1752, Reynolds, the chancellor, told the church-wardens of Doddridge's parish "that he was informed that there was a fellow in this parish who taught a grammar-school, as he supposed, without any license from the bishop," and commanded them, if they found such to be the fact, to present Doddridge, that he might be prosecuted according to law. Nor was such a prosecution in those days an unusual event; for Doddridge tells us that he knew twenty such attempts within less than so many years. Whilst this case was pending in the ecclesiastical court, and at the time of a general election, in which a Jacobite member was returned, a riotous attack was made on Doddridge's house, which was connived at by the mayor of the town.

DODDRIDGE'S HOUSE, NORTHAMPTON.

By the express intervention of George II., who declared that, in his reign, there should be no persecution, the suit was quashed.

Were our volume of a nature which would expand according to the materials which lie before us, it might be interesting to give a detailed account of many recent movements, memorable in the struggle for religious liberty, which we must now pass over in a brief summary.

The doctrine of the alliance of church and state, as understood by the inferior magistrates, proved, on many occasions, no inconsiderable annoyance to the early methodists, although their professed relation to the Church of England, and the decisive measures which were adopted at court, prevented any systematic persecution. It was to the honor of Doddridge, Lardner and other dissenters, that they opposed, in the case of Woollston, the deist, any recourse to the civil power, in order to put down his pernicious opinions. The quakers showed, in a petition to parliament, that they were still liable to severe exactions in consequence of their religious opinions, but failed in obtaining relief. The Test and Corporation Acts still continued. In 1748 a law passed the city of London, enforcing on every person who refused to act as sheriff, when nominated by the mayor, a fine of upwards of four hundred pounds, and six hundred pounds on every one who refused to serve when elected by the common hall. Fifteen thousand pounds were

30

collected by this means, — a sum which was appropriated to the building of the present Mansion House. The speech of Lord Mansfield in the House of Lords, when certain dissenters at length resolved to dispute the validity of this ordinance, will be long remembered to his honor.

The progress of dissenting liberty during the reign of Geo. III. and his successors, the contests respecting the Corporation and Test Acts, and Catholic Emancipation, which were terminated in 1828 and 1829 by the repeal of those oppressive enactments, the bill of Lord Sidmouth, in 1811, which sought to limit "the liberty of prophesying" by demanding securities of dissenting ministers, and which was resisted and defeated by the whole body of the nonconformists, are incidents which belong, indeed, to this volume, but which are matters of such modern history as scarcely to need repetition. The spirit of an establishment is, we thankfully own, becoming every day more enlarged and tolerant; but until — all bounties and penalties apart — the state shall retire within the province which alone she can legitimately occupy, and until the rights of man shall be as distinctly acknowledged in the meanest dissenter who worships in his barn as in the haughtiest churchman who wears his mitre, the war for religious liberty will not be ended.

History has been well designated "philosophy teaching by examples." The reader of the foregoing pages is invited, before he lays down the volume, to glance at the kind of philosophy deducible from its illustrations.

He has seen the civil sword wielded by the magistrate in professed defence of religion, in successive and very different periods. By Romanism, by Lutheranism, by Arminianism, by Presbyterianism, sometimes conjoined with Independency, and sometimes pure; and, since the accession of the house of Hanover, by a system gradually approximating to Erastianism.

He has learned that the state church and the true church are by no means identical. We do not say that the one has never included a portion of the other, but that the one has never been a fair representative of the other. Whatever the reader's religious opinions may happen to be, he cannot but mark certain periods in which error, and not truth, has been armed with civil power. The Romanist cannot believe the state church to be the true church when it is protestant, nor the protestant when it is Romanistic. Whether the reader be a presbyterian, or a baptist, or a unitarian, or a friend, or an independent, he cannot but remember periods in which the state church, so far from being identical with the true church, has done its utmost to weaken and to destroy it, by bounty on the one hand, and by penalty on the other; sometimes by fine; sometimes by imprisonment; sometimes by banishment; sometimes by torture; sometimes by death. Let him, then, remember that a state church, so far from being necessarily a friend to true religion, has been often its most virulent and deadly enemy!

But the reader will see more. If he be a man of candor and piety, he will see that those periods in which a state church has been most dominant are not the periods fixed upon by any party as worthy of the highest complacency. What frank Romanist delights in Hildebrand and Innocent III., or in the memory of Queen Mary and James II.? What pious episcopalian will endorse the acts of Laud and Strafford, of Lauderdale and Sacheverell? What presbyterian vindicates the principles — as a whole — of the covenanters? Just in proportion as the state alliance is a reality, and not a name, men shrink from glorying in it. Can any circumstances be more suspicious, or more suggestive?

On the contrary, with a few distinguished exceptions, the best men of every party have always been those who have either been frowned on by the state church, or else have stood far away from its vortex. Fenelon and Pascal; Wilson, Leighton, Scott, Newton; Baxter, Blackader, Howe, the Henrys; Penn, Fry, Clarkson; Robinson, Nye, Watts, Doddridge; Kiffin, Bunyan, Whitefield, Wesley, were men who, whatever doctrines they avowed, were in no position to exercise civil power for any prolonged period; or, if they were, tarnished by that means something of their lustre. So far is it from being true that a state church is necessary to the vitality of the religious system with which we most agree!

The conclusion is that, so far from the removal of its state machinery being injurious to the true church, that removal is, all other things being equal, the surest means of confirming and advancing it.

Advance, then, we say, advance the true church! Advance it, by displaying its legitimate and spiritual character! Advance it, by disencumbering it of its useless and worthless formalism! Advance it, by removing from its administration men who do not sympathize with its high objects, nor comprehend its gentle spirit! Advance it, by making it the friend of all, and the enemy of none! Advance it, by raising it to an eminence whence, without interfering with their just prerogative, it may observe, and teach and pray, for the powers and dominions of this world! Advance it, that, instead of bearing the mockery of a self-denying name, it may be a sublime reality, comprehending within its range those whom no law can define, and excluding from its bosom those whom no earthly penitence can silence!

We are deeply aware that, to aid in this issue, other and more spiritual processes are requisite. Far be it from us to scorn at them. But, whatever else is important, this surely is: to assert for the religion of the gospel, for it alone can sustain such a demand, a Divine right — a Divine right superior to all human law!

OLD FOUNDERY MEETING, CITY ROAD, THE SCENE OF WESLEY'S FIRST LABORS.

VALUABLE SCIENTIFIC WORKS.

LAKE SUPERIOR : its Physical Character, Vegetation and Animals, compared with those of other and similar regions, by L. AGASSIZ, and contributions from other eminent Scientific Gentlemen. With a Narrative of the Expedition, and illustrations by J. E. Cabot. One volume octavo, elegantly illustrated,..........................cloth,....3,50

The illustrations, seventeen in number, are in the finest style of the art, by Sonrel; embracing Lake and Landscape Scenery, Fishes, and other objects of Natural History, with an outline map of Lake Superior.

This work is one of the most valuable scientific works that has appeared in this country. Embodying the researches of our best scientific men, relating to a hitherto comparatively unknown region, it will be found to contain a great amount of scientific information.

CHAMBERS' CYCLOPÆDIA OF ENGLISH LITERATURE. A Selection of the choicest productions of English Authors, from the earliest to the present time. Connected by a Critical and Biographical History. Forming two large imperial octavo volumes of 700 pages each, double column letter press; with upwards of 300 elegant Illustrations. Edited by ROBERT CHAMBERS,............. .....embossed cloth,....5,00

cloth, full gilt, extra,....7,50

sheep, extra, raised bands,....6,00

The work embraces about one thousand Authors, chronologically arranged and classed as Poets, Historians, Dramatists, Philosophers, Metaphysicians, Divines, etc., with choice selections from their writings, connected by a Biographical, Historical, and Critical Narrative; thus presenting a complete view of English Literature, from the earliest to the present time. Let the reader open where he will, he cannot fail to find matter for profit and delight. The Selections are gems,—infinite riches in a little room,—in the language of another "A WHOLE ENGLISH LIBRARY FUSED DOWN INTO ONE CHEAP BOOK!"

☞ The AMERICAN edition of this valuable work is enriched by the addition of fine steel and mezzotint Engravings of the heads of SHAKSPEARE, ADDISON, BYRON; a full length portrait of DR. JOHNSON; and a beautiful scenic representation of OLIVER GOLDSMITH and DR. JOHNSON. These important and elegant additions, together with superior paper and binding, render the AMERICAN, superior to all other editions.

CHAMBERS' MISCELLANY OF USEFUL AND ENTERTAINING KNOWLEDGE. Edited by WILLIAM CHAMBERS. With elegant Illustrative Engravings. 10 vols.

cloth,.... 7,50

cloth, gilt,....10,00

library, sheep,....10,00

☞ This work has been highly recommended by distinguished individuals, as admirably adapted to Family, Sabbath and District School Libraries.

"It would be difficult to find any miscellany superior or even equal to it; it richly deserves the epithets 'useful and entertaining,' and I would recommend it very strongly, as extremely well adapted to form parts of a library for the young, or of a social or circulating library, in town or country."—*George B. Emerson, Esq., Chairman Boston School Book Committee.*

CHAMBERS' PAPERS FOR THE PEOPLE. 12mo, in beautiful ornamented covers..

This series is mainly addressed to that numerous class whose minds have been educated by the improved schooling, and the numerous popular lectures and publications of the present day, and who consequently crave a higher kind of Literature than can be obtained through the existing cheap periodicals. The Papers embrace History, Archæology, Biography, Science, the Industrial and Fine Arts, the leading topics in Social Economy, together with Criticism, Fiction, Personal Narrative, and other branches of Elegant Literature, each number containing a distinct subject.

The series will consist of sixteen numbers, of 192 pages each, and when completed, will make eight handsome volumes of about 400 pages each.

VALUABLE SCIENTIFIC WORKS.

THE EARTH AND MAN: Lectures on COMPARATIVE PHYSICAL GEOGRAPHY, in its relation to the History of Mankind. By ARNOLD GUYOT, Professor of Physical Geography and History, Neuchatel. Translated from the French, by Prof. C. C. FELTON, with illustrations. Second thousand. 12mo,....................................cloth,....1,25

"Those who have been accustomed to regard Geography as a merely descriptive branch of learning, drier than the remainder biscuit after a voyage, will be delighted to find this hitherto unattractive pursuit converted into a science, the principles of which are definite and the results conclusive."—*North American Review.*

"The grand idea of the work is happily expressed by the author, where he calls it the *geographical march of history.* Faith, science, learning, poetry, taste, in a word, genius, have liberally contributed to the production of the work under review. Sometimes we feel as if we were studying a treatise on the exact sciences; at others, it strikes the ear like an epic poem. Now it reads like history, and now it sounds like prophecy. It will find readers in whatever language it may be published."—*Christian Examiner.*

"The work is one of high merit, exhibiting a wide range of knowledge, great research, and a philosophical spirit of investigation. Its perusal will well repay the most learned in such subjects, and give new views to all, of man's relation to the globe he inhabits."—*Silliman's Journal.*

COMPARATIVE PHYSICAL AND HISTORICAL GEOGRAPHY; or, the Study of the Earth and its Inhabitants. A series of graduated courses for the use of Schools. By ARNOLD GUYOT, author of "Earth and Man," etc.

The series hereby announced will consist of three courses, adapted to the capacity of three different ages and periods of study. The first is intended for primary schools, and for children of from seven to ten years. The second is adapted for higher schools, and for young persons of from ten to fifteen years. The third is to be used as a scientific manual in Academies and Colleges.

Each course will be divided into two parts, one of purely Physical Geography, the other for Ethnography, Statistics, Political and Historical Geography. Each part will be illustrated by a colored Physical and Political Atlas, prepared expressly for this purpose, delineating, with the greatest care, the configuration of the surface, and the other physical phenomena alluded to in the corresponding work, the distribution of the races of men, and the political divisions into States, &c., &c.

The two parts of the first or preparatory course are now in a forward state of preparation, and will be issued at an early day.

MURAL MAPS: a series of elegant colored Maps, exhibiting the Physical Phenomena of the Globe. Projected on a large scale, and intended to be suspended in the Recitation Room. By ARNOLD GUYOT..[in preparation]

KITTO'S POPULAR CYCLOPÆDIA OF BIBLICAL LITERATURE. Condensed from the larger work. By JOHN KITTO, D. D., F. S. A., author of "The Pictoral Bible," "History and Physical Geography of Palestine," Editor of "The Journal of Sacred Literature," etc. Assisted by numerous distinguished Scholars and Divines, British, Continental and American. With numerous illustrations. One volume, octavo, 812pp...cloth,....3,00

THE POPULAR BIBLICAL CYCLOPÆDIA OF LITERATURE is designed to furnish a DICTIONARY OF THE BIBLE, embodying the products of the best and most recent researches in Biblical Literature, in which the Scholars of Europe and America have been engaged. The work, the result of immense labor and research, and enriched by the contributions of writers of distinguished eminence in the various departments of Sacred Literature,—has been, by universal consent, pronounced the best work of its class extant; and the one best suited to the advanced knowledge of the present day in all the studies connected with Theological Science.

The Cyclopædia of Biblical Literature from which this work is *condensed by the author,* is published in two volumes, rendering it about twice the size of the present work, and is intended, says the author, more particularly for Ministers and Theological Students; while the *Popular Cyclopædia* is intended for Parents, Sabbath School Teachers, and the great body of the religious public. It has been the author's aim to avoid imparting to the work any color of *sectarian* or *denominational* bias. On such points of difference among Christians, the *Historical* mode of treatment has been adopted, and care has been taken to provide a fair account of the arguments which have seemed most conclusive to the ablest advocates of the various opinions. The Pictoral Illustrations—amounting to more than three hundred—are of the very highest order of the art.

WORKS ON MISSIONS.

THE MISSIONARY ENTERPRISE; a collection of Discourses on Christian Missions, by American Authors. Edited by BARON STOW, D. D. Second thousand, 12mo, ...cloth,.... ,85

THE KAREN APOSTLE; or, Memoir of KO-THAH-BYU, the first Karen Convert. With Notices concerning his Nation. By Rev. FRANCIS MASON, Missionary. Edited by Prof H. J. RIPLEY. 18mo,..cloth,.... ,25

MEMOIR OF ANN H. JUDSON, late Missionary to Burmah. By Rev. J. D. KNOWLES. A new edition. Fifty-fifth thousand. 18mo,................cloth,.... ,58

FINE EDITION, plates, 16mo,..cloth, gilt,.... ,85

MEMOIR OF GEORGE DANA BOARDMAN, late Missionary to Burmah,—containing much intelligence relative to the Burman Mission. By Rev. A. KING. With an Introductory Essay. By W. R. WILLIAMS, D. D. New edition. 12mo,...cloth,.... ,75

MEMOIR OF HENRIETTA SHUCK; first Female Missionary to China. With a Likeness. By Rev. J. B. JETER. Fifth thousand. 18mo,...............cloth,.... ,50

MEMOIR OF REV. WILLIAM G. CROCKER, late Missionary in West Africa, among the Bassas. Including a History of the Mission. By R. B. MEDBERY. With a Likeness. 18mo,...cloth,.... ,63

A HISTORY OF AMERICAN BAPTIST MISSIONS, in Asia, Africa, Europe, and North America, from their earliest commencement to the present time. Prepared under the direction of the AMERICAN BAPTIST MISSIONARY UNION. By WILLIAM GAMMELL, Prof. in Brown University. With seven Maps. Sixth thousand. 12mo,..cloth,.... ,75

☞ Letters from the Missionaries now in the field, and who are the best qualified to judge of its accuracy, have been received, giving their unequivocal testimony to the fidelity of the work.

HARRIS' WORKS.

THE GREAT COMMISSION; or, the Christian Church constituted and charged to convey the Gospel to the world. A Prize Essay. By JOHN HARRIS, D. D. With an Introductory Essay, by WILLIAM R. WILLIAMS, D. D. Seventh thousand. 12mo,...cloth,....1,00

THE GREAT TEACHER; or, Characteristics of our Lord's Ministry. By JOHN HARRIS, D. D. With an Introductory Essay, by H. HUMPHREY, D. D. Twelfth thousand. 12mo,..cloth,.... ,85

MISCELLANIES; consisting principally of Sermons and Essays. By J. HARRIS, D. D. With an Introductory Essay and Notes, by JOSEPH BELCHER, D. D. 16mo,.cloth,....,75

MAMMON; or, Covetousness the Sin of the Christian Church. By J. HARRIS, D. D. 18mo,.. cloth,.... ,45

ZEBULON; or, the Moral Claims of Seamen stated and enforced. By J. HARRIS, D D. 18mo,.. cloth,.... ,25

THE PRE-ADAMITE EARTH. Contributions to Theological Science. By JOHN HARRIS, D. D. New and Revised edition. One volume, 12mo,..............cloth,....1,00

MAN PRIMEVAL; or the Constitution and Primitive Condition of the Human Being A Contribution to Theological Science. By JOHN HARRIS, D. D. With a finely engraved Portrait of the Author. Third edition. 12mo,.........................cloth.....1,25

"His copious and beautiful illustrations of the successive laws of the Divine Manifestation, have yielded us inexpressible delight."—*London Eclective Review.*

THE FAMILY; its Constitution, Probation, and History; being the THIRD volume of "Contributions to Theological Science." By JOHN HARRIS, D. D. ....[In preparation.

VALUABLE RELIGIOUS WORKS.

THE LIFE AND CORRESPONDENCE OF JOHN FOSTER. Edited by J. E RYLAND, with notices of Mr. FOSTER, as a Preacher and a Companion. By JOHN SHEPPARD. A new edition, two volumes in one, 700 pages. 12mo,............cloth,....1,25

"In simplicity of language, in majesty of conception, in the eloquence of that conciseness which conveys in a short sentence more meaning than the mind dares at once admit,—his writings are unmatched."—*North British Review.*

RELIGIOUS PROGRESS; Discourses on the Development of the Christian Character. By WILLIAM R. WILLIAMS, D. D. Second edition. 12mo,................cloth,.... ,85

"This work is from the pen of one of the brightest lights of the American Pulpit. We scarcely know of any living writer who has a finer command of powerful thought and glowing, impressive language, than he. The present volume will advance, if possible, the reputation which his previous works have acquired for him."—*Albany Evening Atlas.*

"This book is a rare phenomena in these days. It is a rich exposition of Scripture, with a fund of practical, religious wisdom, conveyed in a style so strong and so massive, as to remind one of the English writers of two centuries ago; and yet it abounds in fresh illustrations drawn from every—even the latest opened—field of science and of literature."—*Methodist Quarterly.*

LECTURES ON THE LORD'S PRAYER, By WILLIAM R. WILLIAMS, D D. 12mo, cloth,.... ,85

MOTHERS OF THE WISE AND GOOD, By Rev. JABEZ BURNS, D. D., Author of "Pulpit Cyclopedia, etc." Third thousand. 16mo,.....................cloth,.... ,75

A beautiful gallery of portraits of those who not only were "wise and good" in their own generation, but whose influence, long after they were slumbering in the dust, went forth to live again in their children. A sketch of the mothers of many of the most eminent men of the world, and showing how much they were indebted to maternal influence, for their greatness and excellence of character is given. Works of this nature cannot be too widely circulated or attentively read.

UNIVERSITY SERMONS. Sermons delivered in the Chapel of Brown University. By FRANCIS WAYLAND. Third thousand. 12mo,.......................cloth,....1,00

"The discourses contained in this handsome volume are characterized by all that richness of thought and elegance of language for which their talented author is celebrated. The whole volume is well worthy of the pen of the distinguished scholar and divine from whom it emanates."—*Dr. Baird's Christian Union.*

THE CHRISTIAN'S DAILY TREASURY; a Religious Exercise for every day in the year. By E. TEMPLE. 12mo,....................................cloth,....1,00

THE EXTENT OF THE ATONEMENT, in its relation to God and the Universe. By THOMAS W. JENKYN, D. D. From the third London Edition. 12mo,..cloth,.... ,85

ANTIOCH; or, Increase of Moral Power in the Church of Christ. By P. CHURCH. D. D. With an Essay, by BARON STOW, D. D. 18mo...................cloth,.... ,50

PHILOSOPHY OF THE PLAN OF SALVATION; a book for the times. By an AMERICAN CITIZEN. With an Introductory Essay by CALVIN E. STOWE, D. D., 12mo,— cloth .... ,62½

THE CHURCH MEMBER'S HAND BOOK; a Plain Guide to the Doctrines and Practice of Baptist Churches. By Rev. WILLIAM CROWELL. Third thousand. 18mo, cloth,.... ,38

PRACTICAL COMMENTARY ON PHILIPPIANS, by Dr. A. NEANDER. Translated by H. C. CONANT. With an account of the Closing Scenes of the Author's Life, by RAUH. 12mo,...cloth.

DR. NEANDER'S COMMENTARY ON EPISTLE OF JAMES. [in preparation.]

www.ingramcontent.com/pod-product-compliance
Lightning Source LLC
LaVergne TN
LVHW010146110826
845151LV00002B/440

* 9 7 8 1 4 2 5 5 3 7 1 6 6 *